PROGRESSIVISM

PROGRESSIVISM The Strange History of a Radical Idea

BRADLEY C. S. WATSON

Foreword by Charles R. Kesler

University of Notre Dame Press

Notre Dame, Indiana

University of Notre Dame Press
Notre Dame, Indiana 46556
undpress.nd.edu

Published in the United States of America

Library of Congress Cataloging-in-Publication Data

Names: Watson, Bradley C. S., 1961– author. | Kesler, Charles R.,
    author of foreword.
Title: Progressivism : the strange history of a radical idea /
    Bradley C. S. Watson ; foreword by Charles R. Kesler.
Other titles: Strange history of a radical idea
Description: Notre Dame, Indiana : University of Notre Dame Press, [2020] |
    Includes bibliographical references and index.
Identifiers: LCCN 2019054508 (print) | LCCN 2019054509 (ebook) |
    ISBN 9780268106973 (hardback) | ISBN 9780268107000 (adobe pdf) |
    ISBN 9780268106997 (epub)
Subjects: LCSH: Progressivism (United States politics) | Progressivism
    (United States politics)—Historiography. | United States—Politics and
    government—1901–1953. | United States—Politics and government—
    1901–1953—Historiography.
Classification: LCC E743 . W38 2020 (print) | LCC E743 (ebook) |
    DDC 324.2732/7—dc23
LC record available at https://lccn.loc.gov/2019054508
LC ebook record available at https://lccn.loc.gov/2019054509

PROGRESSIVISM

PROGRESSIVISM The Strange History of a Radical Idea

BRADLEY C. S. WATSON

Foreword by Charles R. Kesler

University of Notre Dame Press

Notre Dame, Indiana

University of Notre Dame Press
Notre Dame, Indiana 46556
undpress.nd.edu

Library of Congress Cataloging-in-Publication Data

Names: Watson, Bradley C. S., 1961– author. | Kesler, Charles R.,
    author of foreword.
Title: Progressivism : the strange history of a radical idea /
    Bradley C. S. Watson ; foreword by Charles R. Kesler.
Other titles: Strange history of a radical idea
Description: Notre Dame, Indiana : University of Notre Dame Press, [2020] |
    Includes bibliographical references and index.
Identifiers: LCCN 2019054508 (print) | LCCN 2019054509 (ebook) |
    ISBN 9780268106973 (hardback) | ISBN 9780268107000 (adobe pdf) |
    ISBN 9780268106997 (epub)
Subjects: LCSH: Progressivism (United States politics) | Progressivism
    (United States politics) — Historiography. | United States — Politics and
    government — 1901–1953. | United States — Politics and government —
    1901–1953 — Historiography.
Classification: LCC E743 . W38 2020 (print) | LCC E743 (ebook) |
    DDC 324.2732/7—dc23
LC record available at https://lccn.loc.gov/2019054508
LC ebook record available at https://lccn.loc.gov/2019054509

About the Declaration there is a finality that is exceedingly restful. It is often asserted that the world has made a great deal of progress since 1776, that we have had new thoughts and new experiences which have given us a great advance over the people of that day, and that we may therefore very well discard their conclusions for something more modern. But that reasoning can not be applied to this great charter. If all men are created equal, that is final. If they are endowed with inalienable rights, that is final. If governments derive their just powers from the consent of the governed, that is final. No advance, no progress can be made beyond these propositions. If anyone wishes to deny their truth or their soundness, the only direction in which he can proceed historically is not forward, but backward toward the time when there was no equality, no rights of the individual, no rule of the people. Those who wish to proceed in that direction can not lay claim to progress. They are reactionary. Their ideas are not more modern, but more ancient, than those of the Revolutionary fathers.

—Calvin Coolidge, 1926

The tradition of Progressive reform is the one upon which I was reared and upon which my political sentiments were formed, as it is, indeed, the tradition of most intellectuals in America. Perhaps because in its politics the United States has been so reliably conservative a country during the greater part of its history, its main intellectual traditions have been, as a reaction, "liberal," as we say— that is, popular, democratic, progressive. . . . In our own day . . . liberals are beginning to find it both natural and expedient to explore the merits and employ the rhetoric of conservatism. . . . This is true not because they have some sweeping ideological commitment to conservatism (indeed, their sentiments and loyalties still lie mainly in another direction) but because they feel that we can better serve ourselves in the calculable future by holding to what we have gained and learned, while trying to find some way out of the dreadful impasse of our polarized world, than by dismantling the social achievements of the past twenty years, abandoning all that is best in American traditions, and indulging in the costly pretense of repudiating what we should not and in fact cannot repudiate.

—Richard Hofstadter, 1955

Contents

Foreword

Charles R. Kesler

In this pathbreaking volume, Bradley C. S. Watson scours the writings of American historians from the 1940s to the present, seeking to describe and to explain their strange reluctance to come to grips with the beginning—and in some ways still the central—phenomenon of modern American politics: the new worldview of the progressive movement. This worldview was asseverated in the title of the journal founded to transmit its insights to mainstream America, the *New Republic*, as well as in the slogans of the movement's greatest political leaders, Theodore Roosevelt's "New Nationalism" and Woodrow Wilson's "New Freedom." The progressives, especially the proudest and most daring of them, longed to begin American politics over again on what they considered a higher ethical and political level, higher, that is, than the eighteenth-century precepts and institutions available to the founders and "blindly" worshiped, as Wilson put it, for a century by their successors of every political party.

Unlike the old republic, however, the new one envisioned by the progressives would dispense with formal moments of founding or refounding in favor of a continual process of adjusting political forms to changing social needs, and so would focus not on a set of enduring institutional safeguards, such as separation of powers or federalism, but on ways of evading or overcoming those precautions in order to empower national efforts to solve national problems. Not revolution, then, but political evolution would be the way forward. Yet the discovery of such problems and the never-ending search, necessarily experimental, for their cure presupposed a new and revolutionary point of departure: the intellectual-cultural breakthrough that revealed the obsolescence of the old nationalism, the old freedom, and the old republic.

Just because they were old, after all, did not mean America's historic creeds and institutions were necessarily obsolete or ill-suited to present-day needs. James Madison had looked forward to "that veneration which time bestows on everything" as an essential ally to good government, "without which perhaps the wisest and freest governments would not possess the requisite stability." He helped to erect a Constitution and governmental system that were *designed* to last or grow old. He founded a Constitution difficult to amend and a government prone (on account of the very institutional safeguards so disliked by the progressives) to check its own destructive excesses. But he hoped, also, that the new Constitution would last because it would deserve to. That is, he hoped its founders had grasped the rights and requisites of human nature well enough to design a system that would conduce over time, as far as humanly possible, to *good government*. A republican government that endured would tend to attract what Madison called the "prejudices" of the people to its side; but to the extent it actually secured justice and the common good, such a government would *deserve* to endure and to be supported even by, *per impossibile*, "a nation of philosophers."[1]

If, as Madison and his colleagues assumed, human nature was unchanging and government itself was "the greatest of all reflections on human nature," then a relatively unchanging constitutional system would be a reasonable conclusion from an essentially unchanging human nature.[2] The system didn't preclude all change, of course, providing in the Constitution itself a method for amending the agreement; but amendments had to be made in accordance with constitutional rules (see Article V), and more broadly and loosely in accordance with the Constitution's general spirit. In fact, the progressives were happy to use the amendment process to open the government to what they considered salutary modernization: the Sixteenth Amendment (ratified in 1913) authorized Congress to pass a national income tax, the Seventeenth (1913) made US senators popularly elected, the Eighteenth (1919) established Prohibition, and the Nineteenth (1920) enacted women's suffrage.

Although designed to nationalize and democratize American politics, and to elevate its moral tone (so they predicted!), these measures did not go far enough. For it was precisely the general spirit or implicit principles of the Constitution that the progressives wanted to reform. They regarded its root assumptions about human nature and government to be wrong, though in a peculiar and revealing way—wrong not simply but relatively. The ideas of unchanging natural rights and law, and of government limited to securing the people's safety and happiness in accordance with such rights and law, had been serviceable in the eighteenth century—appropriate to a nation of dispersed family farms and small businesses, argued progressives like Wilson and Herbert Croly—and therefore true, or true enough, in that age. The founders' mistake, according to these critics, had been to presume these notions were true in every age. Lincoln repeated their error when, speaking of the Declaration of Independence, he honored Thomas Jefferson for inserting in it "an abstract truth, applicable to all men and all times."[3] The progressives charged that Americans hitherto had been blind to the historical relativity of values (a word they did not use in this sense, but we do, alas).

Those founding "truths" were relative then, at best. Some progressive writers—including the historians Charles Beard and Vernon Parrington, ably discussed by Watson in chapter 1—rejected the Constitution's principles not only as time-bound, but as bound to a time that favored property rights over human rights, oligarchy over democracy. In any case, the assumption shared by almost all the leading thinkers of progressivism was that all ideals of right and wrong, good and bad, were children of their age; as the age changed (particularly in its socioeconomic distribution of power), so did the ideals. The only unchanging thing was the process by which the ideals arose, flourished, and decayed, preparing the way for successor ideals. That process was History, with a capital H, and it was the discovery of history in that sense, "the historical sense" alive to the relativity of values, that distinguished the most consistent progressives from the populists and from every school of American political thought before them. History, the process by which ideals came and went, was the only permanent truth.

In place of the old-fashioned view, shared by the founders, of man as an in-between being—between the beasts and the angels—progressivism substituted the view of man as an open-ended being, defined not by an unchanging nature but precisely by how his nature had changed over the centuries in reaction to history's challenges. The most important aspect of human nature, in fact, was its very openness to change. Man's freedom consisted in this indefinite, perhaps even infinite, adaptability. A new kind of idealism, based not on summoning the better angels of our (mixed) nature but on transcending our "nature" (that is, as it had developed so far), began to take wing. Humans, led by the Anglo-Saxon or Teutonic races, had arrived at the moment of self-consciousness, the point at which they could begin to take charge of their own evolution. The past ceased to be a reliable guide to what we might expect of human beings in the future. "Democracy," declared Croly, "must stand or fall on a platform of possible human perfectibility."[4]

Teddy Roosevelt may have doubted that, but plenty of his generation did not. They called themselves progressives for a reason. They believed in History not as teaching an easy-going relativism or agnosticism but as revealing a stern lesson of progress: society (and man with it) was evolving toward greater and greater freedom, justice, and truth. Although modern values were as relative to twentieth-century social conditions as the founders' values were relative to eighteenth-century conditions, for the first time human beings could *understand* that relativity and act on it. The twentieth century had the great advantage of coming later—incorporating all that was valuable in what had preceded it and being closer to the conscious culmination of social and cultural development.

Woodrow Wilson called the old American science of politics "Newtonian," meaning it regarded history as a cycle, eternally retracing the same orbit in obedience to the changeless laws of human nature, especially the law of self-interest. The new political science he termed "Darwinian," implying that human nature and government changed in accordance with the changing social and economic environment, and that the direction of change was, as in biological organisms, from simple to more complex, which in the case of humans meant also from a more primitive to a more advanced morality. The prolific philosopher John Dewey described the key intellectual breakthrough in similar terms, from a static worldview to one that assumed change was normal, pervasive, rational, inevitable, and highly ethical. This was the revelation that marked the progressives' worldview—and their republic, freedom, and nationalism—as something fundamentally *new*.

Their defenders and explicators down to the present, however, have spent more time explaining the progressives' pragmatism (not moderation, alas) than remembering their boldness. This is especially true, as Brad Watson shows herein, of the American historians who have written the history of the Progressive Era and its sequels. How and why did these scholars (almost all progressives of one kind or another in their own politics) become so fond of ironic self-denial, or noble lies, meant to deny or to disguise their forebears' soaring ideological and political ambition?

As such, *Progressivism: The Strange History of a Radical Idea* fills not a gap but a gulf in the literature of twentieth-century American politics. Why have liberals been so reluctant to have a candid discussion of the history of liberalism? By concentrating on some of the biggest names in American history-writing—Charles Beard, Richard Hofstadter, Louis Hartz, Arthur Schlesinger Jr., William Appleman Williams, Gabriel Kolko, Arthur Link, and others—Watson's bold revisionism shows how partial, and how partisan, have been their accounts of the rise, triumph, and (according to some) decline of progressivism. Their "complicity of understatement," to borrow one of his many nice phrases, suggests strongly that nothing could have been more natural, reasonable, and even inevitable than the emergence of modern liberalism as the dominant political allegiance of mid-century America. To most of these writers, it was the predictable, almost boring evolutionary outcome not only of progressivism but of American history as a whole, or at least of its more enlightened parts.

Thus the "living Constitution," as progressives and then liberals came to call it, did not in their view represent a revolution against the original Constitution but simply its grown-up version, adjusted to twentieth-century reality. After all, the alternative to a living Constitution was, in their view, a dead one, or at best a Constitution on life support, fading fast. Conservatives who grasped this point, as many in the pre-Buckley era did and many still do, had to admit that the only way to preserve any remnants of their beloved eighteenth-century Constitution was to incorporate or transfer them into the living Constitution. Accordingly, American conservatives would have to accept their affinity with—more precisely, their subservience to—mainstream, mid-century liberalism. That's how Schlesinger and most of these historians saw it, very conveniently for their own political views, to be sure, though they acknowledged the cost involved: the liberal vanguard would be slowed by its conservative baggage train. (By the late 1950s, the New Left historians, as Watson shows, had begun to denounce this tradeoff as a betrayal of true progressivism.)

Watson breaks with the depoliticized, self-flattering history of these famous historians. Emphasizing the antipathies between the original and the "living" Constitution—antipathies well understood by the progressives themselves—he exposes the ideological, political, and legal conflicts the significance of which the bien-pensants have denied, downplayed, or simply ignored. In this "strange history" (strange because readers of the standard histories will find it mostly unfamiliar), what he calls "the revolt against the Constitution" takes its rightful place, a central place, in the history of progressivism and, by extension, of modern American liberalism. He shines light, too, on the moralism or idealism, the social gospel enthusiasms, and the sublimated religious passions of the progressives. ("We stand at Armageddon, and we battle for the Lord!" T. R. told the Progressive Party national convention in 1912.) Such secular millenarianism continues to pulse through twenty-first-century movements for social and economic justice, but its role in the Progressive Era has tended to be overshadowed. Watson restores its importance in the story, indeed deepens it by discussing some of the unexpected Aristotelian and Catholic roots of the social gospel.

Part of the book's refreshingly clear-eyed view of American history and historians owes to its author being outside the guild. Watson is a political scientist, an expert on political philosophy, American political thought, and constitutional jurisprudence. His eyes are sensitive to theoretical matters and to debates among statesmen, judges, and political thinkers that some historians, at least, have written off as antediluvian. It is a lazy habit of most of the historians he criticizes to associate the past with injustice and error and the future with justice and truth. This is the progressive superstition par excellence—and evidence of how deeply those scholars had been shaped by progressivism's assumptions, whether or not they admitted it. Watson rejects that superstition.

He is aided by his own education as a member of what he calls, in the final chapter, the "Claremont school," well known for its skepticism of all claims that historical Might or success or "owning the future" can make Right. Hence this school is well known for reopening the question of the progressive movement's justice and wisdom as a whole; and for its defense of the Declaration of Independence, the Constitution, and the founders' political science against progressive attacks on them as outmoded and unjust. Because the reader may not be familiar with it, permit me to state a few basic points about Claremont and its place in these debates.

Since the 1980s, a "flood of revisionist scholarship," as Watson writes, has challenged the orthodox liberal account of progressivism. That scholarship arose from many people, places, and perspectives (some of them notably more liberal than conservative, as, for example, Eldon Eisenach), as he notes, but Claremont played a central role in it. "Claremont" refers both to a place and to a school of thought. A pleasant college town east of Los Angeles, Claremont is home to the Claremont Colleges, a consortium of five small undergraduate schools and several graduate institutions. At the heart of the new school of thought were a handful of faculty members, mostly concentrated in Claremont McKenna College's Department of Government but offering courses also at Claremont Graduate University.

The school emerged partly by chance and partly by design. In the beginning were three political scientists hired by Claremont McKenna College (CMC) who overlapped for a few years in the 1960s and early 1970s, though only one, Harry V. Jaffa, would remain in Claremont for decades to come. (Jaffa arrived in 1964 and retired in 1989, though he remained active until his death in 2015 at age ninety-six.) Each had been a student of Leo Strauss, the brilliant scholar who did so much to revive in America the study of political philosophy and who himself spent a short time teaching in Claremont after his retirement from the University of Chicago. Each criticized some aspect of the progressive synthesis. Martin Diamond arrived first, already well known for a series of trenchant essays defending the Constitution and *The Federalist* against Charles Beard's and the progressives' interpretation of them as antidemocratic. (He joined another critic of Beard, the influential historian Douglass Adair, who taught across the street at Pomona College until his suicide in 1968.) Paul Eidelberg arrived last and wrote the first Straussian book critical of Woodrow Wilson: *A Discourse on Statesmanship: Design and Transformation of the American Polity* (1970), which juxtaposed Wilson with Alexander Hamilton, though along the somewhat eccentric lines that the founders had intended to establish a mixed regime and Wilson had set out radically to democratize it.

Jaffa, whose influence in the Claremont school would be the greatest, had already made his reputation as a preeminent scholar of Abraham Lincoln in his *Crisis of the House Divided: An Interpretation of the Issues in the Lincoln-Douglas Debates* (1959). That book was a devastating refutation of the view of the so-called revisionist historians, especially James G. Randall, on the insignificance of the debates and on the folly of Lincoln's moral condemnation of slavery, which led more or less directly, they charged, to the "needless war." Behind the revisionists, however, progressive writers like Albert J. Beveridge and Carl Becker loomed large, and ahead of the revisionists, so to speak, Richard Hofstadter, though friendlier to abolitionism, would still fault Lincoln (along revisionist lines) as a self-promoting propagandist, sham moralist, and inept statesman.

The progressives were not Jaffa's focus in *Crisis*—indeed, he made several favorable references to Woodrow Wilson—but his defense of Lincoln's statesmanship and his revitalization of Lincoln's arguments for natural rights prepared the way, in later writings, for Jaffa to become a thorough-going critic of progressive (and conservative) efforts to abandon nature for history as the ground of Right.

This scholarly circle soon helped to attract scores of graduate students and a handful of other, likeminded professors—notably, William B. Allen, Harry Neumann, James H. Nichols, Ralph Rossum, Mark Blitz, and Joseph Bessette—to Claremont. Two further institutions helped to organize their efforts, to build esprit de corps, and to put Claremont on the intellectual-political map. The Salvatori Center for the Study of Individual Freedom in the Modern World opened its doors as CMC's first research institute in 1969. I arrived as an assistant professor and its associate director in 1983, and served as its director from 1989 to 2008. Mark Blitz succeeded me from 2008 to 2018. It would sponsor countless lectures and conferences over the years on ancient, medieval, and modern political philosophy, on the American founding and constitutionalism, and on progressivism, liberalism, and conservatism. The Salvatori Center welcomed distinguished visiting professors like Thomas G. West and James Ceaser (whose *Presidential Selection: Theory and Development* [1979] was a classic early examination of Wilson's political thought) and provided fellowships for hundreds of undergraduates and graduate students pursuing research.

About a decade later, an independent think tank, separate from the Claremont Colleges though staffed by and serving many of the same graduate students, started up. In fact, the founders of the Claremont Institute for the Study of Statesmanship and Political Philosophy (www.claremont.org) were themselves graduate students at the time—Peter Schramm, Christopher Flannery, Thomas B. Silver, Steve Cambone, and soon Larry P. Arnn. From its inception, the Claremont Institute concentrated a great deal of critical attention on modern liberalism and its predecessor, the progressives. For example, Tom Silver's dissertation soon appeared as a short, powerful critique, *Coolidge and the Historians* (1983), of the liberties that liberal historians, especially Arthur Schlesinger Jr., had taken with the life and presidency of Calvin Coolidge. For forty years the Institute has sponsored scholarly and popular works that have helped to define the Claremont school and to ventilate its insights. The *Claremont Review of Books*, its flagship publication, is a sprightly quarterly (if I do say so) that has appeared under my editorship since 2000.

Brad Watson's *Progressivism: The Strange History of a Radical Idea* is a distinguished addition to the rethinking of progressivism that has been a constant focus of the Claremont school's scholarship. This impressive book argues its case calmly and cumulatively, allowing the author's prodigious research to speak for itself, though with the ready flashes of wit so distinctive of his own voice. In addition, it provides the kind of evidence Americans, both citizens and scholars, need in order to take possession of our past. It encourages us to think for ourselves about how and why our public life, after more than a century of "progress," has reached its present unhappy state.

Acknowledgments

I owe countless debts of gratitude for support, encouragement, and guidance on this book, and on my scholarly career as a whole. None of my work on the progressives—or for that matter the work of many others—would have come to fruition, or even been imaginable, without the inspiration and support of the Claremont Institute for the Study of Statesmanship and Political Philosophy. It is the Claremont Institute, and the scholars associated with it, that have led the effort to reconsider the defining role of the progressives for American political thought and practice over the past century. The Institute has also offered an intellectual home and financial support for my work.

The bulk of this book was researched and written at the Hoover Institution at Stanford University, where I spent a sabbatical year as a William F. Campbell and Rita Ricardo Campbell National Fellow. I am grateful to Hoover for providing immense scholarly resources and an ideal working environment, which allowed me to complete the manuscript.

Most scholars must close a considerable financial gap when they take a year's sabbatical, and I was certainly no exception. Salary replacement and out-of-pocket expenses are no small matters—though much smaller than we political theorists would like. The gap I faced was widened substantially by the necessity of uprooting home and family to move to the Palo Alto area. I could not have done it without the resources of the Center for Political and

Economic Thought at Saint Vincent College. I am grateful to various foundations and individuals who, for many years, have supported the Center, and especially to those that provided funds specifically to make my research on this book possible: the Sarah Scaife Foundation, the F. M. Kirby Foundation, and an anonymous donor. I am also grateful to the H. B. Earhart Foundation for a well-timed fellowship research grant.

Bits and pieces of my argument in this volume have been published elsewhere. Portions of the Introduction, as well as portions of chapter 5, are adapted from the introduction to my recent anthology of contemporary critics of American progressivism, *Progressive Challenges to the American Constitution: A New Republic*, published by Cambridge University Press. Portions of my argument in chapter 1 are adapted from an earlier work, *Living Constitution, Dying Faith: Progressivism and the New Science of Jurisprudence*, published by ISI Books. Some of my commentary on recent books that deal with the progressive phenomenon first appeared in the *Claremont Review of Books* and *Law and Liberty*. I am grateful to Cambridge University Press, ISI Books, the *Claremont Review*, and the *Online Library of Law and Liberty* for permission to adapt my arguments here.

I am also grateful to Ryan Hrobak, a former student at Saint Vincent College, for his work in locating the preliminary sources that helped acquaint me with the daunting volume of historical scholarship on the progressives and helped order my thoughts as to how I might go about sifting and synthesizing it. I undertook preliminary research on this project as a visiting scholar at the Social Philosophy and Policy Center (SPPC) at Bowling Green State University. I'm grateful to Jeffrey Paul and Fred D. Miller Jr. for making my fellowship possible.

Working with the University of Notre Dame Press has been a true pleasure. I am grateful to the director of the press, Stephen M. Wrinn, and to the editor in chief, Eli Bortz, for their confidence in this project and for their professionalism throughout. I am also grateful to the three peer reviewers selected by the press, who were truly the best an author could hope for: sympathetic, knowledgeable, and generous with their time and suggestions. The book is much better for their input.

Finally, on one matter I am in full agreement with the New Left historian William Appleman Williams. More than half a century ago, he felt it necessary to embrace the "somewhat archaic notion that a man writes his own books"—a notion that has grown more archaic since then. A project such as this demands a reconnaissance in force into the scholarly literature. I did not have an army of graduate students and research assistants to undertake such reconnoitering, nor have I ever had the desire to command such an army. But this means— in the fullest sense—that responsibility for errors and omissions is mine alone.

Bradley C. S. Watson
Stanford, California, and Latrobe, Pennsylvania

Introduction

Common experience, and modern psychology, validate the truism that people tend to see what they are looking for. In the professional realm, confirmation bias—that is, the tendency of investigators to seek and elevate that which confirms their preexisting hypotheses— is likely to constrain the gaze of even the most determined and experienced souls, and perhaps especially the most determined and experienced. *Déformation professionnelle*, as the French call it, is a condition that can afflict only the well trained, or at least the long inured.

Economists, meanwhile, use the phrase *regulatory capture* to describe the observable phenomenon of knowledgeable groups with concentrated interests swaying or "capturing" the determinations of regulators who are supposed to act impartially and for the public good. The public's interest, alas, is dispersed. A captured agency might well be more harmful to the public good than no agency at all. Its influence can be pernicious and can go largely unnoticed by everyone except the very few in the know.

Professional academics, nominally dedicated to objectivity, have not proved immune to deformation, or outright capture by professional interests, in their efforts to regulate the ebb and flow of respectable opinion.[1] The American academy, long enjoying various forms of insulation and privilege, is uniquely positioned to generate moral hazard in the realm of ideas. A case in point is the idea of progressivism as it was transmitted by American academics, especially historians, from the middle part of the twentieth century onward. The progressive idea, simply put, is that the principled American constitutionalism of fixed natural rights and limited and dispersed powers must be overturned and replaced by an organic, evolutionary model of the Constitution that facilitates the authority of experts dedicated to the expansion of the public sphere and political control, especially at the national level.

One of the most interesting and talked-about intellectual and political movements of recent years has been the reconsideration, from both scholarly and popular sources, of the progressive intellectual synthesis—culminating in the progressive idea—which has had such a large influence in American political, religious, philosophical, historical, and policy circles over the last century.[2] The progressive synthesis was based on a transformation in American political thought that occurred in the late nineteenth and early twentieth centuries, stemming from the confluence of social Darwinism, pragmatism, and Hegelianism and their metamorphosis into a powerful intellectual progressivism.[3] Elements of this intellectual progressivism were originally exemplified by such thinkers as John Dewey, W. E. B. DuBois, William James, Francis Lieber, William Graham Sumner, and Lester Frank Ward, and such political actors as Theodore Roosevelt and Woodrow Wilson. By the early twentieth century, the historicism at the heart of progressivism came to dominate key academic disciplines, such as law and political science. From Lieber, America's first political scientist, to Woodrow Wilson, the first and only political scientist to become president, the new approach to regime phenomena illustrated the merger not only of disciplines but of "Right" and "Left" under the banners of faith in historical progress and commitment to the political, economic, and social means to bring about progress. This faith and commitment came to be prevalent not only in the universities but also in courtrooms and political and religious offices.

Wilson, for example, argued in various ways against what he understood to be the anachronistic, "Newtonian" Constitution of the American founders that he saw as an obstacle in the path of Darwinian historical unfolding. Political actors since Wilson's time have been less direct in giving voice to overt suspicion of the founders' Constitution, though echoes of Wilson's arguments still resound in both moral-political discourse and constitutional jurisprudence.

My aim in this book is to offer an overview of the scholarly accounts of this progressive synthesis from the 1940s to the present, providing both a historiography and an intellectual history. As Winston Churchill is reputed to have said, "History will be kind to me for I intend to write it." In large measure, the first scholarly interpreters of progressivism were also its intellectual architects, and later interpreters were in deep sympathy with its premises and conclusions. This makes delving into the scholarly literature vital for a fuller political and cultural account of progressivism. Too many scholarly treatments of the progressive synthesis have been products of it, or at least insufficiently mindful of two central facts: the hostility of progressive theory to the founders' Constitution, and the tension between progressive theory and the realm of the private, including even conscience itself. The constitutional and religious dimensions of progressive thought—and in particular the relationship between the two—in effect remained hidden for a very long time. For much of the twentieth century, progressivism was interpreted as a populist or occasionally an intellectual movement that was ultimately assimilable to the basic contours and deepest concerns of the American regime.

Early scholarly interpreters of progressivism contributed much to the definition and influence of the very phenomenon they were describing. Leading progressive historians such as Charles and Mary Beard (*The Rise of American Civilization*, 1927), Harold U. Faulkner (*The Quest for Social Justice*, 1931), and John Hicks (*The Populist Revolt*, 1931) conceived of progressivism largely as a victory for the masses over big business. They were self-consciously part of the progressive intellectual movement. But others—those who began to flourish a generation or so later in the burgeoning industry of American higher education—were not part of the progressive movement, at least according to their self-understanding.

It is these latter scholars, largely historians, who attract my attention in this volume. Writing after the dust had settled and after the

Progressive Era had morphed into the New Deal, leading progressive historians, who fancied themselves historians of progressivism, wrote with the considerable authority that twentieth-century American academia provided. Starting in the 1940s, they were scholars who studied progressivism *qua* progressivism, which is to say they identified it by name, casting long—and longing—glances in its direction. But in so doing they declared it was time for citizens to move along, for there was nothing (or at least not much) to see. And where there was something, it was often a lost promise, an unfulfilled yearning, an unrequited love for an American damsel who too often resisted progressive advances that would in no wise have compromised her integrity. These scholars offered up interpretations and historiographies of the Progressive Era and the strains of political and economic thought that undergirded it, and they cemented in the American mind the image of progressivism as a rather warm and fuzzy movement for change whose time had come and gone. Progressives were but social reformers without legs. The chroniclers more often than not ignored the fundamental constitutional dimensions of progressivism and the relationship of citizens to the state, among other things. And where they didn't ignore such matters, their works trod lightly so as not to leave the barest imprint that might challenge an increasingly conventional wisdom.

For example, Richard Hofstadter's midcentury consensus view of American intellectual history (*The Age of Reform*, 1955) deemphasized the depth of philosophic disagreement that separated the founders of progressivism from the founders of the American regime and from what was then the mainstream of American political thought. And indeed, the continuities in the American tradition, rather than important disjunctions in thought, were emphasized by scholars across the spectrum, from Louis Hartz (*The Liberal Tradition in America*, 1955) to Henry Steele Commager (*The American Mind*, 1950), to Daniel Boorstin (*The Genius of American Politics*, 1953). In these accounts, there was a peculiar mix of understatement and triumphalism, something particularly noticeable in Commager. The progressives' searing constitutional critique attracted surprisingly little attention.

Arthur S. Link (*Woodrow Wilson and the Progressive Era*, 1954) argued for the relatively superficial character of progressive thought, as exemplified by Wilson. The understanding of progressivism as fundamentally a populist rather than philosophic movement was reinforced by historians such as C. Vann Woodward (*Origins of the New South*, 1951). Scholars such as Morton White (*Social Thought in America*, 1949), who dilated especially on the intellectual origins of progressivism, tended to examine leading thinkers in terms of their rejection of formalism in the service of social utility but did not deal with the moral-political and regime-level dimensions of what White called the "revolt against formalism." Henry F. May (*The End of American Innocence*, 1959) even suggested that many progressives represented a basic cultural and political conservatism. Still other scholars, including Robert H. Wiebe (*The Search for Order*, 1967), interpreted progressivism primarily in economic terms, as an effort to bring efficiency and order to the chaos of the marketplace. And for some, including Peter Filene ("An Obituary for the 'Progressive Movement,'" 1970), there was never any "there" there—differences among progressives were so vast as to defy categorization or cohesion.

Broadly speaking, the American historical profession in the twentieth century alternately embraced, rejected, and then embraced again political history—that is, the study of politics, policy, and institutions. Political history had been a central concern of the consensus historians, as well as the New Left historians who followed them in the 1960s and '70s. These political historians were in turn followed by the social and cultural historians who deemphasized political history in favor of new objects of inquiry. The last quarter century has seen a resurgence of political history, as well as the growth of the "American political development" approach within the discipline of political science.[4] But the central thrust of this resurgence and growth has continued to marginalize the progressive critique of the founders' Constitution and relegate it, at most, to a secondary inquiry. It is true that the "new political historians have made a convincing case that government was an important component of the United States long before the Progressive Era."[5]

But government is not identical with the Constitution, which is antecedent to government. The progressives would reject and deny antecedents in their embrace of the future. The presence of an "administration," even in the early republic—checked as it was by congressional control and consent of the governed—never came close to the secular millenarianism informing the modern administrative state. Such differences of degree and kind, premised on the progressives' theoretical assault on the philosophical premises of the founding, have been grasped by a new generation of political theorists more than by political historians.[6]

Even this brief summary suggests that many, if not most, scholarly accounts of progressivism have downplayed its constitutional dimensions and its effect on larger cultural conceptions of the private sphere. One of my claims is that as the idea of a fixed Constitution disappeared as an object of study—and eventually of public veneration—so did the realm of the private and the invisible. The most important forms of social, economic, and political progress came to be seen as depending on the state and on the manipulation by the state of measurable phenomena. Everything, in short—including even the rights of conscience—depends on the demands of politics and their handmaid, social science technique. The downplaying of the realm of conscience is ironic, given the centrality of the idea of individual as well as social flourishing to intellectual progressivism, yet individual flourishing in the progressive dispensation was, and still is, most often seen as an incident of politically engineered growth and transformation. American Catholicism and Protestantism in important ways assimilated themselves to the progressive synthesis in their calls for social solidarity through economic policy. Whether through the Catholic social thought of Fr. John Ryan (*A Living Wage*, 1906) or the social gospel of Walter Rauschenbusch (*Christianizing the Social Order*, 1913), significant portions of religious opinion turned against limited constitutionalism in the quest for more rational and scientific state administration.

Such assimilation of secular thought and theology to the aims of progressivism continues to have important ramifications in the realms of both constitutional interpretation and public policy.

Current controversies over federal mandates on religious institutions are but one example of those ramifications and illustrate the tensions between what might be called the traditional and liberal versions of various Christian denominations, as well as other religions. The link between constitutional and religious understandings in America has not been adequately studied. Such study will enable us to understand more fully the connections between what might loosely be called "liberal" or "conservative" theology and "liberal" or "conservative" politics.

This book is therefore historical and philosophical in nature. It begins by making the case for what progressivism was, in essence, thereby allowing the reader to see the manner in which dozens of post–World War II scholarly interpreters—borrowing the intellectual assumptions and asserting the conclusions of the very phenomenon they claimed to be describing—denied its essence. The story is therefore largely about what happened in the scholarly world after progressivism had painted its gray in gray, shaping American secular and religious conscience from the century's turn through the New Deal and what followed. I do not intend to rehash the many debates over the founding era or to offer a comprehensive account and defense of the founders' constitutionalism.[7] Instead, I offer an account of what the progressives themselves agreed on and what later historians of the progressive era did not report.

Some words on my method are in order. With few exceptions, it is chronological. I am old-fashioned enough to believe in the virtues of chronological history, including a history of history such as this. Relationships among thinkers, scholars, and ideas, including causal relationships, are most likely to reveal themselves when the human mind considers things in a linear way. I deviate from this practice only occasionally: for example, when I consider several works closely related in time or approach, as from a single prolific scholar such as Richard Hofstadter.

It is also worth noting that I am acutely conscious of the sins of commission and omission that might color a book such as this. The former have to do with the delicate matter of interpretation. I have tried to be fair to the scholars I have chosen to discuss, seeking to identify and characterize their awareness, or lack thereof, of the regime questions with which I am concerned. As to the latter, the potential to offend is even greater. Given the enormous amount of scholarship on progressivism, no single work can hope to analyze and synthesize all of it or even do full justice to that portion of it that is the subject of interpretation. I can only say that I have not tried to cherry-pick my examples. I have tried, rather, to give a full and robust sense of the main lines of historical scholarship over the better part of a century. Others will have to judge the extent to which I have succeeded in either of these aims. With luck, my bond with the reader will be tested only on venial matters.

In the first chapter I sketch the philosophic background of intellectual progressivism, offering an outline of what the progressives rebelled against, in order to clarify the depth of their critique of the American regime. This is followed by a chapter on the progressive religious dispensation and its wide-ranging implications. Together, the first two chapters paint a picture of constitutional criticism emboldened and propelled by messianic fervor—a central feature of progressivism that was largely ignored by later historians. The next two chapters offer a decade-by-decade account of shifting scholarly interpretations of the progressive phenomenon, beginning in the 1940s, by which time the New Deal had reified the progressive synthesis at the level of both public policy and consciousness. The chapters also provide an account of the constitutional implications of these interpretations. The fifth chapter offers a discussion of the intellectual consolidation around the progressive synthesis by the latter part of the twentieth century, as well as an account of the recent scholarly pushback against that consolidation. The concluding chapter offers some reflections on what best accounts for the lack of clarity—the complicity of understatement—on the part of the chroniclers of progressivism throughout the twentieth century and for the enduring tensions between the accounts of these historians and a new generation of political theorists.

The progressive line of constitutional (though not so much religious) thought has been the subject of sustained reconsideration over the past decade or so by scholars largely working in the discipline of political science, and particularly the subfield of political theory, and by several journalists drawing on scholarly sources. The tenor of this reconsideration is dramatically different from that of earlier scholarly accounts and suggests that intellectual progressivism amounts to nothing less than a fundamental reconfiguration of the deepest questions of politics and culture.

In light of these interrogations of the progressive synthesis, it is a propitious moment to offer observations on historiography and academic culture. I trust they will be useful for both scholars and citizens who are interested in placing earlier accounts of the progressive synthesis—which generally emphasized the compatibility of progressive categories with the American experience—side by side with more recent critical scholarly treatments. In the course of doing this, I plan to examine more fully the religious dimensions of progressive political thought—or, put another way, the political progressivism that informs much contemporary American religious thought. My ultimate aim is to make clear the power of an idea to penetrate the academic mind and bring into question regime-level politics as well as deep-seated cultural dispositions.

ONE   The Revolt against the Constitution

By the middle part of the twentieth century, historians were reporting that progressivism had never existed. By so doing, they certainly could not be accused of exaggerating its death. In 1971, Peter Filene of the University of North Carolina wrote an obituary for progressivism and for attempts to chronicle a phantom. It was as if scholarly ghostbusters for decades had carefully planted their cameras in the countless rooms of the haunted mansion of American history, only to come up with nothing—or at least nothing clearly identifiable as progressivism once the videotapes had finally been scrutinized by more dispassionate, technically adept observers.

Despite the intentions of scholars to airbrush progressivism from American history, the progressive idea seemed real enough to those who first expounded and developed it. As a recent observer notes, "No one at the time thought Progressivism so various and contradictory as to be meaningless, much less nonexistent, though its adherents battled furiously over its political agenda." Furthermore, each of the three main presidential candidates in the election of 1912 claimed the label.[1]

The reality of American progressivism comes into view only in relation to what it rebelled against, which was nothing less than the American constitutional order and especially the political philosophy on which it rested. Without a sympathetic sense of that order and that philosophy—a sense largely absent from American historical writing over much of the last hundred years—one is hard pressed to see progressivism for what it was and remains, if one can see it at all. In this chapter, we will survey this older political philosophy and its rejection, as well as the work of the early progressive historians who self-consciously understood themselves to be part of the movement whose history they were writing. The point of this chapter and the next is simply to lay the groundwork for the historiography that follows—to give the reader a concise account of the depth and breadth of the progressive idea and therefore to bring into sharp relief the failure of so many twentieth-century historians to give a full account of it, much less to grapple with its implications.

THE OLD ORDER AND THE NEW

In 1863, Abraham Lincoln reminded his listeners that America "was conceived in liberty, and dedicated to the proposition that all men are created equal." Earlier, in his "Lyceum Address," Lincoln had proclaimed that all living Americans are the "legal inheritors" of the "fundamental blessings" bequeathed by the founders—whose principles, institutions, and very names we have a duty to preserve, not because they are old or merely useful, but because they are true. They are true because they are in conformity with the cause of civil liberty and of natural rights. Thus they must shine on, according to Lincoln in his "Temperance Address," in "naked deathless splendor."

The political rhetoric and actions of Lincoln remain among the greatest statements that there are such things as natural rights that do not change with time and that the American Constitution is dedicated to preserving them. For Lincoln, the task of great political actors, while responding to urgent necessities, was to look backward as much as—perhaps more than—forward. For him, the state was more formal than organic, history was not destined to unfold in a democratic direction, and democracy itself, because of its indissoluble link with the passions rather than reason, was always combustible. Moral and political regress were as likely as progress, and perhaps likelier. Furthermore, there were certain fixed principles beyond which progress was impossible. Sharing with Plato and Aristotle the belief that negative regime change is an ever-present possibility, Lincoln was profoundly wary of the very notion of progress. Evolution and growth were not part of his political vocabulary. Government's job, mainly and simply, was to protect the prepolitical rights given us by "the Laws of Nature and of Nature's God."

It is in Lincoln that we can see the culmination of the old understanding of the American constitutional order and the political principles it enshrined. Lincoln's articulation of the nature and purposes of the American regime was perhaps the high-water mark of the old constitutionalism—that is to say, preprogressive constitutionalism. American political thought subsequent to Lincoln has, for the most part, amounted effectively to an attack on Lincoln's conception of American constitutionalism and the philosophical proposition on which it rests. This transformation in political thought, commencing after Reconstruction and running through the Progressive Era of the early twentieth century, undergirds many forms of political thought and action in America to this day.

In the America of the late nineteenth century, the old understanding of the nature and permanent limits of politics was dead or dying. We can summarize this transformation as a move away from the earlier constitutionalism of fixed principles, cognizable words, modest executive and judicial branches, and the limits imposed by federalism, to an organic or progressive constitutionalism in which the very notion of fixity or constitutional principle is something that must be overcome. The transformation rested on the coalescing of two important strains of American political thought: social Darwinism and pragmatism—into a powerful intellectual force that decisively informed institutional and political attitudes and behaviors starting in the early twentieth century.

These closely allied doctrines equally adopted "the basic Darwinian concepts—organism, environment, adaptation," and spoke "the language of naturalism," as historian Richard Hofstadter observed in the middle part of the last century.[2] For social theorist and historian Morton G. White, the doctrines were part of the "revolt against formalism" that defined American social thought in the first half of the twentieth century. White claimed it was a revolt characterized by a good and humane temper, both rational and enlightened, and it was one to which, by midcentury, no successor had been found. It was a temper Americans needed to salvage in order to pave the way for "an adequate social philosophy."[3] At the political level, however, matters were not so simple, and the revolt cut far deeper than Hofstadter, White, or most other twentieth-century historians allowed. But before we can see the significance of what the historians chose to report—and ignore—we have to understand more fully the nature and depth of the progressive critique of America. It was a critique that was at once philosophical, political, and moral.

THE PROGRESSIVE CHALLENGE TO THE OLD ORDER

By the early part of the twentieth century, social Darwinism and pragmatism had merged into the political and intellectual movement known as progressivism, which amounts to the politicization of these doctrines. In the progressive dispensation, intelligent guidance and endless sociopolitical reform are always possible because no problem is understood to be an inherent facet of human nature. This understanding alone is sufficient to distinguish social Darwinism or pragmatism from the political science of *The Federalist*—and the founders' Constitution. Yet progressivism offered even more.

Many of the great progressive thinkers—such as Woodrow Wilson—were rather explicitly contemptuous of the American constitutional order, which they understood as embodying Newtonian, mechanical ideas and institutions that stand in the way of necessary and vital organic growth. Wilson himself advocated, at various times in his life, constitutional revolution, whether in the form of a modified parliamentary system or in a more diluted form of strong executive leadership of Congress. Wilson was the first president to develop an entirely new theory of the presidency—including the chief executive's role as leader of the whole of the

American political system—before taking office.[4] All this was in aid of providing centralized command and control mechanisms which, under the purportedly anachronistic eighteenth-century system of limited and diffuse powers, the system of the founders, could not coalesce and become the necessary vanguard for the direction of an ever-evolving Constitution that must change with History. "This 'new nation,' in Wilson's phrase, lacked a proper State to guide, but also to express, its spirit."[5]

Wilson's reform ideas were at best partially successful. Presidents, and Congresses, have proved not quite powerful enough—and, in the view of progressives, too beholden to populist sentiments that themselves reflect outmoded understandings of politics. In Wilson's memorable phrasing, "public criticism" can too easily become "a clumsy nuisance, a rustic handling delicate machinery."[6]

So as the twentieth century wore on, the judiciary was tasked with taking up the mantle of progressive reform. The shifting institutional allegiances of enlightened thinkers—away from faith in the ability of the executive and legislative branches to be in the vanguard of change and experimentation, and toward faith in the judiciary to do the same job only better—was a residue of the New Deal.

This progressive-historicist view of the Constitution that was central to the New Deal is that we have, of necessity, not simply an interpretable Constitution but one that must be interpreted in light of a particular understanding of the historically situated, contingent nature of the state, the individual, society, and constitutionalism itself. This understanding is in a considerable amount of tension with the earlier American constitutionalism of limited and dispersed powers serving the "Laws of Nature and of Nature's God." As Herman Belz notes, "The conception of the constitution as a formal legal instrument or code giving existence to government and prescribing and limiting the exercise of its powers, rather than as the basic structure of the polity, not consciously constructed but growing organically through history, was one of the distinctive achievements of the American Revolution, and oriented constitutional description and analysis in the early republic toward a legalistic approach."[7]

The modern historicist, as opposed to legalistic, approach has been embraced by elected officials, policy makers, and judicial appointees of different parties, Democrat and Republican, "liberal" and "conservative," since the New Deal. It now forms the unnoticed bedrock and background of American political consciousness. But it grew out of a particular time and place, out of a convergence of particular intellectual currents, especially social Darwinism and pragmatism. And these currents were often commingled, for a while at least, with healthy doses of German idealism.

SOCIAL DARWINISM AND THE POLITICS OF CHANGE

As Hofstadter observed in the 1950s, "In some respects the United States during the last three decades of the nineteenth and at the beginning of the twentieth century was *the* social Darwinian country."[8] According to the social Darwinists and those who would follow in their footsteps, a new social science was indebted to Darwin, whose organic, genetic, and experimental logic could be brought to bear on an array of human problems heretofore considered insoluble or at least perennial. Darwin came to be understood as a political philosopher and political scientist rejecting old modes and orders. No one more clearly explicated the nature of this new science than the philosopher par excellence of the Progressive Era, John Dewey. By the time he wrote his insightful essay "The Influence of Darwinism on Philosophy" in 1909, he was effectively summarizing the intellectual tenor of his times.[9] He was giving an account of the origins of an already regnant pattern of American social and political thought.[10] As Dewey averred, the publication of the *Origin of Species*—the first edition came out in 1859, and over the next dozen or so years five more editions were released—marked a revolution not only in the natural sciences but in the human sciences as well, which could continue in their old form only under the pressures of habit and prejudice. In Dewey's words, "The influence of Darwin upon philosophy resides in his having conquered the phenomena of life for the principle of transition, and thereby freed the new logic for application to mind and morals and life" (8–9). And he needn't have limited himself to Darwinism's influence on philosophy. Darwinian currents quickly engulfed American politics, jurisprudence, and religion — in no small part because *Origin* was so accessible, written as it was in crisp English prose. The same could not be said of social Darwinism's kissing cousin, German idealism.

Darwin, more than anyone else, allows us to move from old questions that have lost their vital appeal, to our interests and needs as we currently perceive them. We do not solve old questions, according to Dewey: "We get over them. Old questions are solved by disappearing, evaporating, while new questions corresponding to the changed attitude of endeavor and preference take their place. Doubtless the greatest dissolvent in contemporary thought of old questions, the greatest precipitant of new methods, new intentions, new problems, is the one effected by the scientific revolution that found its climax in the 'Origin of Species'" (19).

Dewey's Darwin lays hands "upon the sacred ark of permanency" that previously governed our understanding of human beings. Darwin challenges the most sacred cow in the Western tradition, one handed down from the Greeks: the belief in the "superiority of the fixed and final," including "the forms that had been regarded as types of fixity and perfection." The Greeks dilated on the characteristic traits of creatures, attaching the word *species* to them. As they manifested themselves in a completed form, or final cause, those species were seen to exhibit uniform structure and function, and to do so repeatedly, to the point where they were viewed as unchanging in their essential being. All changes were therefore held "within the metes and bounds of fixed truth" (6).[11] Nature as a whole came to be viewed as "a progressive realization of purpose" (6). The Greeks then propounded ethical systems based on purposiveness.

Henceforth, according to Dewey, "genetic" and "experimental" processes and methods can guide our inquiries into the human things. In fact, on Darwinian terms, change is of the essence of the good, which is identified with organic adaptation, survival, and growth. With maximally experimental social arrangements, change in useless directions can quickly be converted into change in useful directions. The goal of philosophy is no longer to search after absolute origins or ends but to study the processes that generate them (13). What is, *materially*, becomes more important than what ought to be, because only the former can be an object of the new empirical science.

In the absence of fixity, morals, politics, and religion are subject to radical renegotiation and transformation. Essences are no longer the highest object of inquiry, or indeed any object of inquiry. Rather, science concentrates on particular changes and their relationship to salutary purposes, which depend on "intelligent administration of existent conditions" (15). Philosophy is reduced from the "wholesale" to the retail level (16). Through the emphasis on administration of concrete conditions, Dewey claims that social responsibility is introduced into philosophy. Instead of concentrating on metaphysics, or even politics in the full Aristotelian sense, the learned are in effect freed to concentrate on policy—or, in Dewey's language, "the things that specifically concern us" (17).

Darwin broke down the last barriers between scientific method and reconstruction in philosophy and the human sciences more generally because of his overcoming of the view that human nature is different from physical nature and therefore requires a different approach. This is contrary to Aristotle's understanding that different methods of inquiry are required for different kinds of beings—for Aristotle, there is no one scientific or philosophic mode of inquiry that applies across the board. Philosophy—the human striving after wisdom or knowledge, including what we now term as science—seeks an understanding of the *highest* things through an examination of *all* things, according to methods appropriate to each.

At one level, Dewey seeks to reintegrate science and philosophy, which were torn asunder by modernity. But he seeks their reintegration on uniquely modern terms: he reduces philosophy to empirical naturalistic science—the *processes*, minus the ends or essences. He insists that philosophical method embrace a kind of obliviousness to the highest things.[12] For Dewey, we must reduce human sciences, including politics, to relatively simple principles, contrary to the Aristotelian view, which held that politics is much *harder* than physics precisely because one must take into account unpredictable behavior, and choice-worthy, purposive behavior toward *complex* ends, rather than more predictable motions and processes toward simple ends. The human sciences, which at the highest level involve statesmanship, are, for Aristotle, more complex than the physical and rely on great practical, experiential wisdom as well as theoretical wisdom.[13] By contrast, for Dewey and his generation, Darwinism seemed to break down the barriers between the human and the nonhuman.

It should be noted that Dewey's elucidation of the utility of Darwinism to social science and the new philosophy of man abstracts from the thought of a number of the major social Darwinist thinkers, including William Graham Sumner, Lester Frank Ward, and W. E. B. DuBois. Together with Dewey, these men provided many of the intellectual categories of their age. And these categories continue to exert a powerful control over political and jurisprudential discourse to the present day. Collectively, they point to a view of society as an organism that, constantly in the throes of change, must grow or die. For the social Darwinists, to look backward—whether to founding principles or to any other fixed standard of political right—inevitably reflects a death wish. While to some degree borrowing Hegelian historical categories, American social Darwinism shares no single rational end point with Hegelianism. Change in itself becomes the end in many instances and is always preferable to its opposite.

In general, we can say that American progressivism was decisively . . . American. While it is true that Hegelian/Marxist philosophical categories ran through and through various progressive understandings—especially those held by men educated in Germany or, like Wilson, influenced by German-educated scholars—social Darwinism and pragmatism were largely American inventions. And it is fair to say that it is their influence that endures in American political thought, rhetoric, and constitutional interpretation. By contrast, the era of high (by American standards) Hegelianism died with Woodrow Wilson in 1924.

In summary, we can say that on the foundation laid by the social Darwinists and those in allied philosophical movements, many of the most influential American political thinkers and actors came to share, from the early part of the twentieth century onward, six core, overlapping understandings of the nature of politics and constitutional government:

First, there are no fixed or eternal principles that govern, or ought to govern, the politics of a decent regime. Old political categories are just that, and Lincoln's understanding of the founders' Constitution, to the extent it is worthy of any consideration at all, is a quaint anachronism.

Second, the state and its component parts are organic, each involved in a struggle for never-ending growth. Contrary to the Platonic ideal of *stasis*, and contrary too to the Aristotelian notion of natural movement toward particular ends, the new organic view of politics suggests that movement itself is the key to survival and what can perhaps loosely be termed the political "good."

Third, democratic openness and experimentalism, in the economic but especially in the expressive realms, are necessary to ensure vigorous growth—they are the fertilizer of the organic state. Such experimentalism implies a particular sort of consequentialism or utilitarianism when judging institutions and laws.

Fourth, the state and its components exist only in History, understood as an inexorable process rather than a mere record of events.

Fifth, some individuals stand outside this process and must, like captains of a great ship, periodically adjust the position of this ship in the river of History—to ensure that it continues to move forward, rather than run aground and stagnate. Politics demands an elite class, possessed of intelligence as a method, or reason directed to instrumental matters rather than fixed truth. This elite class springs into action to clear blockages in the path of historical progress, whether in the form of anachronistic institutions, laws, or ideas. These blockages will form in the path of the ship of state when openness or experimentalism proves inadequate. The brain-trusters and jurists become the philosopher kings of the new age.

Sixth, and a direct corollary to the strong historicism just mentioned, moral-political truth or rightness of action is always relative to one's moment in History, or the exact place of the ship in the river of time.

PRAGMATISM AND PROGRAMMATIC LIBERALISM

While social Darwinism came to define so many of the terms of American intellectual discourse by the turn of the century, the distinction of being known as the quintessential American philosophy belongs to pragmatism. But the connections between pragmatism and social Darwinism are broad and deep, and indeed it is impossible to understand pragmatism without understanding its relationship to social Darwinism.

William James's early twentieth-century reflections in "What Pragmatism Means" elucidate these connections.[14] Even though James rejected the Hegelian/Darwinian historical categories that were never far from the thinking of his fellow pragmatist and younger contemporary John Dewey, the two shared a thoroughgoing skepticism of the tradition of absolutes, a faith in progress, and an emphasis on the process, rather than essence, of human life and activity. With Darwinism, pragmatism rejects what James calls the "rationalist temper" that is ossifying rather than instrumental, and it accepts the displacement of design from scientific consciousness.[15] According to James, all ideas must be interpreted in light of practical consequences, rather than purposes or metaphysical underpinnings. There are no important differences in abstract truth that do not express themselves in concrete fact—no principles, absolutes, or a prioris can govern the pragmatic method, which is an attitude of casting one's glance away from first things toward last things, emphasizing all the while the "fruits, consequences, facts" of life.[16]

It is arguably the very protean nature of pragmatism—its willingness to assimilate *anything*—combined with its democratic ethos and faith in scientific intelligence, that has made it an enduringly popular doctrine for Americans, politicians and jurists no less than private sector entrepreneurs. Indeed, in the pragmatic understanding, it seems any idea or pursuit can be justified if it serves this ethos and this faith. The fact that versions of pragmatism are today espoused in all branches of American government—though they were not at the time of the founding—is significant for the development of our constitutional understanding.

Many have noted the movement in twentieth-century political rhetoric away from discussions of the Constitution or constitutionalism and toward discussion of policy.[17] This move is partly a reflection of the hold of pragmatism on the American political imagination. Darwinism and pragmatism are oriented toward the empirical, secular, relativist, contingent, and democratic.[18] Although each of these orientations had existed in one form or another for a long time, and each might, in the wrong hands, be a dagger at the heart of constitutionally limited government, it took the progressive intellectuals of the late nineteenth and early twentieth centuries to weaponize them. Dewey in particular brought pragmatism and social Darwinism together as a compact set of political ideas, while showing their mutually reinforcing character. Dewey's pragmatism in some respects follows James's, but it remains reliant on the intellectual categories of "Left" social Darwinism. James's purer pragmatism all but did away with the categories of nature and natural law that were still central, albeit only in a materialist sense, to the Darwinists.

Dewey's pragmatism, by contrast, re-injects natural forces and a strong sense of historical unfolding with which any method must comport itself. It is in Dewey that we can see how social Darwinism and pragmatism together become an intellectual and political force to be reckoned with: a modern liberalism whose goal is to help History—with a capital H—along its democratic path, relying on the intellectual inputs of an elite vanguard that need not directly consult the people or ask for their consent.

While still a graduate student at Johns Hopkins, Dewey had fortuitously heard the Left social Darwinist Lester Frank Ward give his paper entitled "Mind as a Social Factor."[19] Dewey was deeply antagonistic—as was an increasing proportion of the intellectual class of his day—toward classical economics and philosophical individualism. Like Ward, Dewey conceived of human beings as having the capacity and responsibility for choices aimed at directing organic social and individual growth that is stifled by outmoded notions of competition and individual rights. Such choices and the policies that flow from them are always provisional responses to the flux of life, but their ultimate end is a more democratic society. Ideas grow and survive, not because they are true or transcend human experience, but because they respond to it most effectively. "Social action" is called for once we understand that scientific intelligence can in fact superintend the unfolding of History.[20]

In his short book *Liberalism and Social Action*, based on a series of lectures, Dewey offers a history of liberalism, an analysis of the crisis it faces, and its prospects for a renaissance that will cement it as the guiding force of social life. As reason becomes purely instrumental, no longer concerned with ultimate truths but only with "concrete situations," liberalism comes into its own.[21] This new liberalism is far from its outmoded earlier version because it makes itself relevant to the problems of social organization and integration of various historically situated forces. In fact, the lack of a historical sense on the part of earlier liberals blinded them, according to Dewey, to the fact that their own interpretations of liberty were historically conditioned, rather than immutable truths. Historical relativity finally frees liberalism to recognize that economic relations are the "dominantly controlling" forces of modernity and that they require social control for the benefit of the many (42). Free competition and removal of artificial barriers are no longer enough. Instead, the individual's powers must be "fed, sustained, and directed" (40) through cooperative control of the forces of production (59). Individuality itself does not simply exist but is attained through continuous growth (46).

In Dewey we see a dominant theme of American progressivism and the New Deal but also of twentieth-century liberalism more broadly: the belief that there is an intelligence, or "method of intelligence," that can be applied to solve social problems, which are themselves primarily economic in nature. It is this intelligence, which makes no pretense to knowledge except as a result of a pragmatic experimentation, that captures the spirit of democracy more than any philosophical or institutional analysis (80). While all social relations are historically situated and in flux, there is one constant: the application of intelligence as a progressive ideal and method. "For the only adjustment that does *not* have to be made *over again* . . . is that effected through intelligence as a method," Dewey says (55–56). It is the only simulacrum of God in an otherwise desiccated world of process, evolution, and growth.

Dewey rounds out his discussion by giving us insight into the nature of a "renascent liberalism" (61). Growth must be physical, intellectual, and moral, and all classes and individuals must benefit. This of course means a vast state mechanism must be constructed that is confidently dedicated to ensuring growth by means of progressive education, the welfare state, and redistribution of capital. The older political science of the founding era, including that of *The Federalist*, is easily swept aside by Dewey. While the exact contours of public power and policy are not necessarily the same for him as they are for progressive political actors such as Theodore Roosevelt, Woodrow Wilson, or FDR, all agree that there are no inherent limits on state power. Like the progressive presidents, Dewey's political theory is impatient with constitutional restraints and institutional forms. Separation of powers is a doctrine rooted in stasis and therefore political death. And to concern oneself with constitutional forms and formalities is to give to institutions an abiding character they do not deserve. In Dewey one finds scant— or no—concern for such forms and formalities. Such considerations are subsumed to the newly political categories of change and growth. Long before "the courage to change" became an effective presidential campaign slogan, Dewey helped ensure that "change" would have a central position in American political rhetoric.

While Dewey seems concerned about the exercise of *arbitrary* power, he evinces no concern for the aggregate power of the state. The cure for a powerful democratic state seems to be constant evolution in the direction of more democracy. The key to the perpetuation of our political institutions is far removed from either the constitutionalism of the founders or the statesmanship of Lincoln. Offering a powerful encapsulation of social Darwinism, progressivism, and contemporary liberalism, Dewey claims, "[Flux] has to be controlled that it will move to some end in accordance with the principles of life, since life itself is development. Liberalism is committed to an end that is at once enduring and flexible: the liberation of individuals so that realization of their capacities may be the law of their life" (61).

Human life therefore *is* nothing in particular beyond a continual unfolding and advancement, and liberalism is dedicated to its liberation through social policy. When the economic necessities are provided, individuals may pursue the higher life according to their spiritual needs, whatever they might be, and however they might change. And change they will. Dewey's vision of liberalism is ultimately of an individual free of the various constraints that were previously thought by so many to be necessitated by a sometimes dangerous, and eternal, nature. This vision of liberalism is a version of Marx's notion that truly free men may fish in the afternoon and criticize after dinner. Although Dewey sees the constraints of his day as largely economic in nature, he is pointing less to materialism than to growth toward freedom as the heart of modern liberalism.

THE SCHOLARSHIP OF THE NEW DISPENSATION

The new evolutionary and experimental approach to historical and social phenomena was shared across the progressive intellectual spectrum. It was quickly adopted and woven into the fabric of American self-understanding by the great progressive historians — prime among them Frederick Jackson Turner, Charles Austin Beard, and Vernon L. Parrington. Each of them did much to influence and define the intellectual temper of the very phenomena they chronicled.

Turner had taken his PhD at Johns Hopkins in 1891 under the German-educated Herbert Baxter Adams. Throughout his own influential academic career, Turner spread the then characteristically German "scientific" approach to historical analysis, which emphasized development and change over principle and continuity—and organic, evolutionary development over the determining power of regime politics. Turner's famous "frontier thesis," first advanced in 1893, was but one expression of his overall concern with the particulars of time, place, and material conditions, as opposed to institutions and political principles, and his concern with what would come to be known as social history.[22]

According to the frontier thesis, the essentially American traits—the most important of which were expressions of rugged individualism—were created and conditioned by the expansive frontier across which settlers on the new continent continually poured, and to which they gradually adapted. Social, economic, and political transformation followed the evolution of frontier ideas and the satisfaction of frontier needs in continually higher stages of development. A rejection of—even scorn for—old modes and orders accompanied each development.

For Turner, institutions and constitutional forms are constantly shaped and reshaped by "vital forces," rather than vice versa. As the geographic frontier closed, the new frontiers of the industrial age—opened by education and technical expertise—had to be crossed. Viewed broadly, and in terms congenial to the progressive imagination, Turner's work suggested that no historical truths might be found. Rather, historical interpretations (including his) were always contingent on what was important to the present age. The frontier metaphor carried through to the New Deal and beyond, with FDR among others emphasizing the need for Americans to keep crossing new frontiers to solve social, scientific, and economic problems.

Two decades after Turner first presented his frontier thesis, his younger contemporary Charles Austin Beard published his celebrated book *An Economic Interpretation of the Constitution of the United States*.[23] In it, he argued that the Constitution itself was the product of class interests and was designed to reflect and protect the interests of those who drafted it. The votes of members of the

Constitutional Convention were contingent upon their landed or business interests, and the Constitution served in effect to roll back the democratic gains of the Revolution. While his class conflict model was highly reductionist and deterministic, Beard maintained that it could offer a comprehensive explanation of the development of American political institutions and the broad currents of American history, from the revolutionary moment forward.[24] Beard adopted the progressive stance of scientific realism, seeking to find the roots of institutional development and change in the grubby economic motives of the founders. In Beard's socioeconomic account of the founding, interest group politics and financial incentives could better account for America than political theory and high statesmanship, which were at best epiphenomenal. With such a low starting point, there was nowhere to go but up. Progressives quickly seized on his arguments—and one might say his ethos—to advocate everything from urban reform to national economic planning.

But it was Vernon L. Parrington's sweeping three-volume study *Main Currents in American Thought* that came to be recognized by scholars in the second half of the twentieth century as the magnum opus of progressive history.[25] With the first two volumes appearing in 1927 and the third appearing posthumously three years later, Parrington had the benefit of hindsight on the Progressive Era itself. Drawing portraits of America's great figures with an unquestionably poetic pen, Parrington sought to demythologize. For him, ideas were mostly a function of deeper economic and social forces and could not be understood or appealed to in their own right. In fact, no appeal to philosophic principles—principles that transcend historical circumstance—could help Americans make sense of their regime. Political, social, and economic horizons were delimited by time and chance rather than by reflection and choice. The key for the historian was to uncover the "real" that underlay the high-toned rhetoric of America: to recognize that American history was little more than a long masquerade ball.

Parrington subjected to particular scrutiny the Gilded Age— the "great barbecue" to which not all were invited. But those who

were invited received political favors aplenty. The result, in Parrington's vision, was the end of the frontier and the beginning of a
standardized machine culture and mass psychology that would have
been unrecognizable to Jefferson, Jackson, or Lincoln. The struggle
for democracy and for a liberalism of and for the common man
was destined to be ongoing and always subject to the vicissitudes of
economic forces poised to sweep away incremental gains. Yet history marches forward, ever forward, on the wings of an idealism
neither despairing nor blind to social realities.

Once the relationship between economics and politics had been
clearly discerned by the sages of progressivism, progress beyond an
inherently undemocratic Constitution was possible. Through scientific realism, we could mold the existing environment into the
shape of a new Jeffersonianism. This vision informed the thinking
of not only the philosophers and historians of the progressive age
but a new generation of social scientists: economists, political scientists, and sociologists. For economists like John R. Commons,
E. R. A. Seligman, and Thorstein Veblen, economic reform and
social action seemed to be the point of the newly "scientific" economic analysis and study of economic history. In political science,
Arthur F. Bentley and J. Allen Smith laid the groundwork for a
discipline that was to be at once value-neutral, empirical, realistic,
and reformist. Meanwhile, in sociology, E. A. Ross committed his
scholarship to social action and social growth, even at the price of
eugenics.

For all these scholars, government seemed unlimited in principle—and it certainly could not be limited by a dusty eighteenth-
century Constitution based on a flawed theory of a "fixed" human
nature. Banished from the new scholarship was Madison's understanding of the perennial problem of faction in free society. It was to
be replaced by the progressive fixation on the problem of interests—
which must, and could, somehow be tamed and reconciled by intelligent political and economic superintendence.[26] Very different
from mere populism, progressivism was future oriented rather than
nostalgic, scientific rather than ad hoc, and deeply concerned with
the purported inadequacies of the Constitution itself, something

pointed to by Beard and Smith.[27] Experts, rather than "the people," would lead America to the brave new world, which was several steps removed from the old constitutional order for which the people still had too much reverence. In fact, "Nothing separated Progressivism from Populism, or for that matter from all previous American democracy, more sharply than this faith in the presumptive expertise, integrity, and political authority of the academic mandarins."[28] The progressive conception of leadership "began almost immediately to marginalize . . . [the] whole conception of fidelity to constitutional forms. . . . Into their place stepped the leader's sympathy with the people, his reliance on them as his indispensable connection to the Spirit of the Age."[29]

THE PERMANENCE OF THE PROGRESSIVE STATE

This new progressive constitutionalism that swept the intellectual classes almost immediately after the Age of Lincoln led, in turn, to the constitutionalism of the New Deal. Indeed, by 1932, things had changed politically in a manner that would have been unrecognizable not only to the founders but even to Calvin Coolidge, who, a mere six years before, had praised the deep "spiritual insight" that had led the founders to proclaim the true and "final" principles of the Declaration of Independence. By contrast, Franklin Delano Roosevelt in his Commonwealth Club address, delivered on the campaign trail, called on Americans to engage in a "a reappraisal of values." Not one to let a good crisis go to waste, Roosevelt reconceived the Democratic Party as the party of modern liberalism, while never eschewing the word *progressive*.[30] He told Americans that the "earlier concepts" of the American constitutional order had to be adapted—ever adapted—to suit the conditions of the day. In the course of doing so, he relied on a striking reconfiguration of the founders' constitutionalism. He told his audience that "the Declaration of Independence discusses the problem of Government in terms of a contract. . . . Under such a contract rulers were accorded power, and the people consented to that power on consideration that they be accorded certain rights. The task of statesmanship has always been the re-definition of these rights in terms of a changing and growing social order." In this formulation, rights themselves are decidedly political rather than prepolitical: they are the gifts of government, not God, and therefore are eminently . . . *negotiable*, according to the exigencies of the age—the changing and growing social order. He also told Americans that their "task now is not discovery . . . or . . . producing more goods. It is the soberer, less dramatic business of administering resources and plants already in hand . . . of adjusting production to consumption, of distributing wealth and products more equitably." He announced that the "day of enlightened administration has come," in aid of "a more permanently safe order of things."

And in words that sound remarkably contemporary, FDR went on to proclaim that

> every man has a right to life; and this means that he has also a right to make a comfortable living. . . . Every man has a right to his own property; which means a right to be assured, to the fullest extent attainable, in the safety of his savings. . . . If, in accord with this principle, we must restrict the operations of the speculator, the manipulator, even the financier, I believe we must accept the restriction as needful, not to hamper individualism but to protect it. . . . The responsible heads of finance and industry, instead of acting each for himself, must work together to achieve the common end. They must, where necessary, sacrifice this or that private advantage; and in reciprocal self-denial must seek a general advantage. It is here that formal government—political government, if you choose—comes in.

Extending progressive thought to its logical political conclusion, FDR insists that rights must be understood as collective rather than individual—a notion utterly alien to the founders. Social welfare, rather than liberty or justice, is the end of government.

A few years later, during his first term as president, Roosevelt gave an address to the Young Democratic Clubs of America, where he offered equally contemporary reflections on the political economy of the American republic. He claimed that this

> modern economic world of ours is governed by rules and regulations vastly more complex than those laid down in the days of Adam Smith or John Stuart Mill. . . . Our concepts of the regulation of money and credit and industrial competition, of the relation of employer and employee created for the old civilization, are being modified to save our economic structure from confusion, destruction and paralysis. . . . Government cooperation to help make the system of free enterprise work, to provide that minimum security without which the competitive system cannot function, to restrain the kind of individual action which in the past has been harmful to the community — that kind of governmental cooperation is entirely consistent with the best tradition of America.

Nowadays, when presidents echo such lines, they ring true — or truer — than they did in FDR's time. Federal government "cooperation" to restrain individual action seems consistent with the tradition that has existed in America at least since the New Deal. However, such a tradition did not consistently predate the New Deal: hence FDR's much greater boldness and inventiveness in speaking with a straight face about such a "tradition," compared to subsequent presidents' more platitudinous invocations of that tradition.

And in his famous "Four Freedoms" speech of 1941, FDR assured us that we were moving rapidly toward a future that promised to look like the one in Tolstoy's legend of the green stick, on which words were written that would bring universal happiness and ease. For FDR, the millenarian hopes of mankind could be attained with the denouement of History. Universal freedom of speech and worship, and freedom from want and fear, were, in FDR's words, "no vision of a distant millennium. It is a definite basis for a kind of world attainable in our own time and generation."

With the advent of the New Deal, the progressive intellectual synthesis began to bear real fruit that would ripen in five different but overlapping ways:

1. The substitution of purported governmental expertise for the invisible hand of the marketplace
2. The growth of federal projects, and more significantly, programs. Whereas TR's "New Nationalism" and Wilson's "New Freedom" were not essentially programmatic, the New Deal decidedly was
3. The administrative state in all its manifestations
4. The erosion of federalism and state sovereignty
5. The growth of national executive power, and, finally, judicial power at the expense of republican lawmaking

These developments came to the fore in the name of superintending social and economic forces and ensuring that the change enlightened thinkers hoped for—and believed that History required—was in fact the change that would come about. In all of that, the founders' Constitution could be relegated to an afterthought, to the extent it would be thought of at all. The country had moved far and fast (a mere three score and seven) from the natural rights republicanism of Abraham Lincoln to the visionary politics of FDR.

As a consequence of the progressive synthesis—the melding of social Darwinism and pragmatism—the age-old question of "what works" politically, or what should be given a chance to prove itself, was increasingly divorced from a sense of constitutional restraint, as it was informed by an organic conception of a state unlimited in principle, whose only end was growth and development under the aegis of experts committed to ever-shifting conceptions of "democracy." America was bequeathed a very new deal indeed.

TWO The Real Presence of Christ

As progressives mobilized intellectually and politically around the inadequacies and injustices of the founders' Constitution and the modern economic order, they did so with a fervor for, and faith in, the social sciences, which they thought could remedy injustice. The intensity of their fervor and faith can be traced to the influence of religion.

At the dawn of the Progressive Era, American Christianity still buttressed the constitutional order by linking human fallenness to the need for political moderation, individual rights and responsibilities, and limited government, which in turn reflected what historian Johnathan O'Neill refers to as "the long-established view that maintenance of a political regime involves ideas and sensibilities associated most readily in the Western tradition with religion."[1] Scholars have also shown that this view of religion and morality, pointing to fidelity to a Constitution embodying immutable truths, informed the thinking and constitutional interpretations of pre-progressive Supreme Court justices.[2] So for the progressives, regime change necessarily meant religious change, and vice versa. Christian progressives held that a new era had dawned, based on a new conception of religious obligation. A reconstituted worldly Christianity called for the expansion of the state in the name of moral and theological progress.

This reconstitution accounted for the zeal of many progressives, confident as they were not only of the direction of history but of their own rectitude. As Christian progressives directed their minds to what they saw as the new problems confronting America, they exhibited various degrees of millenarianism, which accounted for the power of their thought and its ability to capture the hearts and minds of a growing cadre of true believers. Throughout the Progressive Era, religious language was common at political gatherings at the local, state, and national levels, including even national conventions. But the fervor of Christian progressivism was unlike that of prior American religious awakenings. Instead of concentrating on individual moral failings and the especial need for individual reformation, Christian progressives concentrated their gaze almost exclusively on matters of social and economic justice.[3] By the first decades of the twentieth century, both Protestant social gospelers and Catholic reformers were vigorously attempting to shift the center of gravity of mainline Christianity toward applying what they claimed to be true Christian ethics in the here and now. It was clear that they understood their project to be both radical and political, and a very sharp break from the Christianity of their fathers. They "prided themselves on having freed Christianity from the shackles of the past—asceticism, dogmatism, and ceremonialism—and on having transformed it into a message befitting the future—brotherly love in a truly democratic society."[4] For these progressives, Christian churches placed too great an emphasis on the salvation of souls and the life of the world to come. The real presence of Christ came to take on whole new meaning.

Historians of progressivism have occasionally observed this phenomenon but have been divided on its origins and significance. Some have noted that, along with more purely economic notions like "antimonopolism" and "efficiency," the language of "social bonds" ran through most strains of progressivism and was juxtaposed against *homo economicus*, and especially the notion of man as the autonomous wielder of property rights.[5] This was the language "most tightly attached to the churches and the university lecture halls. Its roots stretched toward Germany and, still more importantly, toward the social gospel. When progressives talked of society and solidarity the rhetoric they drew upon was, above all, the rhetoric of socialized Protestantism."[6] Richard Hofstadter goes so far as to trace the roots of progressivism to Protestant guilt and the need to atone:

> In evangelical Protestantism the individual is expected to bear almost the full burden of the conversion and salvation of his soul. What his church provides him with, so far as this goal is concerned, is an instrument of exhortation. In Catholicism, by contrast, as in some other churches, the mediating role of the Church itself is of far greater importance and the responsibility of the individual is not keyed up to quite the same pitch. A working mechanism for the disposal and psychic mastery of guilt is available to Roman Catholics in the form of confession and penance. If this difference is translated into political terms, the moral animus of Progressivism can be better understood.[7]

But such psychological and theological reductionism cannot adequately account for what Protestant progressives claimed was the essentially social and political nature of the Christian enterprise, or for the strains of progressivism that animated leading Catholic thinkers—including, for example, Fr. John Ryan. In *A Living Wage*, Ryan, like his Protestant counterparts, sought human solidarity and heavenly justice through economic policy.[8] And in this quest, he sought to turn Catholicism—as the social gospel movement had turned Protestantism—against the American system of constitutionally limited government, private property, and capitalism, in the search for a more rational scientific state that would support nothing less than the Kingdom of God on earth.

The roots of the modern administrative state thus run deep in the soil of Christian progressivism. But one might go further and argue that religious reformers drew on notions of moral duty running from Aristotle through the medieval Catholic intellectual tradition, albeit often infused with an antiprudential Kantian moralism. And as a practical matter, Protestant progressives allied with both Catholics and Jews, whose understandings of law and morality antedated modernity. While rejecting the natural rights tradition of the American founders, religious progressives—unlike their secular confreres—at least formally asserted versions of a natural moral order, and even natural rights, which purported to be time-less.[9] They were not willing to reduce "nature" merely to physical or biological laws.

In short, one needs to take religion more seriously than many historians have been prepared to do. The centrality of serious and wide-ranging religious sentiment to progressive ideology should not be underestimated. Christian progressives joined forces with economists like Richard T. Ely and political scientists like Wood-row Wilson against what they claimed were the new economic and social realities that had been fully unleashed by the modern indus-trial age. They generally glossed over, and sometimes deliberately understated, the fundamentally anticonstitutional character of their arguments and the reforms to which they pointed. Secular and Christian progressive thinkers together pressed for an expansion of state power, and especially national state power, at the expense of constitutional limits. And in the case of the theologians, it was also at the expense of the sacred, even as the essential revelations and rituals of Christianity were of vital importance to them. Theirs was a natural law that did not limit government in principle but rather vouchsafed its protean expansion as it simultaneously reduced Chris-tian faith to a set of economic and political demands.

From a contemporary perspective, it seems ironic that social Christianity of both the Protestant and Catholic varieties helped lay the foundations for the modern administrative state, as nowa-days religious faith is frequently associated with political conser-vatism and opposition to progressive goals. But it was not always so. And to the extent that a secularized millenarianism is evident in the rhetoric of contemporary liberalism, it can trace its origins to the rather insistent piety of the early progressive religious thinkers.

RICHARD T. ELY ON THE BORDER LAND

In the thought of Richard Ely—progressive economist and ex-pounder of the social gospel at the end of the nineteenth century—

one can find a compact explication of the overlapping intuitions and arguments that the new breed of social scientists shared with Christian theologians. Ely was a professor of political economy first at Johns Hopkins—the institution that most channeled German Hegelian understandings onto American intellectual shores—and then at Wisconsin, which would become a bastion of progressive thinking throughout the twentieth century. Along with his intellectual antagonist William Graham Sumner, Ely was arguably the most influential economist of his age, laying the intellectual groundwork for, and anticipating the reforms of, both the Progressive Era and the New Deal.[10] But it was in the views of Ely the armchair theologian that the era—if not the century—that he foreshadowed was most comprehensively limned. Not only did he decisively influence both the social gospel of Walter Rauschenbusch and the Catholic social thought of Ryan, he also served as practical exemplar and theoretical explicator of the power of faith to move social science, as well as the obligation of faith-based social science to move the levers of power. As the twentieth century wore on, the faith that animated social science and justified governmental power shifted from its roots in Christianity to a fully secular millenarianism. But the leap was perhaps not that great once American elites had fully internalized the worldliness of Ely's version of Christianity—what he called Christianity's inherently "manward" side.

Ely concentrates on the ethical obligations of Christians in the industrial age. He makes clear that his writings deal with the "border land" where theology, ethics, and economics meet. He claims that only Christianity can provide the Archimedean point on which a proper political and economic ordering can rest.[11] Christianity—albeit with a new worldly emphasis—provides immeasurable advantage to those committed to social change. It is the most powerful social force known to man; it need only be harnessed and directed toward its proper end (20).

Ely recognizes that modern social science cannot provide answers to normative questions, and he claims it leaves "too much in the air" to give progressive thinkers a firm or confident motive for their reformist ambitions (15). Enter Christianity, which Ely claims is unique among religions in the nature and extent of the civic and secular obligations it imposes. Remarking on Matthew 22:34–40, where Christ reduces the law to loving the Lord and loving thy neighbor as thyself, Ely says no merely human teacher would place the duty to man on an equal plane with the duty to God. He claims that such a juxtaposition of duties exists in no other religious system.[12] Personal salvation is not the end of religion, though it is the beginning: only when the individual Christian is in right relation with God can he get on with the ultimate task of being in right relation to his fellows. Christianity alone provides a stable ground for humanitarianism (*Social Law*, 250).

The history of ethics, according to Ely, confirms the view that Christianity is unique: classical philosophers did not know of benevolence. Benevolence, for Christians, is a form of divine service, and piety is identified with pity.[13] Prior to the Reformation this fact was obscured, and the separation of "right life" from religion was a scandal to the church. "Some have gone so far as to make salvation consist in ceremonies, obedience to the dictates of priestcraft, in some sort of magic, or in a feeling of the emotional nature . . . even in intellectual assent to a species of metaphysics. What have all these things to do with conduct?" ("Church," 64). But Ely argues there is much work still to be done, and much that Protestants can learn from Catholics, for the Church of Rome provides the greatest opportunities for renunciation and sacrifice of the self, thus overcoming one of the errors of Protestantism (*Social Law*, 102).

Ely elsewhere notes with regret that modern hymns are almost exclusively oriented to individual rather than social salvation. So different are they from the Psalms, which tend to be "social and national" and don't "contain an *I* or *me* except when the words are put into the mouth of the Lord."[14] The hymns thereby deny or downplay our common humanity, united in God, of which we are reminded by the visible witness of Baptism (*Social Law*, 110). Likewise, the Lord's Supper, though it draws us to heaven, reminds us of the "manward" side of Christianity in the food and drink — bread and wine — that so sublimely express human fraternity (*Social Law*, 112–13). And yet even this sacrament is degraded by the use of individual communion cups. Ely asks, "Is our earthly life so precious that it must be so saved at all hazards?" (*Social Law*, 117).

The rituals and revelations of Christianity point to our unity and interdependence in the tribulations of this world. All of Christ's words must be read in light of the doctrine of "social solidarity," which makes us all responsible for the sin and suffering of our fellow men. An entire city is guilty of a murder that occurs in one of its slums (*Social Law*, 127–33). This is a truth confirmed by social science, which can show us the determining power of heredity and environment (*Social Law*, 135–36). We develop true "individuality" only by bringing ourselves into harmony "with the laws of social solidarity" (*Social Law*, 140).

Christ separated good men from bad on the basis of their respective performance of "social duties," which makes true Christianity unique in the extent to which man serves God by serving man. Other religions tell men they may serve God by injuring their fellows ("Social Aspects," 5). Christianity, by contrast, exalts man (*Social Law*, 30). Through his second great commandment to love your neighbor as yourself, Christ introduces sociology, or the science of society, to the world ("Social Aspects," 8). It is therefore incumbent on the church to embrace research in social science; her failure to do so has encouraged communism to become infidel, and socialism to become materialistic rather than spiritual ("Social Aspects," 10). Ely goes so far as to suggest that half the time spent in theological seminaries—which should be the intellectual centers of sociology—should be devoted to social science education ("Social Aspects," 17). While social science cannot point to ends, it can provide the means to achieve them. As political scientist Luigi Bradizza argues, Ely's social science "becomes practical Christianity," and its confident pursuit is an implicit rejection of the inherent imperfection of this world.[15] But the twentieth century would provide ample evidence that social science, on Ely's terms, could not long serve Christianity. The table would soon be turned, and Christianity swept from it.

For Ely, the welfare of man is the point of the "most fundamental laws" of the church, and social utility is their test (*Social*

Law, 45). There is, Ely insists, only one law taught by Christianity on its "manward" side: that is the law of love, which finds expression through social service and its test in social welfare. "Christianity and ethical science agree perfectly" (*Social Law*, 81). Ely tends to ignore biblical passages that cut against a worldly Christianity, or at least he glosses them to support it.[16]

In a statement that is characteristic of the progressive mind, Ely expresses profound confidence in the power and utility of expertise, so long as it is wielded by the right sort of people. "Philanthropy," he claims, "must be grounded in profound sociological studies. Otherwise, so complex is modern society that in our efforts to help man, we might only injure him. Not all are capable of research in sociology, but the church should call to her service in this field the greatest intellects of the age."[17] The purpose of the American Economic Association, of which Ely was a founder, is nothing less than "to study seriously the second of the two great commandments on which hang all the law and the prophets, in all its ramifications, and thus to bring science to the aid of Christianity" ("Social Aspects," 25). Ely goes on to express something approaching bewilderment that not one in ten Christians would contribute to the association (a fact of which he had personal knowledge as its secretary).

Because of the indifference of Christians to the second great commandment, wage workers feel increasingly alienated from the church, Ely notes with regret. This is destined to be, so as long as the church fails to understand its true mission and fails to see that "nearly everything in the words of Christ applies to the present life" ("Church," 55). Ely makes many arresting claims, but perhaps none more than this: "Christianity is primarily concerned with this world, and it is the mission of Christianity to bring to pass here a kingdom of righteousness and to rescue from the evil one and redeem all our social relations" ("Church," 53).

At the end of the nineteenth century, Ely was pointing to the similarities between early Christianity and socialism. Each appealed mainly to the masses, grew rapidly, and had an international, cosmopolitan character. Each demanded universal dominion, neither had been slowed by persecution, and each commanded of its adherents a religious devotion.[18] Ely claims that socialism is attractive not for its materialism but for its ethical ideals, which parallel Christianity's, and which inspire "fiery zeal" for labor and sacrifice on behalf of the masses. While the influence of the Bible on the average Christian has waned over the centuries, socialism retains a power to guide the lives of its followers similar to that of early Christianity. In fact, socialism is Christianity for the modern age insofar as it promises to realize the brotherhood of man by creating a social system dedicated to the maxim "One for all; all for one" (*Socialism*, 145–48). Christian socialism arises out of the belief that Christianity must be real and vital, applying in the marketplace as well as the pews, and recognizing the fact of social solidarity: that all interests are intertwined and that the prosperity of any one depends on the prosperity of all (*Socialism*, 89). In this context, it must be understood that private property is a useful and exclusive right but never an absolute one, for property has a "social side." Individual claims, essential to "thrift and industry," must nevertheless give way to social claims on the understanding that all property is a trust to be administered in accordance with the will of God (*Socialism*, 306–7). The land of Israel was not the property of the nation, let alone of the individual, but remained always God's property, assigned to the use of families "under national regulation" (*Social Law*, 67). It remains the task of just societies to find some political mechanism to make the Christian doctrine of stewardship real. In practice, this involves "public agencies" exercising regulatory power (*Socialism*, 309). In fact, passing "good laws" in the cities is as much a religious service as preaching the gospel ("Church," 73).

Despite Ely's assertion of a right to property, it seems clear that title to property creates a social obligation more than a right to exclusive use. Ethical behavior, from a Christian point of view, depends much on coercion, or at least law that attracts true believers as it cajoles those who need guidance. Drawing on the insights of classical political philosophers, Ely sees law as education as well as force, enlightening the conscience. The subjects that Ely imagines the law might effectively compass and the lessons he imagines it might teach are in no way limited to those matters over which

reasonable men might, after due deliberation, agree. Law is unmoored from any grounding in nature and is instead directed at
moving—more or less in unison—the consciences of men toward
particular policy conclusions concerning the regulation of the conditions of industrial life (*Social Law*, 182–83). Ely's view of property relations, like economics as a whole, is distinctly historicist: all
policies must change depending on time, place, and cultural particu-
larities. And government, animated by the essential moral teaching
of Christ, is the primary agent of change and direction.[19] The progressive state is valorized along with the things of the world.[20]
With the growth of such an understanding, the only things on
which the morally earnest man need concentrate are those things
that are within the purview and control of the state—those that
can be manipulated through the application of law and administrative expertise.

To further these ends, lawyers and judges must become social
scientists in order to do away with the messiness and corruption of
American republican institutions. Well before it became a commonplace observation, Ely recognized that judges in effect exercise
legislative authority, but he saw little problem with that so long as
it was well exercised. Judges should be selected with explicit reference to their social and economic philosophies and should decide
the limits of police powers in a scientifically (as opposed to constitutionally) appropriate manner.[21] Unlike Tocqueville, Ely was not willing to sacrifice some order, along with predictability and high conceptions of moral propriety, for the sake of self-government. Viewed
retrospectively, Ely's understandings of judicial competence and
power seem refreshingly honest, if not exactly true to the American
constitutional and common law tradition. But if they were articulated as clearly and honestly today, such understandings might at
least have the benefit of preventing judicial confirmation hearings
from turning into the comic kabuki dances they have become.

In language that sounds remarkably contemporary (save perhaps for its grounding in the duty of Christians), Ely stresses the
importance of fulsome tax payments, for he who neglects to pay
his "fair share" does so on the backs of the "weaker elements in

society, such as the widow or orphan" (*Social Law*, 175). A "great body" of "attractive laws" must be formulated by thinking Christians to keep the ways and means flowing toward the government without complaint, paving the way to a brighter future (*Social Law*, 189). Private philanthropy will not suffice for this comprehensive task, for the "great lines of social reform must be the concern of agencies which work steadily and persistently" (*Social Law*, 205). Property distribution must be manipulated by the state for the good of all, though not all property must be owned collectively. So Ely, while no friend of capitalism, was not strictly speaking a socialist, or at least not a very comprehensive one. Distribution and regulation of private property, however, must be undertaken fairly regularly, and without the counterproductive and artificial constraints that would be imposed by traditional constitutional understandings. A constitution grounded in natural rights and expressing limitations on government power is an obstacle to social Christianity. So what might be called the default position of the founders' regime—that a central purpose of government is to protect property as a natural right, rather than to distribute it as a contingent one—is flatly rejected by Ely.[22] And in this he seems to ignore the possibility of factional conflict over governmental distribution of spoils, not to mention the dangers posed by the imperial overreach of ambitious politicians and the consequent discrediting of government itself.[23]

A developed, innate moral sense of social obligation is something for which Ely hopes, but he believes it is not something on which he, or his fellow Christians, can rely. Freedom is not absence of restraint but is found in service to others and therefore eschews self-interest.[24] And this freedom needs external guidance. Our individuality must be directed toward others—rather routinely, one might say—in a manner that is contrary to both the letter and the spirit of the founders' Constitution. This is so because of Ely's implicit denial of Madison's observation that the causes of faction are sown irreducibly in the nature of man and that the simultaneous unleashing and checking of unequal interests, opinions, and passions can conduce to the public good far better than the high-minded moralism of the state. For Ely, rather, freedom comes in pursuing the common rather than individual good and in overcoming what Madison calls self-love, which routinely limits and degrades man's higher faculties.

Ely is confident that man shall know the truth and that the truth shall set him free to concentrate on social goals. In the words of Bradizza, "Ely does not fully acknowledge the daunting character of the Christ-like love and self-sacrifice he asks of men. Ironically, Ely diminishes the prospect of actual human excellence among the talented few, while he simultaneously asks for a level of blessedness men might never reach."[25]

THE STATE AND SOCIAL ETHICS

Ely claims his conception of the state is derivative from Christian social ethics, which rejects the "English" philosophy of individualism. A proper reading of the Old Testament confirms that the nation, in its law-making capacity, is nothing less than "God's instrument for the establishment of universal righteousness" (*Social Law*, 57). God consistently deals with nations and reaches individuals only through them (*Social Law*, 58). Ely insists that this "co-operative institution" of the state is merely the means to a proper political economy that is in harmony with religion.[26] In Ely's scheme, the practical morality man needs is the morality embodied in and expressed through the state. At best, this seems to result in muddying the relationship between ethical ends and means.

Ely understands the state to be an organic whole rather than a product of the conscious will of man. No social contract created it, nor can it be dissolved through the deliberate choices of men. Christ himself recognized the state's divine character, with powers ordained of God (*Social Law*, 165–67). Ely strikingly insists that yet another outcome of the Protestant Reformation was "the exaltation of the state," overcoming the Roman Church's insistence on the distinction between the cities of God and man (*Social Law*, 168). With poor laws and the curtailment of the functions of the ecclesiastical courts, Protestant nations achieved something analogous to the merger of English courts of common law and equity, each with their own bodies of substantive law, but overlapping and interconnecting at various points. In each case, the goal was unity under a higher, more complete understanding of justice. The clergy and the special prerogatives of the church gave way to universal law expressed through the sovereign unity of the state, which is a truer representation of God's will. Ely goes so far as to make the arresting claim that "religious laws," broadly understood, "are the only laws which ought to be enacted" (*Social Law*, 173).

So the state must be understood to be divine in idea and intention, if not in practice (*Social Law*, 171). To the extent that the political life of the United States is "unworthy," it is because "the nature of offenses against the purity of political life as offenses directly against God has not in recent years been adequately emphasized" (*Social Law*, 171). The state is not quite God—but woe unto that man through whom offense to the state cometh.

Although the New Testament replaces the nation with a "worldwide" society and extends our duties accordingly, the nation-state is still, practically speaking, the instantiation of universal Christian truth. As Moses said nothing of the future life, so Christ, even in his resurrection and immortality, reminded us that "eternal life begins in this world" (*Social Law*, 68). Even the injunction to render unto Caesar is nothing more than an admonishment to submit to sovereign authority, even if it is established by conquest (*Social Law*, 72). Christ condemns not the world but the worldliness of self-interest and seeks always national righteousness:

> We must have a feeling for our city, for our country, like that which is inculcated in the Bible. Our Jerusalem must be so dear to us that we can say with the psalmist, "If I forget thee, O Jerusalem, let my right hand forget her cunning.
>
> "If I do not remember thee, let my tongue cleave to the roof of my mouth; if I prefer not Jerusalem above my chief joy."
>
> When we reach this point, then we shall attain civic reform; then our commonwealths will be regenerated; then shall we see our nation a new nation, exalted by righteousness. (*Social Law*, 276)

Ely was routinely bold to pray, "Thy Kingdom come, thy will be
done on earth as it is in heaven."

WALTER RAUSCHENBUSCH AND THE SOCIAL GOSPEL

Walter Rauschenbusch was a Baptist minister, social worker, theology professor, armchair political theorist, and adviser to Theodore Roosevelt. By the early 1900s, he was bringing to theological
prominence and respectability—making gospel—what Ely, the
layman, had advocated in the economic and moral realms at the
end of the previous century. Rauschenbusch also drew inspiration
from liberal preachers such as Josiah Strong and Washington Gladden. Strong had emphasized the importance of missionary zeal in
fighting social sins and fostering moral regeneration, while Gladden had decried biblical literalism and infallibility as he advocated
workers' rights. Rauschenbusch, more than any other single figure
in America, spoke the words of blessing at the formal union of liberal economics and theology.

Rauschenbusch addressed himself largely to the Protestant
churches, which, in his estimation, were calcified in their attachment to moral, political, and economic individualism. Nothing
symbolized and reinforced this fact more than their concern for
personal salvation at the expense of broader economic and political
concerns. For Rauschenbusch, sins were social as well as individual,
and salvation was as much a matter of collective mobilization as the
proper ordering of the soul. Society as a whole must prepare itself
for the final judgment. And "Thy will be done in earth, as it is in
heaven" was the prayer to which Rauschenbusch, like Ely, repeatedly repaired, understanding it as a demand for social justice as well
as a call to social action. For Rauschenbusch, all Christian doctrines
and dogmas must be interpreted or modified so that they comport
well with the central truth of Christianity: the realization of the
Kingdom of God, as manifested in the coming Christ. As early as
1892, in a public address, he offered some "plain" and "candid"—
if sweeping—remarks on the matter: "My first proposition is that

the whole aim of Christ is embraced in the words 'the kingdom of God'; that this ideal is for this side of death, and not for the other side; that it is a social ideal and not an individualist ideal; and that in that ideal is embraced the sanctification of all life, the regeneration of humanity, and the reformation of all social institutions."[27] The church is the organ of this great project and must preach on such moral questions before they become political questions—that is, before they have become partisan, for the ideas that underlie them transcend partisanship and should be a source of incontrovertible union rather than wrangling. The church must see itself as the vehicle for social solidarity rather than individual salvation.

Rauschenbusch insists that there can be no happy escape to the afterlife but through the purification of the present through the realization of God's will on earth. Otherworldliness must take a back seat to immanentizing the eschaton, to borrow the formulation of political theorist Eric Voegelin. And a true Christian ethic calls for social, if not socialist, transformation. Rauschenbusch and his students from Rochester Theological Seminary went forth to proclaim the necessity for the salvation of society first and foremost, and with and through it the regeneration and rehabilitation of the individual Christian.

Which was the chicken and which was the egg, was not always clear, nor was it as important to Rauschenbusch as the proclamation of his central message, which prioritized the social: society must be born again, washed clean, so that all might experience the Kingdom, and this in turn required that individuals be "thoroughgoing Christians," which is to say committed to social transformation.

Such transformation was possible given Rauschenbusch's belief in the inevitability of evolutionary progress, a belief he shared with most progressives, secular and religious. The question was how to nudge the human conscience, and with it, History, in the right direction. Darwinian scientific precepts formed the inchoate, optimistic backdrop against which Rauschenbusch's thinking developed. Unlike more conservative evangelical Protestants, Rauschenbusch and the social gospelers took a sanguine view of evolution as a scientific doctrine because it could provide an account and indeed an argument for the movement of Christian churches away from a more primitive, individualist past. The "social Darwinism" of the social gospel shared the liberal, intellectual, reformist bent of Lester Frank Ward. In its confidence that evolutionary change could be seen as the working out of God's plan for the social order, it also showed the influence of Hegelianism.[28]

Rauschenbusch saw the Protestant churches' earlier evangelism at home and abroad as pious and patriotic, as it had been from the beginnings of the American experience, but without sufficient concern for forward motion in the sense of establishing the rule of political and economic righteousness—and with it the kingdom of God in the here and now. The perfect had become the enemy of the good. The highest things had to be renamed—and human eros redirected—in order to support proper action. Moral failings had to be redefined as failures to engage in socially conscious political action, as if sin itself could be washed away by the pure waters of politics. Why wait for kingdom come, when the kingdom can be realized now?

BOUNDLESS HORIZONS

Rauschenbusch published his influential *Christianity and the Social Crisis* in 1907, close to the pinnacle of progressive political aspirations. In that year, President Roosevelt was becoming known as a "trustbuster," new consumer protection laws were coming into effect, child labor and welfare were national concerns, corporations were being held to account in both courtrooms and the media, Eugene Debs was rising to prominence as a political candidate and critic of existing institutions, and a concern with civic vice animated both religious leaders and the public conscience.

Christianity and the Social Crisis was the first in a series of books that attempted to bring American religion down from clouds, purporting to convert theology into a comprehensive political and social ethic, one that would arouse the conscience so that Christians would go forth and solve human needs in this world rather than concentrate first and foremost on the next. In it, Rauschenbusch insists that religion is neither "ritual and sacramental" nor "personal."[29] Ethical conduct must replace sacramental obsession. Social reform, through labor and governmental action, takes precedence over individual reform, though there is a symbiotic relationship between the two. In a revamped social order, men and women could devote their time and strength not to eking out a subsistence living or — the only other alternative under existing arrangements — piling up excess wealth but to amassing leisure whereby they might engage the "higher pursuits of the mind and the soul" to live the life that Jesus desired (341).

The "Kingdom of God," the center of Christ's teaching, must be interpreted to mean the coming to be of God's justice in the nation-state rather than merely "internal blessedness." This meaning was lost "as Christianity passed from the Jewish people and found its spiritual home within the great Graeco-Roman world." The Greek world held no national aspirations or religious hope like that of the Jews; the only trace of the phrase's original meaning persists "in the millennial hope and in the organic conception of the Church" (55). Protestantism has long since abandoned withdrawal and monasticism and has chosen to live in this world and indeed to change it. As the Reformation freed the church from the clutches of the state, so it freed its inner democratic logic to reform the state. Morality, rather than ritual, can finally speed the pace of evolution toward perfectibility of human nature (421–22). In this neo-Hegelian account there is no room for stasis and no possibility of satisfaction, for perfection's demands depend on time, place, and economic circumstance. "The Kingdom of God is always but coming" (421).

A proper theology would recognize that it is the social order, not the individual, that must be saved.[30] "The Church runs to tradition and dogma; the Kingdom of God rejoices in forecasts and boundless horizons" (*Theology*, 115). Indeed, no Christian can be a conservative, for "If a man wants to be a Christian, he must stand over against things as they are and condemn them in the name of that higher conception of life which Jesus revealed. If a man is satisfied with things as they are, he belongs to the other side"

(*Christianity*, 90). Jesus was not only the first socialist but the first humanist, the first "real man" (*Christianity*, 91). Rauschenbusch is emphatic in insisting on the choice that must be made in the modern, postascetic age: the church must condemn the world as it is or conform to it (*Christianity*, 342). He does not entertain the possibility that this is a false choice.

Strikingly, Rauschenbusch goes on to posit other related, highly reductionist, choices: the embrace of social justice is the only way for contemporary Christians to "gain the crown of martyrdom," and the only rival to God is Mammon (*Christianity*, 418). The believers' "everlasting pilgrimage . . . is better than contented stability in the tents of wickedness" (*Christianity*, 421). He puts to rest any doubts about the radical nature of the church's task: "Primitive society was communistic. The most valuable institutions in modern life—the family, the school, and church—are communistic. The state, too, is essentially communistic and is becoming increasingly so. During the larger part of its history the Christian Church regarded communism as the only ideal life. Christianity certainly has more affinity for co-operative and fraternal institutions than for competitive disunion. It should therefore strengthen the existing communistic institutions and aid the evolution of society from the present temporary stage of individualism to a higher form of communism" (*Christianity*, 414). Rauschenbusch then takes Ely one step further by averring explicitly that a working relationship between the church and labor is needed to ensure that workers own the means of production.

What Rauschenbusch repeatedly refers to as the "social crisis" is bound up with the clash between "concentrated wealth" and the "common people" (*Christianity*, xi). This theme has periodically recurred in American politics and has found new voices more than a century after Rauschenbusch wrote. But for Rauschenbusch, a religious fervor is necessary to ensure that History moves in the right direction. "Unless the economic and intellectual factors are strongly reinforced by religious enthusiasm, the whole social movement may prove abortive, and the New Era may die before it comes to birth" (*Christianity*, xii). The prophets of the Bible were public men with the conviction that God demands righteousness in public affairs (*Christianity*, 8–9). "The prophets," according to Rauschenbusch, demanded social morality rather the private morality of "detached pious souls" (*Christianity*, 11). Alas, social morality was enforced in Old Testament times only by the lowly and debased priests and scribes, who did not share the spirit of the prophets.

MANLINESS AND FAITH

Social reform therefore becomes in the first instance a matter of faith, for only faith has the necessary power to move hearts and minds toward reconfiguring the social order. It is then made real through political machinery. And in this observation, Rauschenbusch himself appears a prophet for the twentieth and twenty-first centuries. Nowadays, the faith of public individuals has lost its specifically Christian grounding—something arguably accelerated by the very worldly outlook of Christian progressives. As the Kingdom of God was steadily dropped from consideration by the heirs to the early progressives, America was left only with millenarian political rhetoric and public policy professionalism directed at seemingly endless reformation and improvement through the mechanisms of the administrative state.

Rauschenbusch's critique of mainstream American religious sensibilities, and of the Protestant churches in particular, echoes Theodore Roosevelt's critique of the modern polity: each was in danger of effeminacy. Rauschenbusch remarks that while women face inward and nurture individuals in the home, men should face outward and deal with public questions. In a remarkable presaging of the contours of present-day social activism, including its distinctly self-righteous edge, Rauschenbusch carves out an elevated role for the unmarried and childless: they have a special opportunity, and therefore duty, to devote their time and resources to sacrificial service to the Kingdom of God (*Christianity*, 420). They should view "the whole coming generation" as their own. As he writes elsewhere, they may even postpone marriage to serve the common good.[31] And college-educated men and women have a unique obligation. To realize "the social principles of Jesus," they must do what they can to ensure the fusion of modern social science with the moral teachings of Christianity.[32] "For the first time in history," Rauschenbusch writes, "the spirit of Christianity has had a chance to form a working partnership with real social and psychological science" (*Theology*, 107). It becomes unclear just who the senior partner is, but Rauschenbusch offers a clue with his claim that the partnership puts the "democratic spirit" in control of the church itself (*Theology*, 107).

The very nature of "individualistic religion" has "helped to feminize our churches" and make them less political than they should be (*Christianity*, 367). Ministers are to be useful when it comes to solving the "social problems" of the "present crisis." In fact, the church has much for which to atone, for it "has riveted the attention of the people on other aspects of life hitherto and thereby has diverted their attention from the social problems. It ought to make up for this" (*Christianity*, 368). One of the minister's most important jobs is to fill the workers with "moral enthusiasm" so that they do not see the economic struggle as merely a "stomach question."

Rauschenbusch does not pause to wonder just what is left of the realm of spirit if the "spiritual force of Christianity should be turned against the materialism and mammonism of our industrial and social order" (*Christianity*, 369). Yet in his more restrained moments he does ask a question that was as genuinely pressing for Christians then as it is now: "How ought industry to be organized in order to protect and foster the family, the human individual, and the Christian life?" In the twenty-first century, the liberal wings of mainline Christian churches seem to have discovered this question anew.

His answer is more explicit and radical than many Christians would accept: "socialistic political economy," which, he claims, puts man before wealth and is therefore more genuinely Christian than "the orthodox science has been." An "anthropocentric" political economy is a "Christocentric" theology, and vice versa (*Christianity*, 371–72). According to Rauschenbusch, religion must remind people of the primacy of soul over body. Yet in the amount of time it must spend dealing with the concerns of the body, one cannot help but wonder how much is left over for the soul.

PROPHECY AND POLITICS

By the end of the first decade of the last century, social gospel had come into its own. In 1908, the Federal Council of Churches — precursor to the National Council of Churches — was formed. Along with the governing bodies of some existing denominations, it started to take cognizance of, and advocate social action on, seemingly secular matters, including especially those surrounding organized labor. By this time, Rauschenbusch was a widely quoted and widely sought-after lecturer in churches, seminaries, and Christian service and labor organizations. In 1910, he published *Prayers of the Social Awakening*, as a "religious expression" of the new social consciousness.[33] His introduction to that volume, entitled "The Social Meaning of the Lord's Prayer," offers a pithy summary of his understanding of the relationship of the personal to the political in religious matters. The opening of the prayer, according to Rauschenbusch, evinces the yearning of Jesus for the reign of God on earth and the ultimate perfection of human life, based on a "divine revolution."[34] Of the subsequent petitions in the Lord's Prayer, the prayer for daily bread establishes the primacy of the economic basis of life and the means to sustenance that responds to needs rather than the desire for excess.[35] Economics need not be the dismal science after all but the language of earthly solidarity and salvation. To be "religiously right," we must be "socially right." Piety toward God must coexist with mercy toward men, expressed politically and materially.

A few years after the publication of *Prayers*, Rauschenbusch delivered "A Social Litany" of prayers at a national Episcopal convention, beseeching God to deliver the nation from a variety of worldly impositions, including "From the fear of unemployment and the evils of overwork, from the curse of child labor and the ill-paid toil of women," and "From the luxury that enervates."[36]

Rauschenbusch's *Christianizing the Social Order* was published in 1912, the same year that Roosevelt bolted from the Republican Party after the tumultuous Republican convention to form the Progressive Party, thus ensuring the election of Woodrow Wilson. Rauschenbusch had read the speeches of both Roosevelt and the populist Democrat William Jennings Bryan, who by 1912 had become the most popular speaker on the evangelical, progressive Chautauqua educational circuit. The symbiotic relationship of the social to the personal ran through and through Rauschenbusch's book, and the paramount goal was always social change through economic reformation. A new economic system would revamp the conscience, but a revamped conscience and strengthened faith were necessary for economic reform to take place (459–60). The idea of faith in or knowledge of God for its own sake is never present in the work. The social order needs to be Christianized, but mere Christianity is never the end game. "Seek ye first the Kingdom of God . . . and the salvation of your souls will be added to you. . . . Our religious individuality must get its interpretation from the supreme fact of social solidarity" (465).

According to *Christianizing the Social Order*, a man needs a great cause to which he can surrender in order to live a life doing the will of God. Fortunately, we can—with the advent of social science (and only with its advent)—effectively confront the greatest task ever confronted in the history of Western civilization. "We now have such scientific knowledge of social laws and forces, of economics, of history that we can intelligently mold and guide the evolution in which we take part. . . . Former generations were swept along more or less blindly toward a hidden destiny; we have reached the point where we can make history make us." The only thing we need provide is will, to "marshal the moral forces capable of breaking what must be broken. . . . Our 'moral efficiency' depends on our religious faith" (41).

Faith comes to sight as that which serves "efficiency" of social action. And once this is granted, it is but a small step to a comprehensively de-Christianized willfulness, which takes the form of unshakable belief in the efficacy and self-sufficiency of human beings as they confront and remake the human prospect through political action. Rauschenbusch is explicit: the new task of Christianity is not individual salvation but the alteration of antiquated and immoral economic systems, laws, and customs from an "evil" and "despotic" past (41). Christianity must concentrate its gaze not on the next world but on this, making the earth "clean and sweet and habitable" (42). The setting of this task is dependent on the great progressive confidence that it can be performed well by mere mortals, albeit mortals possessed of the new scientific methodologies.

Jesus himself was misinterpreted for too long when he said his kingdom was not of this world. We must have love, but it is "socialized" love that is called for in the present age (44). Such love cannot rely on merely imploring the consciences of individual businessmen to spend their money faithfully, though a truly Christian business-man would see that his obligation is not to own resources but to be a steward of them and that his fortune consists of unearned and unjustly obtained money (469). Any movement of conscience must be backed up by force of law expressing "modern democratic feeling" and "economic knowledge," which is precisely where the Golden Rule proves woefully inadequate (45). Living Christ-like as individuals cannot transform society, for it creates no doctrine, or what Rauschenbusch tellingly calls "collective enthusiasms" (46).

The book makes clear Rauschenbusch's hostility to the natural rights foundations of the American republic in his far-reaching claim that all the evils of civilization are traceable to private property, which leads, ipso facto, to exploitation (392). He claims that any hostility between the church and socialism is epiphenomenal and that American socialist leaders have committed an enormous tactical mistake in portraying socialism as antagonistic to Christianity. They should instead take advantage of the moral fervor that religion makes possible for their purposes, recognizing "what an equipment for propaganda lies stored in the Christian churches" (399). Echoing Tocqueville, Rauschenbusch reminds his readers that Christianity is a very different institution in America than in Europe, where it has a history of being bound up with state power and therefore in constant tension with democracy. Here, in its

Roman or Protestant varieties, it exists, as it were, in its natural environment, which puts it in a position to be the vehicle par excellence for spreading democracy and supporting the interests of the
common man. Unlike Tocqueville, however, Rauschenbusch equates
democratic change with socialism. In fact, socialism and Christianity
can be seen as two religions (or two sides of the same religion) with
one objective: "The Socialists are not nearly as unbelieving as some
of them try to make us believe. Their theories may make everything
turn on 'economic class interests'; they may scoff at moral ideals, and
insist that it is all a 'stomach question'; but they appeal to men to
act contrary to their economic interests on behalf of humanity, and
they themselves labor with a moral enthusiasm and a power of self-
sacrifice which look most suspiciously like religion" (401). Indeed,
the sacrificing atheist is nearer to God than the self-interested church
member (401). The goal is to make the potential menaces of socialism manageable and the blessings of socialism great. Such would be
merely the latest blow against the Roman Catholic Church's arro-
gance, following naturally on the Protestant Reformation—each directed at the realization of God's ends (403–4).

   In his *Theology for the Social Gospel,* published at the end of
World War I, Rauschenbusch notes that social gospel continues
the work of the Reformation in its intelligent hatred of oppression.
He tells the story of a God who is immanent in humanity—in the
very dirt of human existence, to borrow a phrase from William
James—rather than a being on high (121–22). Rauschenbusch
insists elsewhere that the central problem of the age is that love has
failed between classes and that workers feel no identity of interests
with employers and possessors.[37] "Rich men are almost ruled out
of the Kingdom," and rich churches are not spiritual churches.[38]
Social solidarity—of and for the lower classes—becomes a simulacrum of God's all-encompassing love.

   By 1917, Rauschenbusch was not merely writing theology. He
was celebrating the dawn of a new world. He insisted, with considerable justification, that "social gospel has become orthodox," everywhere except in the most backward communities (*Theology*, 105).
Indeed, most mainline churches were by then offering open sup-

port for a variety of social causes and slogans, including, most comprehensively, "making the world safe for democracy." At the very least, various strains of social gospel rhetoric were commonplace by America's entry into World War I, even when no dogmatic changes could be identified. Modern theological liberalism, at least in mainline churches, had been born.

Again identifying trends that would become more and more pronounced throughout the twentieth century, Rauschenbusch insists on the need for churches to "hold audiences" by stressing the social relevance of their teachings, for the college educated in particular will be "listless" in the face of religion without social content (*Theology*, 106). War, and particularly the Great War, dwarfs all other issues and has a way of concentrating minds on "disarmament and permanent peace" (106).

Far from advocating separation of church and state, Rauschenbusch suggests their merger, albeit for largely secular purposes: "The two must somehow interpenetrate. . . . The state must be built on righteousness. Its very purpose is to exercise righteousness among men, and its ultimate goal is to be merged in the Kingdom of God which is to come on earth. . . . This is the ideal of the state."[39]

It is worth noting again that such a view of the power and reach of the state could not be further from the view of America's founders, who were willing to accept the political consequences of original sin. Indeed, they incorporated responses to it into the Constitution, through such devices as separation of powers and the decentralized structure of a large republic. As James Madison asks in *The Federalist* 51, "What is government itself, but the greatest of all reflections on human nature?"

Rauschenbusch does not ignore the question but makes radical arguments about human nature that the sober Enlightenment rationalism of the founders, or the traditional biblical accounts of original sin, do not, and cannot, support. As Madison went on to argue, "If men were angels, no government would be necessary. If angels were to govern men, neither external nor internal controls on government would be necessary. In framing a government which is to be administered by men over men, the great difficulty lies in this:

you must first enable the government to control the governed; and in the next place oblige it to control itself." Controls on government are unnecessary only if that fixed conception of human nature—that men are but men, as they were in the beginning—is rejected. And for this rejection to appear plausible, both reason and revelation must be dramatically reconfigured to allow for the second coming of man.

FATHER JOHN RYAN AND A ROMAN CATHOLIC POLITICAL ECONOMY

Like his friend Rauschenbusch, Father John Ryan offered a theology of political economy. Also like his Protestant counterpart, he was an influential scholar, professor, and activist with an overriding interest in matters of economic justice, resting on a belief that religion, ethics, and economics could not be divorced. He taught first at St. Paul Seminary, and then at the Catholic University of America. Unlike Rauschenbusch, he attempted to ground or at least embed his arguments in a larger natural law theory. And he rejected, at least formally, the idea that the church's primary objective should be anything other than the salvation of souls. Also unlike Rauschenbusch, he lived through and directly influenced the New Deal period, so he was able to see his moral theology come to fruition in very concrete ways. New Deal initiatives like minimum wage laws, social security, and labor legislation are all enactments of various elements of Ryan's plan. And Ryan was a political actor himself when circumstances called for it. In several states, he testified in favor of the passage of minimum wage laws. The Progressive Party platform of 1912 incorporated his "living wage" language. And by the 1930s, he became a vehement supporter of the New Deal, on the basis that it found a Christian middle ground: "neither individualism nor socialism."[40]

Ryan's most influential contribution to the intellectual ferment of his times was his argument in favor of a living wage. But it would be a mistake to construe his efforts narrowly. His case for the living wage amounts to a social welfare version of the natural law, as well as an argument against what he sees as the rampant individualism of the American polity. His doctoral dissertation was first published in 1906 as the book *A Living Wage* and was widely reviewed in America and abroad. The book was introduced by none other than Richard Ely, whom Ryan had first read as a young seminarian and to whom he sent a prepublication copy.[41]

In the book, Ryan shared Rauschenbusch's confidence that a new day was finally dawning in Americans' understanding of the ends, and injustices, of their economic system. In his 1919 preface to a revised edition, he asserted what he claimed was almost "universally accepted" by "all intelligent and disinterested persons": a laborer has a distinct moral claim to a decent living wage.[42] And Ely, in his introduction, suggested the main purpose of the book was to stimulate the conscience of Christians as to their palpable duties, including supporting a Christian doctrine of wages. But the book's subject matter was yet broader than that, according to Ely. It was in fact "the first attempt in the English language to elaborate what may be called a Roman Catholic system of political economy."[43]

In the words of Ryan's mid-twentieth-century biographer Francis L. Broderick, "More than any other single figure in the Catholic Church in America, he is responsible for the progressive stands adopted by official Catholic spokesmen in our time. Some of these men are former students of his; many were trained in an atmosphere he helped create."[44] When, in 1919, the American bishops issued their "Program for Social Reconstruction," Ryan in effect enjoyed the support of the American Catholic hierarchy for the reforms he had long championed. The document, for Ryan's purposes, "created another standard to set beside *Rerum novarum* when he appealed to the conscience of Catholic America."[45] The effect was to shift the burden of proof on economic matters—more or less permanently, as it turns out—from progressives to conservatives within the church. The American church, while making room for conservative clergy and laymen, has itself spoken the language of economic progressivism, in its official voice, since Ryan's time.[46]

Insisting on his Christian bona fides, and, beyond that, his religious orthodoxy and commitment to the Holy See, Ryan is at pains in *A Living Wage* to state the influence of Pope Leo XIII's 1891 encyclical *Rerum Novarum* as the document that "converted the Living Wage doctrine from an implicit into an explicit principle of Catholic ethics."[47] Opposing socialism and materialism as well as exploitation of labor, Leo argued for the dignity of workers and wage justice, as well as for a wide sphere of state action—things that accorded with Ryan's views even before he read the encyclical.[48] Ryan notes that Protestantism, in its individuality, has less pronounced and uniform teachings on these matters, but it is nonetheless true that Protestant denominations have never signaled approval of "unlimited bargaining" (50). And he also notes that the Federal Council of Churches had just made a formal demand for a living wage enforced by the state (49–50). Paradoxically, despite his orthodoxy, Ryan, like most progressives, could never escape his fascination with modern science and its tendency to direct human attention away from eternity and toward the here and now.[49]

Ryan wastes no time in arguing that his notion of a living wage is derivative from natural law. In this sense, his work is less dependent on a parsing of the Gospels than is Rauschenbusch's. Ryan asserts that the labor question cannot be solved without religion, but "Neither will religion suffice in the absence of a detailed application of moral principles to the relations of employer and employee" (180). With Rauschenbusch, Ryan recognizes that men might be religious in a conventional sense but blind to moral wrongs because of their false commitment to an individualist, competitive ethical code. In fine, business ethics instead of Christian ethics govern their lives. Clergymen must therefore give more attention to preaching a living wage and less to "other duties that are no more important." Moral and religious suasion—including using one's ecclesiastical position to "deprive recalcitrant employers of the church privileges that are ordinarily denied to persistently disobedient members"— are important, but they are not all (181). For Ryan, philosophical reason looms much larger as a source of influence on Christians than it does for Rauschenbusch.

The laborer, Ryan emphasizes, has an individual natural right to a living wage that belongs to him personally, not simply to him as a member of society. It is something he possesses at birth and is in no way a creature of the positive law. The "absoluteness" of the right is meant in the sense it does not depend on the will of another, not that it cannot be subjected to reasonable limits. Or, as Ryan puts it, it is absolute in existence, though not in extent. Men's natural rights are equal in number and embrace a minimum of goods, which minimum is determined by the reasonable needs of human "personality." The catalog of natural rights to which Ryan refers includes not only life, liberty, and property but livelihood, marriage, religious worship, and education (3–7).

But rights are not ends in themselves; they are means to the end of the "welfare of the person," which is an inviolable fact of the natural order. Happiness and dignity are alternative expressions of this welfare. And in turn it is the "development" of "personality" that allows for welfare to be achieved. As we are morally obliged to order our lives to pursue human welfare, so we have a natural obligation not to interfere with the natural rights of others (8–13). We know what conduces to human welfare by knowing first what constitutes man's nature—"his essential constitution, relations and end" (22). Ryan claims that academic opposition to natural rights doctrine is a result of the doctrine's "exaggerated and anti-social form"—its Rousseauist form—which can be found among both European and American theorists (though Ryan's tendency is to conflate the two). According to this form of natural rights theory, *nature* refers not to what is permanent in man but to what can be found in his primitive state. "State of nature" theory for Ryan seems always to point to a denial of nature that allows the strong to oppress the weak through legal mechanisms (23–24). He seems therefore not to allow that a robust natural rights theory—one that is self-limiting and oriented toward protecting the rights of the minority from the tyranny of the majority—is embedded in a social contractarian view of government.

He claims his doctrine is the antidote to the dangers of anti-social natural rights theories, a middle ground between revolutionary, fundamentally Rousseauist views and legal positivism. Individuals must be understood to be endowed by nature, and God, with rights that are requisite to the development of personality. The extent of the rights must be worked out in time, according to social circumstances. No right can be understood to interfere with the state's obligation to adjust conflicting claims in the name of social welfare (24). "The true formula is, that the individual has a right to all things that are essential to the reasonable development of his personality, consistently with the rights of others and the complete observance of the moral law" (25). Ryan claims this middle ground will guarantee that man does not become a mere instrument of the state.

Following Pope Leo, Ryan argues that the right to property is in fact natural rather than conventional but that it is also contingent. Private property is a right not for its own sake but insofar as it conduces to the satisfaction of genuine human needs, and especially the needs of the family. It is, again, a means rather than an end. It best enables the realization of the primary right of man to use nature for the development of personality—physical, intellectual, moral, and spiritual (33). "Adjustment" is necessary because, though men are equal "generically," they are unequal "individually," each having different powers and needs. A decent livelihood varies from time to time, place to place, and individual to individual. Hence the need for elasticity and, most importantly, expertise in determining just what constitutes such a livelihood (35–39). During his time teaching at St. Paul Seminary, Ryan tellingly devoted more than a quarter of his course in moral theology to economic history and political economy.[50]

The difficulties of making such complex economic determinations, while daunting, should not deter. The right to a living wage can be asserted only against members of the industrial community where the worker lives, which is something Ryan admits can be defined only approximately. But the complexity of modern economies, while serving to obscure economic rights, should not halt confident action (70). Even traditional rights doctrines interfere with a proper understanding of natural rights, which are more akin to the Christian doctrine that private ownership is not absolute but a form of stewardship (72–74). The capaciousness of Ryan's understanding of stewardship is notable. He favored using the "superfluous" goods of the wealthy to subsidize the needs of the poor—from labor unions, to education, to hospitals and housing.[51]

In an early version of equal pay for work of equal value, Ryan observes that women deserve the same living wage as men, assuming their efficiency is the same. But he grounds this in a concern not only for distributive justice but for the family. Paying women less than men would tend to drive the latter out of an occupation and thereby increase the proportion of female workers, which he does not see as a good (76). As man by nature needs the permanent love and companionship of the opposite sex, a living wage must be sufficient to support family life. In an interesting admixture of what might be called contemporary individualist and Catholic communitarian arguments, Ryan claims the majority of men cannot achieve appropriate "self-development" outside the conjugal state. For the average man "celibacy is not normal" and cannot be the measure of his natural rights (85–86). But, in his search for some limiting principle, Ryan claims that a laborer cannot in justice demand a wage to support his parents because in the normal course of things parents should have taken precautions to secure themselves financially. Rights, he asserts, "are not to be interpreted by the abnormal and exceptional exigencies of existence" (87).

And again, in his efforts to make economic life compatible with the life of the nuclear family, Ryan argues that the family living wage is due to every male laborer, based on "average" rather than exceptional circumstances. Even those who are unmarried are due this wage, for to deny it to them would create an increased demand for their labor, to the ultimate destruction of the family. It would place a premium on "a very undesirable kind of celibacy" (88). The basis for estimating the family living wage is in relation to a family containing the average number of children found in a working-man's home—about four to five (88–90). While Ryan admits this formula is not perfect, this is the best that can be done in present circumstances to preserve "the intrinsic worth and sacredness of personality" (109).

Writing elsewhere—shortly after President Theodore Roosevelt warned Americans, in 1903, that its best citizens were insufficiently fecund—Ryan echoed TR's concerns that moral decadence and demand for luxurious living were leading to a dangerous decline in the birth rate.[52] In *A Living Wage*, Ryan goes further to argue that aversion to marriage fosters selfishness that leads to indolence and inertia, and therefore that arguments for "sexual self-restraint" as a means to aid the working class are misplaced. They are "immoral and anti-social," bad for both society and the individual personality (165). What is needed is not misguided moralizing—exhortations directed at encouraging fundamentally unnatural lives—but "social action," especially in the realms of government regulation and labor organization (155–56). Positive rather than negative freedom is needed. In a summative statement of his conception of the social order—which is at once rights based and organic—Ryan states that

> the obligation to pay a Living Wage falls upon the employer as a reasonable consequence of his position in the economic organism. From this responsibility he cannot free himself by appealing to the labor contract or to the productivity of labor; for the former is consistent with extortion, while the latter is usually unknowable, and is always inferior to needs as a canon of distribution. Inability to perform the obligation suspends it, but inability must not be so interpreted as to favor the superfluous needs of the employer at the expense of the essential needs of the laborer. The employer's right to obtain interest on the capital that he has invested in his business is subordinate to the laborer's right to a Living Wage. (129)

The state therefore has both a "right" and "duty" to require a living wage, for its very purpose is "social welfare," or assisting the individual in attaining earthly ends. And this state activity can perforce be thought of as protecting natural rights (170–71). A minimum wage law is both an urgent necessity and a dictate of natural law reasoning, and the Constitution—long thought to protect freedom of contract—cannot remain a barrier to natural rights. While the expression of these rights is new, they are rights that in Ryan's estimation predate and supersede the flawed Enlightenment conceptions of negative liberty so mistakenly elevated by America's founders.

Ryan considered his 1916 book *Distributive Justice* to be his most important work, though it was lesser known in his own day, and subsequently, than *A Living Wage*. The relative obscurity of the former is no doubt due to its being both drier and considerably more ponderous than the latter. It attempts to discuss "systematically and comprehensively the justice of the processes by which the product of industry is distributed" among landowners, capitalists, businessmen, and laborers—all with an eye to the morality of the processes and outcomes.[53] Based on a sweeping survey of the morality of private land ownership, private capital, profits, and wages, the book reiterates familiar themes. The role of the state is substantial, and little to no regard is given to questions of legal or constitutional constraint. On the whole, Ryan was guided by Ely's view that socialism could be severed from materialism and that elements of the socialist program—if not complete public ownership—were essential to a Christian commonwealth.

Ryan claims private ownership of land is preferable to socialism, but the landowner's right to rent is a moral claim no stronger than the capitalist's right to interest, and neither is as strong as the tenant's right to live decently or the laborer's right to a living wage. Public ownership of valuable lands should be maintained or expanded, and increases in land value should be severely taxed, to the point of breaking up exceptionally large or valuable estates (*Distributive Justice*, 426–27). With respect to capital and interest, it is wrong to claim, as the socialist does, that the capitalist has no claim to interest. But the right to collect it is conventional: "The State is justified in permitting the practice of taking interest" (428). The "right" exists only when it is socially useful. The best practical hope for reducing the "burden of interest" is wider diffusion of capital through cooperative associations in key fields like banking, agriculture, distribution, and manufacture.

When it comes to profits, "needs, efforts and sacrifices, productivity, scarcity, and human welfare" must be taken into account. Only businessmen who use "fair methods of competition" have the right to all the profits that come their way. And Ryan predictably claims that "remedies for unjust profits are to be found mainly in the action of government"—in the form of public ownership and legal regulation of monopolies. Ryan also believes progressive taxation and inheritance taxes play an important role. His book was written just three years after the ratification of the Sixteenth Amendment, granting Congress broad powers to lay and collect taxes on incomes.

Finally—and almost incidentally—"The possessors of large fortunes and incomes could help to bring about a more equitable distribution by voluntarily complying with the Christian duty of bestowing their superfluous goods upon needy persons and objects" (429). With respect to laborers, a living wage is a right to be vouchsafed through minimum wage laws, unionization, and cooperative enterprises in which workers have a substantial voice in the conditions of their employment. Ryan concludes with a reiteration of the importance of faith: "For the adoption and pursuit of these ideals the most necessary requisite is a revival of genuine religion" (433).

In a 1922 book entitled *The State and the Church*, Ryan attempts to set out a comprehensive account of the Catholic Church's teachings concerning the state, with an eye toward specifically applying that teaching to contemporary circumstances.[54] Consisting of a series of commentaries by Ryan and others on Pope Leo XIII's 1855 Encyclical Letter "Immortale Dei," concerning the Christian constitution of states, the book emphasizes—not without foundation—the church's view that the state is an organic, ethical whole ordained by God to conduce to the general welfare of man. But Ryan explicitly rejects classical and Hegelian accounts (buttressed by more recent theories of sovereignty and legal positivism) of the state as the final end of individual striving, with the unlimited ability to subordinate all interests and purposes to itself. The state cannot combine both church and state into a single entity, which would have the effect of reducing individual citizens to mere means to the ends of the state, rather than vice versa.[55] Ryan sees his doctrine of natural rights as an antidote to the idea of state as an end in itself. Individuals must be understood to have rights that are not subject to the determination of the earthly sovereign.[56] He emphasizes that the state can never be considered apart from the individuals composing it, lest it become a "mere abstraction."[57]

But he insists this rejection of idealist political philosophy cannot be allowed to devolve into a cramped, Enlightenment version of individualism whereby the state is constrained to guarantee only negative liberties, rather than required to provide positive ones. The notion of the state as the guarantor of human welfare means that men must not simply be protected from injustice but have their needs for religion, morals, education, and health catered to.[58] Although originating in a theory of natural rights, practically speaking individual welfare must be pursued through corporate action. It is best promoted when the state deals "with men as groups, through their most important group relationships; therefore, as members of families, and as members of social classes. When it provides for the needs that are common to members of these two fundamental forms of association, it benefits most effectively the whole number of its component individuals."[59] For it is not only life, liberty, and property that must be safeguarded by the state but "livelihood, good name, and spiritual and moral security."[60] The second paragraph of the Declaration of Independence does not explicitly enumerate all rights to which men are entitled, but it embraces them implicitly, including marriage and family life.[61]

Ryan's view of the Declaration is at once expansive, partial, and particular. He sees republican government as but one means among many to pursue social welfare and therefore claim the mantle of legitimate government. But he fails to note the apparent incompatibility of this view with the limited and precise conception of natural rights found in the Declaration, which stems from what Jefferson claims to be the self-evident truth of human equality. According to Ryan, democratic forms can claim legitimacy along with monarchic or aristocratic ones, depending on circumstances.[62] And even in democracies, the people are not the source of political authority but only its depositories.[63] Linked to Ryan's gloss on political equality is his view that the state should ideally recognize the one true religion, that professed by the Catholic Church, and prevent the introduction of new forms. He allows that Catholic states where other denominations are already established, should generally tolerate them as a matter of prudence.[64] But no rights are absolute in the sense of being ends in themselves, including freedom of speech. All aspects of the state should be understood to be the means to human welfare.[65] And so Ryan leaves to the good judgment of Christian rulers vast amounts of discretion as to what constitutes public welfare, even in matters of conscience. And he appears to deny that freedom of conscience is, in principle and nature, an essential incident of human welfare. It therefore easily follows that he would view lesser things—such as the right to property—as not to be entitled to inviolable protections, despite their apparent grounding in what he understands to be nature.

When the purpose of government is seen in such broad terms—that is, the furtherance of the general welfare of man in light of God's purposes—natural rights are bound to be understood as less natural, less fixed, and less protective of irreducible spheres of human thought and activity than would have been acceptable to America's founders—on grounds of either principle or prudence. In the language of contemporary academic discourse, we can say that Ryan's Catholicism, while not hostile to republican government, is in tension with it. In less couched terms, we can say it is indifferent to it.

THE LIBERAL MILLENNIUM

And so we have come full circle. Over the last two chapters, we have seen how progressive theorists, statesmen and theologians alike, embraced a notion that material and spiritual fulfillment can be found in and through the good graces of the state. They shared a sense of the possibilities for an organic political wholeness that was coupled with a deep suspicion of anything they saw as too individualist—or, in other terms, too Newtonian or Lockean. All this represented, in theory and practice, a stunning transformation of American politics, morality, and constitutionalism.

Ely's "ethical ideal" of political economy led him to advocate "'such a distribution of economic goods' as would nurture the 'growth of all the higher faculties,'" including even love itself, as seen in religion, art, and literature.[66] The heavenly city on earth was indeed a possibility, if only the Gospels were understood to condemn individualism, and individuals could be made to act on this teaching.[67]

For his part, Woodrow Wilson tried to Americanize his Hegelianism and tame his social Darwinism through comforting versions of an increasingly familiar Christian theology. "Wilson, whose father was a Presbyterian minister and his mother the daughter of a Presbyterian minister, fluently incorporated religious language and sentiments in his Progressivism. That was the era of the Social Gospel movement, a tributary of Progressivism, so it was common to encounter millenarian religious longings translated into calls for social work and social justice."[68] Even Wilson's emphasis on the patriarchal origins of the Aryan races is very revealing as to his view of the relationship of politics to Christianity (not to mention what it says about the race consciousness of leading progressives). His claim that the state is the family writ large is the precursor to contemporary liberalism's assertion that it takes a village to raise a child.[69] For Wilson, the order and authority of the patriarchal family is the analogue to the order that the modern administrative state provides. As a contemporary scholar has noted, this understanding, at once an old and new dispensation, suggests that "we need not fear government's increasing power to be our keeper . . . because it operates as merely the most efficient instrument of our brotherly and sisterly duty to care for one another."[70] And according to this political theology, our duty of care extends less to concern for the soul, but neither is it limited to mere life. Instead, it encompasses most facets of human existence that can be touched by the brave new world of centralized administration. In fact, concern for the soul is not the proper purview of the state, for spiritual progress is not measurable, whereas material progress—in the form of material equality—is. The state concerns itself only with those things that it can measure and manipulate, or that can be measured and manipulated by the expert scientific classes on which it relies for guidance.

Man becomes a creature of the state, rather than a political animal free to order the state according to his deliberative choices. To the Protestants and Catholics who were influenced by such a teaching, religion became an enemy of natural rights and limited government and a friend to the state. "Conscience," far from being threatened by an unlimited state, could instead be followed—but only by influencing the mechanisms of the state in the interests of social justice. Christian progressives seemed unconcerned that, in a larger sense, the realm of conscience—not itself measurable or manipulable by the state or by modern social science—seemed by those very facts destined to play second fiddle to all those things of which the modern state could take cognizance and thereby directly superintend. What after all can be the status of Christian conscience to those who know the trajectory of History, including what will be revealed to every good Christian in the fullness of time? No one should be free to reject true progressive enlightenment, for to do so would be a form of slavery. When the fullness of time was come, God sent the administrative state.

And so, while the early progressives were motivated by faith, their children and grandchildren became increasingly secularized. One can see a distinct and unbroken line of descent from progressivism, to the New Deal, to the Great Society. But as each of these waves of liberalism crested, it became apparent that the underlying force and motivating energy of each was different. The millenarianism of the early progressives was driven, thanks to Rauschenbusch and others, by a genuine if idiosyncratic sense of Christian purposes. This Christian sensibility was already on the wane by the 1930s. Franklin Roosevelt in effect secularized the phenomenon while maintaining some degree of recognizably Christian language: "When Roosevelt, as sensitive a barometer of his times as could be imagined, expressed the higher ethical life to which liberalism pointed, he did so in relatively unassuming, vaguely Protestant and vaguely Progressive terms that could appeal to almost everyone."[71]

The Great Society, by contrast, was characterized by its all-encompassing confidence in the power of government to do pretty much anything and everything. And so its premises sowed the seeds of its demise. "Its soaring expectations, its utopian promises, could not be fulfilled in ten years or a hundred years. What it proffered was the satisfaction, in principle, of all material and spiritual needs and desires. But human desires are infinite. They cannot be satisfied, unless first governed or moderated by reason and morality."[72] And certainly by the late 1960s, the spiritual needs for which people demanded satisfaction had lost even the attenuated connections to the next world that could be seen in the longings of the early progressives.

But these insights, and more, would not play a role in most scholarly accounts of progressivism until well into the twenty-first century. They had to await a new generation of political theorists to bring them to the surface. The historians of the twentieth century had very different stories to tell.

THREE   Gray in Gray

The Strange History of Progressive History
in the 1940s and 1950s

By the time the progressive intellectual synthesis had come to fruition in the politics of the New Deal, there was plenty for historians to report. The first three decades of the twentieth century had witnessed a sea change in American political thought and practice, all converging around the progressive idea. Understanding the extent and depth of this change requires the channeling of a rather large river with many tributaries. And it was this very challenge—the most important one in the realms of American intellectual history, political science, and public policy analysis—that scholars were not up to.

In his *Philosophy of History*, Hegel famously claimed, "When philosophy paints its gray in gray then a shape of life has grown old." By this he meant it is the province of philosophy—at least prior to his own—to apprehend its time in thought and decipher its meaning for the age, but not for the ages. And even this is possible only when history has reached a certain state of maturity and is, in effect, ready to be understood. The process of revealing the meaning of history, of bringing to the surface its details in some intelligible and orderly fashion, is preeminently a philosophic enterprise when this state is reached—when the reflective glance of philosophy is positioned to capture history's meaning. History itself is understood as a mere record of events, an actuality without reality, until that reality is given by the ordering mind of the philosopher.

Historians are not philosophers, to be sure. But for twentieth-century Americans they performed some of the same functions that Hegel suggested were the lot of philosophers. American philosophers had long since lost sight of, or rejected outright, the ancient role of philosophy as the comprehensive pursuit of wisdom. And they had for the most part rejected the even more limited role contemplated by Hegel. They became instead small cogs in an increasingly compartmentalized academic machine, leaving to the discipline of history—or sometimes to the amateur or popular historian—the job of making sense of things, if only for the time being. It was largely American historians—particularly historians who achieved public intellectual status—who gave order and meaning to the vast congeries of events, ideas, and characters that constituted the American experience.

The leading Progressive Era historians like Turner, Beard, and Parrington had looked back on all of American history to paint complementary pictures of corruption and the necessity for dramatic evolutionary growth and change in the political order, though in the course of doing so they exaggerated both. Later, the historians who looked back on the Progressive Era tended to defang progressive ideas and arguments, making them appear more compatible with the American experience and constitutional order than they in fact were.

Historiographers have only occasionally hinted at the problematic nature of this assimilation. According to Ernst Breisach, America lacks the long historical continuities of Europe and has tended to be forward-looking. By the late nineteenth century, the nation found itself in need of a new sense of itself—a new version of history's promise—to keep up with modernity. The early generations of professional historians therefore set off to reconstruct America's past according to the spirit of the scientific age.[1] Timeless elements, "sanctioned by God or natural law," had to be jettisoned (15). Progressive history represented an "experiment in modernization" (38). This experiment carried with it certain tensions from the get-go. Progressive historians had to strike a balance between downplaying the individual in the face of the dominance of evolutionary forces beyond anyone's control and at the same time spurring individuals to action (45–46). They also had to be objective, yet align themselves with what they knew to be history's course (59). And in replacing—with mere pragmatism and progress—the older understanding of the American project as the realization of timeless truths, they faced an ambivalent public (64–65). They were reformers without solid moral, political, or historical ground to stand on. Progressive historians had tried to "lift the heavy weight of tradition from modern people. They understood this task as depriving the past of any significant role in the shaping of the present and the future" (214). The core elements of this progressive history continued with minor adaptations and innovations after World War II (205).

This commitment to modernization ran broad and deep, as legal historian Edward A. Purcell Jr. noted in reference to the radical critique of constitutionalism and formal lawmaking undertaken by the legal realists of the 1930s, who went so far as to question whether a government of known, standing laws was even possible, much less desirable.[2] Although legal realism was an adjunct of intellectual progressivism, Purcell was examining it in the context of the growth of "scientific naturalism" rather than progressivism per se, and his observations were outliers in a historical profession in which the progressive band played on.

Openness, innovation, and interpretive democracy are rarely hallmarks of academic associations. As the iconoclastic cultural historian John Higham argues of the professionalization of history, "The guild-enclosed historian could not escape the standardization of goals and activities that is inherent in organizational life."[3] Higham suggests that "scientific history" was the "formative orthodoxy" of early professional historians, incorporating a new evolutionary realism that discredited reliance on "ideal, transcendental principles." Two ideas—skepticism of truth and faith in progress—were at once the birthmarks and the driving forces of modern American history.[4] Furthermore, the early guild historians felt pressure to make their work "excitingly contemporary," as the social scientists were doing at the beginning of the twentieth century.[5]

The original sins of American historians were transmitted to their descendants. We are reminded of them whenever we survey the fallenness of the profession. This is a topic to which we shall return in the last chapter, but for now suffice it to say that American historians shared key assumptions: the utility of statism, the chimerical status of natural rights in the face of Darwinian and pragmatic criticisms, and the anachronistic nature of a constitution rooted in political thinking that could not be squared with such modern developments. The constitutional perspective is absent or downplayed, not so much because other things are seen as having greater importance to the preferred narratives of progressivism, but because such a perspective would be quaintly irrelevant. Taking seriously the constitutional order would simply have been intellectually and professionally antediluvian for a serious historian. In short, the radicalism of the progressive project was lost on historians who, with rare exceptions, chose to emphasize very different matters.

Furthermore, as constitutional historian Herman Belz argues, there was a sense in which constitutional critics, including some erstwhile realists, closed ranks in the era of World War II and the Cold War around amorphous commitments to "constitutionalism." But they made their promises with fingers crossed. Ruthless legal realism—which claimed to demythologize and delegitimize constitutional norms—simply had to come to terms with political reality. By the 1930s, "The challenge of European totalitarianism began to introduce new forces into American intellectual life. The principal impact among students of law, politics, and government was to stimulate a reconsideration of traditional constitutionalism. Those who insisted on the importance of the rule of law spoke with a new immediacy which, by the end of World War II, made neo-constitutionalism a major ideological force." Nazism and Soviet communism abroad and, in the 1950s and '60s, civil rights turmoil at home cried out for at least some normative commitments—a "vital center" to which Americans could repair for stability and guidance.[6] This supposedly Archimedean point turned out to be vital but not much of a center, as neoconstitutionalists themselves often embraced a very living constitution, protean enough to encompass all manner of economic manipulation, state expansionism, and innovative civil rights theory.[7] Nonetheless, such political concerns probably account for at least some of the historians' blindness, both willful and inadvertent, to the nature and degree of progressive rejections of formal constitutionalism. Twisting Jefferson's observation that every difference of opinion is not a difference of principle, the historians often maintained that no difference of opinion is a difference of principle. Whatever reasons they had for circling the wagons, circle the wagons they did.

The tone for what was to come was set by Harold U. Faulkner of Smith College in his book *The Quest for Social Justice: 1898–1914*.[8] Published in the transition period between the Progressive Era proper and the New Deal, the book marked his contribution to the twelve-volume "History of American Life" series, edited by progressive notables Arthur M. Schlesinger Sr. and Dixon Ryan Fox, with consulting editors including Carl Becker. The editors' foreword proclaims the truths that were self-evident to the progressive mind: democracy was imperiled by the growth of giant industry, corruption was rampant, and unalienable rights "had become the despair of an ever larger proportion of average humanity." The editors immediately deploy the American founders to make their case seem as American as apple pie and as postpartisan as it was possible to be. Individualism and competition were relics of a distasteful past, according to Schlesinger and Fox, and a new "Hamiltonian exertion of governmental power had become necessary in order to restore Jeffersonian conditions of equal opportunity."[9]

Viewed in retrospect, the book seems tailor-made to establish what would become a preferred narrative of progressive history. Faulkner's work is a straightforward morality play: as America gained the whole world, she was in danger of losing her soul. The book sports an epigraph from Herbert Croly's *The Promise of American Life*, proclaiming the fact that the "national Promise" is not destined for automatic fulfillment but must become a national purpose, the subject of conscious work on the part of reformers. The author opens by appealing to an imaginary "thoughtful visitor" to America at the turn of the century, who would have seen a land full of curious contradictions—as thoughtful people seemingly do. Without a hint of irony, Faulkner notes that in no nation was the status of women and children higher than in America, yet social legislation "was far behind that of other progressive nations." Though the successful businessman was an American ideal and people were "lost in a scramble for wealth," there was a "mighty drive" afoot to achieve "some degree of social justice." The "essential soundness" of this chaotic civilization became manifest only in the decade and a half following the century's turn, as the social consciousness of the people rose to direct "national energy" in fresh and nobler directions (26).

Faulkner's story goes on like this: as the nineteenth century drew to a close, big business grew bigger, industrial activity moved from producers to bankers and stockholders, private wealth and power became concentrated, and the necessity to curb them became the challenge of the age (51). State and local politics were corrupt, and states constantly tinkered with their constitutions in an effort to curb legislative abuse. (Interestingly, the federal Constitution merits almost no mention in his book.) Laissez-faire and "money madness" were glorified, as they had been since the Civil War, though laissez-faire had outlived its usefulness (111, 129). Teddy Roosevelt was willing to translate this crisis into the language of political theology: "'We stand at Armageddon, and we battle for the Lord,' shouted Roosevelt in concluding his keynote speech to a convention which in its fervor resembled an old-time religious revival" (107). And in doing so, he "represented the aspirations of the common man" (109).

Faulkner, unlike later historians, does not ignore the religious dimensions of progressivism but instead celebrates them. Religious leaders wisely turned their attention away from theology and doctrine and toward the role of the church in "the new society." Disparate Christian denominations attempted to unify around liberal theology and social concern—evolutionary theory and higher criticism within the seminaries dealt hammer blows to "old-fashioned" theology. Students issued forth from "the centers of advanced theological thinking" to man the pulpits of the nation, finding sympathetic ears among college-educated congregants as they concerned themselves with physical and intellectual well-being rather than matters of the soul (204–18).

Social science too marched forward—ever forward—under the influence of pragmatism, directed by the "virile leadership" of sociologists, economists, political scientists, and lawyers drawn to the new dispensation and committed to realism in American history.[10] And of course, the story would not be complete without mention of the fact that during this period it was courts, grounded in outmoded eighteenth-century philosophy, that stood in the way of social legislation—that is, until judges finally yielded to the humanitarian impulses of the times, their minds "touched by the new spirit of the age" (80).

A NOT-SO-DISTANT MIRROR: PROGRESSIVE HISTORY AND THE HISTORY OF PROGRESSIVISM

By the 1940s, the dust of progressivism had settled, and American scholarship on the Progressive Era had come into its own. Alas, objectivity was not the strong suit of American historians. The discipline had long struggled with what University of Chicago historian Peter Novick has called the "objectivity question."[11] History as a discipline had come to understand itself as historicized: that is, proclaiming only tentative judgments, doubtful of the possibility of arriving at transhistorical truth. Notwithstanding the moral and disciplinary skepticism that led to this disposition, historians could not help but transmit, directly or by implication, strongly preferred interpretations, if not the truth itself. And this was especially the case when it came to the momentous changes wrought by the progressives, in the realms of both ideas and action. Historians generally underplayed or distorted these changes in a manner that made them seem nonthreatening or inevitable, or both, to the point of making them almost unrecognizable.

In the middle part of the twentieth century, few academics could claim greater status as a public intellectual or political historian than Columbia's Richard Hofstadter. He was also the preeminent scholarly chronicler of the Progressive Era and the ideas that animated it. His 1944 work *Social Darwinism in American Thought* marked his first book-length foray into the central currents of the progressive age. In a revised edition published fifteen years later, he began by noting that Darwinian evolutionary theory was unique in the extent to which it affected not only the internal development of science but the patterns of thought in almost all fields. In his account, it comes into view as a profoundly conservative force, supporting the laissez-faire status quo.

It fell to Lester Frank Ward and the pragmatists to wrest control of evolution away from the conservatives and put it to progressive uses.[12] William Graham Sumner was a "social Darwinist" (51), while Ward was a "critic" (67) who comes across as a hero for anticipating social planning and liberating American thinking from the conservative uses of science (84). The social gospel movement too arose as evolution made converts out of clergy, secularizing them and turning their attention away from "abstractions" to "social questions." Religion suffered less from "insularity" as the Kingdom of God seemed attainable on earth (107–8). Meanwhile, social theorists, exemplified by men like Turner and Beard, came to see the need for "empirical research and accurate description" rather than "theoretical speculation" as they eschewed "ancestor worship." The goal everywhere was change and improvement, rather than maintenance of the existing system and the outmoded ideas that supported it (169).

While Hofstadter admits that both Right and Left social Darwinists—the latter being "critics" in Hofstadter's language—shared a belief in the transforming power of evolutionary ideas, he does not attempt to make clear how that shared belief aimed a dagger at the heart of the Constitution and at the idea of the separation of the religious sphere from the ever-expanding concerns of the state. In fact, even though the "state was conceived by all reformers to be an indispensable instrument of the new reconstruction" (121), the Constitution gets nary a mention as a serious limitation on that reconstruction, or as a document that might aim at substantive human goods not amenable to evolutionary change.

By the late 1940s, Hofstadter had published his influential and oft-reissued *The American Political Tradition*, which emphasized a consensus view of American political and social history, albeit a consensus too far to the right for the author's tastes.[13] According to Hofstadter, Americans like to see where they've been more than where they're going, and they typically adopt a passive, noninquisitive posture toward their own history. In the post–World War II era, their insecurities led them to search for a past that acted as comfort food for the mind and soul. They sought a golden age that seemed attractive in the face of war, corporate concentration, and a decline in traditional faith (v–vi). And they were not without precedent in being backward-looking. Both Lincoln and the progressives harkened to simpler times and cried out to recover the glories of bygone ages. But forward or backward looking, what most Americans have in common is an attachment to property rights and the preservation of the principles and practices of competitive striving. The Constitution itself coincided with the rise and spread of industrial capitalism.

In the twentieth century, it was not until Franklin Roosevelt that America had a forward-looking statesman who embraced novelty on a scale with the founders, albeit one that did not cling as much to the sanctity of private property. These facts made him different in kind from the progressives who went before him. Woodrow Wilson, like Teddy Roosevelt, was a "conservative" liberal. Both men, being from "socially secure" backgrounds, were late converts to progressivism and never questioned conventional laissez-faire arguments. Wilson, according to Hofstadter, was only slightly influenced by the German historical school and the economics of Richard Ely. He never abandoned "the conservatism of his formal political writings." Wilson's conservatism envisioned government as mediator, seeking the mean between extremes, and looking out for the common interest (238–49). That this brand of "conservatism" was something very different from the founders' constitutional conservatism is a fact that Hofstadter does not admit. As Wilson entered the political arena, his speeches adopted an aggressive note, demanding change, but always change that was in accordance with past conceptions. They amounted to nothing but the "collective wail" of the middle class (254–55). In terms of his constitutional politics, Hofstadter's Wilson comes across as an eminently mainstream thinker.

With FDR's death, liberalism became "rudderless and demoralized" (vii). Hofstadter therefore finds the time is ripe by the late 1940s to salvage the recent past of the New Deal for the sake of the future. The American national consensus around individualism, capitalism, and isolationism must again be put into serious question in "a corporate and consolidated society demanding international responsibility, cohesion, centralization, and planning" (x). It is simply the case that no one abreast of modern science can believe in unchanging human nature as the founding fathers did. Our goal is to transcend notions of conflict and property rights that the Constitution took to be eternal (16–17).

Hofstadter's writing is characterized by more than a little reluctance to deal with constitutional matters on their own terms, a fact made clear again in his 1950 article on Charles Beard's influence on our understanding of the Constitution. Hofstadter concentrates on the "context" for Beard's work rather than "evaluation" of it.[14] The sources of Beard's economic interpretation are several, according to Hofstadter, and include the purported economism of James Madison and other leading statesmen of the eighteenth and nineteenth centuries. Also playing a role were populism, with its emphasis on sectional struggle and class conflict, and progressive intellectualism broadly speaking, represented by such works as J. Allen Smith's *The Spirit of American Government*, which attempted ultimately to reduce the Constitution to a compromise of democratic and undemocratic interests associated with class cleavages (198).[15] Finally, Beard was influenced by parallel changes in academic disciplines, especially the social sciences, including the new realism of sociological and historical thinking and the concomitant move away from formalism toward theories of interest. These changes began to define law under the influence of Oliver Wendell Holmes and Roscoe Pound, economics under the influence of Thorstein Veblen, philosophy under John Dewey, and political science under the influence of Frank Goodnow and Arthur Bentley (199–200).

"It is clear," writes Hofstadter, "that by 1913 the time was ripe for a thorough presentation of the new thesis on the American Constitution" (203). Hofstadter pauses to lament that the "vistas" opened by Beard's methodology—the bringing to bear of empirical data on the social and economic backgrounds of those who make history—never really took off in historically oriented social science investigation in the decades following Beard's effort. He identifies the two major historical works of the 1920s as Charles and Mary Beard's *Rise of American Civilization* and Parrington's *Main Currents in American Thought*, each containing versions of Beard's thesis on the economic origins of the Constitution (208–9).

As Beard directed his attention away from domestic concerns and class conflict toward foreign despotism in the 1940s, his scholarship became concerned with constitutional maintenance and allowed for the virtues of civilian rule and decentralization. He came to view the Constitution less as an undemocratic imposition of aristocrats and more as a prophylactic against despotism (211–12). The shift is explicit, according to Hofstadter, when one compares the emphases of the *Rise of American Civilization* to those of the Beards' 1944 *Basic History of the United States*, where class consciousness recedes in favor of a broader view of the backgrounds, purposes, and accomplishments of the founders (212–13). But by the time the Allies rode tilt against Hitler's legions, the enduring intellectual damage to America's decentralized, natural rights republic had already been done—something not even hinted at in Hofstadter's "contextual" analysis.

In 1955 Hofstadter published his comprehensive account and gentle critique of populism and progressivism, entitled *The Age of Reform*, which covered the era from the 1890s to 1940.[16] Unlike Morton White in *Social Thought in America*, Hofstadter aims his gaze downward, to what he claims is the "most characteristic" thinking in America rather than the best, with a concentration on "middlebrow writers" rather than "high culture" (6). He begins with a telling observation: "The tradition of Progressive reform is the one upon which I was reared and upon which my political sentiments were formed, as it is, indeed, the tradition of most intellectuals in America" (12). Since, according to Hofstadter, America lacks a conservative intellectual tradition, progressive thinking exists as a highbrow reaction to political conservatism—it is the safe house to which scholars repair, never having to fear a serious assault on their commodious living. Quoting Lionel Trilling approvingly, Hofstadter claims that conservatives resort only to "irritable mental gestures" rather than ideas. Conservatives have simply been "out of touch with the main lines of thought" and with the "primary public" they would like to reach (13). His criticisms of what he deems the Populist-Progressive tradition are therefore, by his own admission, mild and oriented toward attempting to free it of complacencies (15). Strikingly, the possibility of a genuine constitutional conservatism—stretching from the founders to Lincoln and reasserting itself in the very period that is the subject of his book (through William Howard Taft and Calvin Coolidge, among others)—remains beyond Hofstadter's ken.

In Hofstadter's telling, the desire for reform was more psychological than political, best understood as rising less from a will to promote ideas than from a reflex to defend against economic and emotional insecurities, including a certain nativism. He sees progressivism as the quest of the essentially well-off classes to maintain status in an era of socioeconomic challenge. Men of the "Mugwump type—the old gentry, the merchants of long standing, the small manufacturers, the established professional men, the civic leaders of an earlier era" (137)—were suffering not so much economic deprivation as declining influence and prestige in the face of increasingly concentrated economic power. As deference to these morally upright, mostly northeastern Protestants waned, their political consciousness waxed. The sons of Mugwumps found a following as they eschewed their fathers' faith in laissez-faire and embraced a flexibility toward popular government (135–43). The mere existence of plutocracy was their bane (147). Pride and insecurity were the mothers of their discontent.

Of course, they also embraced a flexibility toward the Constitution and their religion that might have made their fathers blush. And this means progressivism was much more than an "impulse toward criticism and change" (5) that Hofstadter claims had manifested itself by century's turn, when agrarian and middle-class concerns merged into a demand for social and economic reforms. *Reform* is a very mild descriptor for the kinds of change Hofstadter describes as he ranges from the agrarianism of the 1890s, to progressivism proper, to the New Deal. He in effect describes an age of political reform and secular millenarianism so mild that it is relatively easy to assimilate to the main currents of American history. Populism merges with progressivism in a way that threatens almost nothing: "When the farmers and the gentlemen finally did coalesce in politics, they produced only the genial reforms of Progressivism; and the man on the white horse turned out to be just a graduate of the Harvard boxing squad, equipped with an immense bag of platitudes, and quite willing to play the democratic game" (93).

Hofstadter claims both far too much and far too little when he argues that progressivism amounted to (merely) "a rather widespread and remarkably good-natured effort of the greater part of society to achieve some not very clearly specified self-reformation" (5). He barely notes the progressive reconfiguration of religion, save for what amounts to little more than the asserted moralism of mostly upper-class Protestant do-gooders, a kind of political redemption through civic responsibility and engagement (9, 11). The mistake progressives fell into, for Hofstadter, was not moral relativism or historicism but moral absolutism and the setting of "impossible standards" (16). He never quite makes clear what those standards are, or whether, in the impulse toward criticism and change, the word *standards* even had meaning.

Hoftstadter claims that in the 1870s and 1880s the respectable opinion-making classes—lawyers, professors, journalists, Protestant ministers—argued for the conservative status quo, which he identifies with "the conservative apologetics of social Darwinism" (148–49). In light of the fact that social Darwinism had only just burst onto the scene in that time period, it is more than passing strange that he identifies it as the "conservative position." His argument implies that the ideology of social Darwinism was more deeply rooted in the American experience, and American principles, than in fact it was. He goes on to claim that by the 1890s the opinion-making classes had shifted their allegiance to "liberal dissent." This claim suggests that, if anything, the move from "Right" to "Left" social Darwinism was not really that significant after all and was likely a function of intellectuals sharing fundamental premises about evolutionary change—and fundamental hostility to the founders' Constitution—and coalescing around a different version of the most fashionable idea of their age. The "age of reform" starts to look more like the stampede of herd animals.

Even if the opinion-making classes in fact shared "a common sense of humiliation and common grievances against the plutocracy," Hofstadter's psychologically and materially reductionist account at best diverts attention from the shared premises of those on the "Right" and "Left" at the turn of the century and masks just how radical each faction was in relation to the principles of the American founding and to the mainstream of Christian thinking prior to that point.

It is worth noting that Hofstadter's fascination with psychological reductionism can be seen in many of his other writings, including his well-known essay "The Paranoid Style in American Politics," where he claims American political life has been an arena "for uncommonly angry minds." In his essay "What Happened to the Antitrust Movement?" he again blurs distinctions by claiming the conservatives of his day (the mid-1960s) inherited their favorable views of small business from the progressives. Hofstadter repeatedly assimilates antitheses to a mainstream American view that is never quite where it should be but never really that radical either, for there is no Archimedean point to which it might be fruitfully compared.[17]

Even if it were the case that "the general decline in deference to the ministerial role was shown nowhere more clearly than in the failure of the lay governors of Protestant congregations to maintain the standard of living of their pastors under the complex conditions of urban life," this says nothing about church teachings (*Age of Reform*, 152). The social gospel for Hofstadter simply becomes a means to an end: an attempt to restore "authority and social prestige that clergymen had lost" (152). The chaplains of progressivism are depicted as liberals revolting against a personally and professionally threatening "conservatism," rather than creators of a new kind of faith—the harbingers of a bold secular millenarianism.

Lawyers, meanwhile, "turned to public service with a sense of release" (162). Muckraking journalists "acquainted the Protestant Yankee with what was going on around him" and shifted his thinking from individual responsibility to social concern (205). Professors could "complain against their position" by relying on the criticism of "vested interests" launched by the giants of academic progressivism—John R. Commons, Richard T. Ely, E. R. A. Seligman, and Thorstein Veblen in economics; Charles A. Beard, Arthur F. Bentley, and J. Allen Smith in political science; E. A. Ross and Lester Frank Ward in sociology; John Dewey in philosophy; and Roscoe Pound in law (154). Ideas don't have consequences—or even intellectual roots. They spring from "social-psychological tensions" and are themselves epiphenomena of something more fundamental (153).

In the end, Hofstadter's progressivism is rooted in a certain kind of conservatism: a general status discontent among "native"—essentially Anglo-Saxon—Americans, who desired to keep reforms always "genteel, proper, and safe" (185). It amounts to little more than "an effort to realize familiar and traditional ideals under novel circumstances" (215). Especially in Eastern states, it "was a mild and judicious movement, whose goal was not a sharp change in the social structure, but rather the formation of a responsible elite, which was to take charge of the popular impulse toward change and direct it into moderate and . . . 'constructive' channels—a leadership occupying, as Brandeis so aptly put it, 'a position of independence between the wealthy and the people, prepared to curb the excesses of either'" (163–64). Hofstadter even assimilates the progressive idea of concentrated political power—especially in the executive—to "Mugwump traditions" without mention of Wilson's radical new theory of leadership (265).

Of course, there is truth to the observation that some did not appear to seek "sharp" change. But whether there is anything "mild and judicious," "familiar and traditional," or even constitutional about leadership that is prepared to curb the factionalism that invariably arises in a large republic is a question Hofstadter elides, advertently or inadvertently. And he does so with particular fluidity. "For Hofstadter and later critical historians, what was impressive about the progressive period was the fact that despite its rhetoric and apparent successes, it failed to bring about significant changes. . . . If the progressives were as successful as first appeared, the New Deal would have been unnecessary. . . . The fact that the goals of the progressives were chiefly psychological explains why they failed to achieve meaningful reforms. They were content to obtain power and pass weak laws that served as 'ceremonial' solutions."[18]

By contrast, Hofstadter portrays the New Deal as a radical break with all that had gone before, including progressivism. Far from being a second wave cresting after the progressive swell had reached shore, it was as if the storm had only begun brewing in 1929. "The New Deal was different from anything that had yet happened in the United States: different because its central problem was unlike the problems of Progressivism; different in its ideas and its spirit and its techniques." While the progressives were concerned with democratizing the economy, the New Dealers were concerned about managing it (*Age of Reform*, 306). While the progressives were principled, FDR was practical, opportunistic, and flexible (306–11). Moralism in the face of dislocation and discomfort gave way to economic experimentation in the face of necessity (316–17). Philosophy gave way to workable public policy (325). In this account, progressivism is reduced to a kind of political conservatism that did not lay the groundwork for the more radical, ad hoc, and utilitarian reformism that would follow.

Compared to Hofstadter, Harvard's Arthur Schlesinger Jr. found in the New Deal something a good deal more ennobling. Schlesinger Jr.—son of the previously mentioned Progressive Era social and urban historian Schlesinger Sr.—was a major public intellectual throughout the twentieth century. His fame was linked largely to his full-throated defense of the New Deal, which he began to make as the embers of World War II were barely cold. Schlesinger gives an old progressive theme—the "pressures of industrial society"—a new treatment. For him, the New Deal fills "the vacuum of faith" inherited from the "cynicism" and "complacency" of the America that came on the heels of the Progressive Era.[19] New Deal liberalism provides an intellectual and moral compass that allows America to work its way through the anxieties of the postwar era, when "unhappy people" see that both communism and capitalism have dehumanized workers and destroyed personal and political liberty (2).

Echoing the central theme of the progressives, while seeming to dismiss their romanticism, Schlesinger observes matter-of-factly that the "problem remains of ordering society so that it will subdue the tendencies of industrial organization, produce a wide amount of basic satisfaction, and preserve a substantial degree of individual freedom" (171). Failures of the Right and Left threaten the "vital center"—the New Deal center—that must, somehow, hold, especially in the face of the totalitarian threat. The Right, "obsequiously" serving the business community and rejecting the "Hamiltonian" progressivism of Teddy Roosevelt, is incapable of producing the leadership necessary to save a free society (chap. 2). The progressive Left, whose ideas are superior in practice, nevertheless clings too much to a mere sentimentality in politics and culture (chap. 3). The Jeffersonian Wilson must give way to the Hamiltonian Roosevelt. The "positive state," latent in the American tradition since Hamilton, must continue to serve democracy (158–59). The powerful nation-state *is* the vital center of American politics; any doubts, from left or right, must be resolved in its favor. "The New Deal completed the exorcism of Jeffersonian inhibitions about strong government, committing liberals ever after to the Hamilton-T. R. faith in the state as a necessary instrument of social welfare" (181). As we shall see later in this chapter, Schlesinger would have more to say about these matters.

THE INVISIBLE CONSTITUTION: HISTORICAL SCHOLARSHIP OF THE 1950S

The 1950s seemed a propitious time for historians to take stock of the whirlwind of events that had defined the American century, and the scholarly floodgates opened as American universities boomed. Henry Steele Commager's midcentury study entitled *The American Mind* offered another leading public intellectual's interpretation of the Progressive Era.[20] A central thrust of Commager's claims is that progressive calls for reform rested on moderation, common sense, and even inevitability, given the fundamentally changed political and economic landscape of the early twentieth century. In other words, his historian's interpretation coincides with the self-understanding of his subjects. This makes it difficult for him to see the real radicalism of their work, even as he, unlike many who would follow, allows that it has important constitutional dimensions.

Commager argues that Walter Rauschenbusch was a man given to religious orthodoxy but economic heterodoxy. For Commager, there is nothing radical about Rauschenbusch's view that sin is social rather than individual, supported as it was by social scientists such as E. A. Ross. The "revolution in economy as well as in morals" that Rauschenbusch called for seems to Commager not to include a revolution in politics or constitutionalism, much less theology. It was simply an expression of the phenomenon of "socialization" that was in accord with the pragmatic temper of the times in a wide variety of professional and educational fields—and especially in philosophy (173–76).

Commager notes that the Declaration of Independence, the Constitution, and the great body of American law as understood by John Marshall and Joseph Story rested on understandings of the nature of the universe and the eternal verities it disclosed. He laments the fact that the "artificial" principles of the founding, resting on a "Newtonian" conception of the laws of nature, were translated into constitutional law, thus preventing them from giving way to concepts "more harmonious" with the realities of the American experience. Thus did a formal, eighteenth-century government of laws rather than men come to exercise sovereignty over the American mind and American political practice. By the 1890s, this system was "cracking at the joints" (312–16). Fortunately, the new "science of society" pursued by Lester Frank Ward came into conflict with such formalism, and Woodrow Wilson's administration took this new science in a moderate direction, providing a formula whereby government could be put at the service of humanity, but in a manner not dangerous to the liberties of men and not involving undue centralization (199–219). In general, Newtonian principles in law and politics were destroyed and replaced by "evolution, pragmatism, the recognition of the economic forces and psychic factors"—each a facet of the historical approach that had been accepted on the Continent. Separation of powers and "fear of government" were creatures of a particular time and place and had no place as the new century dawned. Expansion of government was simply a reflection of the fact that government was made for man's instrumental uses, whatever they might be. Wilson in particular sagely and pragmatically viewed the Constitution as a Darwinian "vehicle of life" that did not impose on men any "preconceived pattern of political conduct" (320–26). Aided by Oliver Wendell Holmes, Roscoe Pound, and Louis Brandeis in the legal field, "dynamic, progressive ideas" would win the day in all areas of American life (374). The progressive synthesis is the story of unalloyed triumph. It overcomes the embarrassing views of America's founders and bestows on all citizens a newfound respect and longing for the inevitability of state power:

> What populism and progressivism, the New Freedom and the New Deal, meant in terms of political philosophy was the final repudiation of laissez faire and the explicit recognition of government as a social welfare agency. What it meant in terms of constitutional theory was the unqualified triumph of the doctrine of broad construction. The pernicious notion that there was some inevitable conflict between man and the state had long embarrassed American politics. Distrust of government, inherited from the Revolutionary era, approved by Jefferson, endowed with perverse rationalization by Herbert Spencer, gave way at last to the realization that government was man organized politically, and that vigilance— still the price of liberty—was not synonymous with paralysis. The "necessary evil" of Thomas Paine had become so necessary that it was no longer evil. (338)

The year 1951 was particularly fecund for scholarship on progressivism. Historian Daniel Aaron of Smith College—who would go on to found the Library of America—published his influential *Men of Good Hope*. Aaron, unlike Hofstadter, made it his explicit task to resuscitate the progressive tradition from the desuetude into which it had fallen in the postwar period. For him, progressivism was Jeffersonian in its pursuit of government by the people and the happiness that ensues from such government, and evangelical in its relationship to reformed Protestant Christianity. He claims that progressivism was defined by its visionaries, not simply its techniques, and thus enjoys a moral superiority over the liberalism of his own day. It was the early, romantic progressives—not the political imposters like Theodore Roosevelt or Woodrow Wilson—who saw the emptiness of American life and sought an achievable utopia the likes of which could not be captured in the "sublimated rhetoric" of Wilson, and which did not excite the New Dealers or Truman's Fair Dealers. According to Aaron, both liberal and antiliberal voices among his contemporaries were trying to make progressivism a shabby thing, when in fact it was the thought of the present that was grim.

He argues that liberalism requires moral righteousness, idealism, and ethics—a faith as well as a strategy. And those who laid the groundwork for the progressives displayed such things in spades.[21] The book's epigraph, from Emerson, sets its tone: "They speak to the conscience, and have that superiority over the crowd of their contemporaries, which belongs to men who entertain a good hope." Emerson was a precursor to the progressives in his vision of "transcendental democracy" with its Jeffersonian and Jacksonian overtones. His was a spiritual and intellectual disposition—one might say an aesthetic preference—that placed human values over materialism and property rights and helped to cultivate a class of reformers who "never deserted the leaderless majority to whose cause they had consecrated themselves" (3–20). The "protean" Emerson in turn inspired a host of "spiritual sons and daughters," including the political reformer and "transcendental systematizer" Theodore Parker (21). The Unitarian minister and abolitionist provided the language of evangelical fervor to a group of reformers who shared his belief that competitive labor markets imposed more costs than benefits and that the state had a positive duty to nurture its children—that is, its citizens (49). Politics must become the religion of the nation, and economics applied Christianity. "Industrial democracy" would prevent the capitalist from occupying, in Parker's words, "'the chief seat in our Christian synagogue'" (50).

In the footsteps of these precursors came the "prophetic agitators" in the form of political economist Henry George, utopian writer Edward Bellamy, muckraking journalist Henry Demarest Lloyd, literary critic William Dean Howells, and sociologist and economist Thorstein Veblen. George captured the spirit of his age in a single book, *Progress and Poverty*, which channeled the "unconscious mass awareness of the community that it was being endangered by inhuman social forces" (56). George, according to Aaron, combined the agrarian radicalism of Jefferson with "humanitarian transcendentalism" in aid of a still valid criterion for a good society, namely one in which nonprogressives do not "dam up mental energy and where monotonous labor does not deprive man of his 'godlike power of modifying and controlling conditions'" (91). Bellamy meanwhile also pursued a vision of individual fulfillment as he favored a nationalism that carved a space for higher, nonmaterial activities, a secular "religion of solidarity," which was the title of one of his early essays. Echoing Emerson, man was both individual and universal, and must at some level be as one with other men and nature—something that only politics, rightly and broadly conceived, could deliver (127–28). Lloyd too recognized that progressivism had a religious dimension, requiring a political faith similar to that of Victor Hugo or Henry James Sr. "The religion of progressivism" universalized rather than individualized Christ, making him a symbol of humanity and making religion a public rather than private affair. Communion with God depended on communion with other men (133). Darwin had taught men "to look ahead instead of behind," and Lloyd was an attentive student (145). Howells marked the transition from the "journalism of exposure" to the "literature of exposure" and the "social gospel of the novel," embodying the economics and ethics of the progressives in fiction, capturing the middle-class radicalism that was by now native to the American experience (172). Veblen marked the end of this period of romantic progressivism, using the academic monograph to express the same sentiments as the other prophetic agitators, condemning the decadent and ignoble business model's penetration into all areas of social life (217–25).

In comparison to this spiritually elevated line of thought, the Roosevelt-Croly program was merely "pseudo-progressive," offering cooperation with, and regulation of, big business. No longer animated by the dream of democratic fulfillment, it was motivated by fear of social revolution. The New Nationalism could not capture the hearts of "the progressive crusaders who sang 'Onward Christian Soldiers' at the Progressive party convention in Chicago." A split in progressive ranks became inevitable as the men of good hope were supplanted by mere political operators (251). Though Wilson shared a somewhat "closer kinship to the spirit of progressivism" than TR, he too was motivated by political expediency and clung to the idea that change must be orderly and regular and must unfold within established bounds (282). His vision was too constrained, and his living Constitution not quick enough for Aaron's tastes. With the coming of Franklin Roosevelt and the New Deal, the fervor of the true progressives was deadened all but completely. Private enterprise was embraced in principle, though not the graft of the insiders, and reform became a technical rather than moral question. Makeshift and "reconstructive rather than radical," the New Deal made peace with its enemies and spent much of its time—as good liberal movements must—on "undoing the work of accumulated stupidity." But such an effort invariably dilutes the promise of true reform (292–94). The New Dealers dropped "the ethico-religious baggage of the old progressives" and in so doing downplayed the idea that citizens had obligations as well as rights and that reform must be a continuous process (295).

Aaron thereby embraces a progressivism that is at once more intellectual, radical, and millenarian than that of its leading political advocates. And yet he does so in a manner that never directly confronts the constitutional status of the reforms he envisions or the theological legitimacy or plausibility of the secularized Christianity on which his vision relies.

Also in 1951, intellectual historian David W. Noble of the University of Minnesota offered a chronicle of the idea of progress as depicted by the house organ of progressivism, the *New Republic*.[22] Concentrating on the founders of the magazine—Herbert Croly, Walter Lippmann, and Walter Weyl—Noble traces the manner in which World War I undermined the salutary "faith in progress" shared by progressive intellectuals. Noble notes their heavy reliance on evolutionary and instrumental modes of thought and their concomitant belief in the power of experimentation to reveal the nature and extent of change that American government and society constantly needed to move forward toward ever greater, and eventually perfected, democracy. By overcoming the constraints of individualism and a formal, legalistic conception of government, social growth, cooperation, and welfare could finally be achieved. Noble notes, but only in passing, the need to discard constitutional checks and balances in favor of a strong executive and administrative state that could overcome the centrifugal forces that the judicial and legislative branches brought to bear.[23] He also points to the necessary plasticity of the approach to private property in a world with absolute or unchanging laws. For the editors of the *New Republic*, a spiritual regeneration was on the horizon, and faith in progress took on a religious tone. In their minds, they were standing at the beginning of a millennium, but one not determined to unfold strictly along the lines of scientific materialism, or likely to be created by the soft and reactionary liberalism of a Woodrow Wilson or the sporadic progressivism of a Theodore Roosevelt.[24]

Their belief in activism and internationalism eventually moved the editorial position of the *New Republic* toward confident support for the war and for Wilson's bold articulation of international ideals. If nothing else, war requires social cohesion at home—something that the progressive vision of democratic collectivism would require to further social progress.[25] But with the Democratic Party's poor showing in the election of 1918, and Woodrow Wilson's failure to bring either the allies or the American people on board with his ambitious plans, the progressive, humanitarian optimism of the *New Republic* waned and its editorial stance devolved into warnings of class warfare. Noble's analysis in the end reads as something of a tragedy, as progressive utopianism was brought up short by the realization that irrationality and selfishness were motives as powerful as their opposites, as winsome faith was dashed on the rocks of despair.

Noble continued this line of analysis a few years later as he concentrated more squarely on Herbert Croly's relationship to progressive thought and in particular the changes in his thinking in the years leading up to the founding of the *New Republic*.[26] In 1909, Croly presented himself as the anti-Jeffersonian in his book *The Promise of American Life*, from which TR borrowed the phrase "the New Nationalism." In Croly's take on the progressive unfolding of history, steeped as it was in a grim Hegelian conception of the nation-state as the reflection of the absolute, the individual played only a subordinate role. Five years later, with the publication of *Progressive Democracy*, Croly had softened and Americanized his progressivism with an elevated conception of the individual and a stronger sense of the reciprocal relationship between the evolution of the individual and the state. The latter view, taking cues from the Christian populism of Lloyd, was a species of Left social Darwinism and Christian progressivism, and it allowed for more spontaneous acceptance by the American people of the progressive democratic ideals of solidarity and social freedom.

Furthermore, evolutionary psychology, at least as put forth by social psychologists such as Charles H. Cooley and James M. Baldwin, was leading people away from mere self-regarding individualism toward the possibility of love of neighbor and social solidarity. Such new social science supported the reality of a shift in the American mind, which in turn shifted Croly's political thinking toward the view that individual reformation and progress were possible without heavy reliance on the superintending structures of society—and that they would in fact further the growth of those structures. *Progressive Democracy* was therefore both more progressive and more democratic than the book written only a few years earlier. Ironclad laws gave way to flexibility and continuous adaptation to the environment. In Noble's words, "Reliance on freedom and participation replaced the emphasis on discipline and imitation found in *The Promise of American Life*."[27]

It was this evolutionary and pragmatic view, rather than his Hegelianism, that led most clearly to Croly's hostility to the Constitution, exhibited in *Progressive Democracy*. As Croly moved away from his top-down belief that institutional forms and traditions were necessary to guide the progress of the individual, he came to argue that only a capacious "living" constitution could keep up with evolutionary change. The executive would be more a reflection of public opinion, a legislator-in-chief and someone who would channel opinion through the expertise of a class of professional administrators, rather than via established constitutional mechanisms.

Alas, with the seeming dissolution of the possibility of utopia in the face of World War I and its aftermath, Croly's ability to undertake further positive political thinking was destroyed, according to Noble. Progressivism's advances in social theory would lie discredited in the eyes of the next generation.[28] As we shall see later in this chapter, Noble would have more to say about the relationship of progressivism to American political development and political liberalism as he reacted to the flurry of scholarship throughout the 1950s.

C. Vann Woodward—widely recognized as the preeminent historian of the American South—offered a sectional and qualifiedly populist account of progressivism.[29] Sharing Hofstadter's view of class angst being at the root of an essentially conservative reform movement, Woodward claimed that southern progressivism was an urban, middle-class phenomenon led by professional and business interests, occasionally allying with agrarian interests to battle monopolies. Distinctly sectional, the enemies for southern progressives were "foreign" business interests, especially in the form of northeastern-based railway, insurance, and oil companies. In the course of opposing these interests, southern progressives ended up opposing Democratic machine politics and favoring direct primaries, initiatives, referendums, recalls, and various forms of corrupt practices legislation. At the gubernatorial level, southerners adopted positions similar in tone and substance to those of northern progressive governors, such as La Follette in Wisconsin and Cummins in Iowa.[30] Marked alternately by political burlesque and political violence, southern progressivism was perhaps more rough and tumble than its northern counterpart, but it "had its day in the South as elsewhere," eventually failing to satisfy its political aspirations.[31] Woodrow Wilson, preeminent son of the South during the Progressive Era, was not clearly identifiable as a radical or conservative but was something in between. His administration represented a geographical revolution in Washington rather than an ideological or constitutional one.[32]

In 1952, Princeton historian Eric F. Goldman came out with *Rendezvous with Destiny*, his history of modern American reform.[33] Typical of many leading historical works of the day, it sought to come to terms with postwar American liberalism, claiming that the word was "headed toward semantic bedlam." Such bedlam, according to Goldman, makes writing a work about reform difficult but worthwhile, precisely because such a study can clarify the jumble that is modern liberalism. Identifying himself with the liberal tradition he sets out to describe, Goldman claims from the outset that he seeks to defend the New Deal and Fair Deal as reactions to urbanization and industrialization. While defending liberalism from charges of socialism, he does not think it necessary—indeed, the reader suspects it never crosses his mind—to defend it from charges of anticonstitutional bias (vii–ix). The most he is willing to allow is that progressives were "men in a hurry" compared to the populists and were more willing to seek centralization of power—in terms of both federal and executive action. The efficiency of the "good man" was prized by progressives, and they viewed checks and balances with suspicion, seeking instead restoration of lost opportunity—a relatively anodyne description of their indifference to constitutional restraints (79–83).

In fact, the problem as Goldman sees it lies in the Constitution having been elevated in public esteem, and the Declaration of Independence lowered, by late nineteenth-century conservatives (87). With "naïve" Americans so "awe-struck" by a conservative interpretation of the Constitution, it seemed only natural that someone might come along and knock that interpretation—though not the Constitution itself—down a peg. Reform Darwinism comes to sight as the vehicle by which "conservatism's steel chain of ideas" could be dissolved away (94). Law could be understood as "a constantly evolving set of ideas," and the Constitution could be toppled "off the pedestal of eternal truth by making an economic interpretation of the way it was written and of the purposes for which it was written." And all this could somehow be accomplished without doing any real violence to the document itself or to the regime it created—certainly nothing in the nature of revolutionary violence. The burden of proof now simply rested on those inclined to think in a "pre-Darwinian way" (133–34). All law, including fundamental law, is conventional rather than natural, and reformers must elevate the equalitarian Declaration over the conservative Constitution—the Laws of Nature and of Nature's God apparently excepted. The Constitution is dead—long live the living Constitution!

Goldman rightly sees Teddy Roosevelt not as a pseudoprogressive but as someone riding the main current of progressivism in the first decade of the century. Reform sentiments dominated the White House, and progressives of all stripes could take heart that social change was the topic du jour, allowing for ebullient discussion "about the goodness, the inevitability, the sheer fun of re-doing America" (186). Even relative radicals like Herbert Croly—who rejected the Jeffersonian notion of equal rights leading to equal opportunities and with it any desire to "restore" a glorified past—could find succor in such a climate. For Croly's belief in "powerful officials operating a powerful state" makes virtue the principle of democracy (198). As the age of Roosevelt bled into the age of Wilson, and despite the "conservatism" of the latter, an important constant was their favoring of executive leadership. Discussions of human goodness and possibilities, rather than fallenness and constraints, were the soil in which all strains of intellectual progressivism could flourish.

Goldman insists that American liberalism is not without its internal contradictions, stemming from the relativism inherent in "Reform Darwinism" and its alternating dependence on "the people" and administrative centralization. Yet Darwinism is the only ideology likely to take hold of the American mind that is also potent enough to dissolve the "steel chain of ideas." So in the end liberals must live with contradictions and tensions (452–53). And despite the retrenchment of the 1920s—when the wrong sorts of leaders undertook leadership—the American liberal has a rendezvous with destiny based on his "momentous tradition" stretching from the founding era "to the sidewalk heresies of Harry Truman." The modern American reformer has been the nation's gadfly and conscience, its heart and its mind (461). And so for Goldman the band of progressive reform continues to play its marching tune, rarely pausing for a break, always harmonizing with itself, and never playing a note that is discordant with what is best in America.

Although betraying a more conservative sensibility than Goldman's book, Daniel J. Boorstin's 1953 *The Genius of American Politics* continued the consensus tradition in American historiography. For Boorstin, the genius of American politics lies in the lack of any American philosophy, and Americans' concomitant "lack of interest in political theory."[34] Americans, unlike Europeans, are of the land, not of the world of ideas or abstractions. They see their institutions as organisms rather than conscious creations (6).[35] The founders are best understood as ciphers into which we can, and do, read our present preferences (15). Any assault on them, even one as radical as that of Charles Beard, is therefore destined to be met with rejection— because the founders in effect are who we are at any given moment (18). Not even a Lincoln or an FDR offered a political theory. The "experimentation" of the New Deal could not be understood as a rejection of a founding moment dedicated to transcendent truths, because such a moment never existed (20, 21). Turner's frontier thesis comes close to capturing the essence, such that it is, of American constitutionalism insofar as it insists that "vital forces" lie behind constitutional forms, which are invented, and then adapted, in response to them (25–26). American institutions have a "givenness" that is at once organic and malleable according to present needs.

Aversion to ideas, and with it continuity rather than change, has characterized American politics since the beginning, according to Boorstin (34–35). From the Puritans onward, "Mastery of nature depended on the ability to understand rather than on the ability to persuade," and glittering generalities and "dogmatism" have never been true to the American experience (64–65). Even "in the era of our Revolution, a political theory failed to be born" (66). The Declaration was not a declaration of rights, but of independence, and therefore lacking in "cultural self-consciousness" (70). And certainly *The Federalist* cannot be read as if it had a "single logical structure" (97). The Civil War was not an argument over "a new vision of society" and was in no way "theoretical" (103, 131). Secessionism, and the Revolution, were merely "surface breaches in a firm federal framework" (125). Likewise, in religion, Americans have long been unconcerned with "basic doctrinal issues" (140). Leading progressives cannot therefore be understood to be reacting against anything particularly American, except perhaps the lack of political philosophy itself (167–68). And such a quixotic pursuit can't be expected to succeed. Even the New Deal appears as an organic growth rather than a sharp break (178). Americans never deny preceding ages and stages of American history. For Boorstin, the genius of American politics seems to rest on the lack of genius and originality of its founders and interpreters.

In 1954, Arthur Mann, then of MIT, and later of Smith and Chicago, wrote a history of reform in microcosm, offering a thick description of the Boston area in the two decades prior to the turn of the twentieth century. Mann, who would become known as one of the preeminent chroniclers of reform politics in America, thereby set out to describe some of the precursors to the full-blown progressive movement. He made it part of his mission to establish that "modern liberalism owes its beginnings to the city as well as to the farm" and thus to an intellectual sensibility and to the character of a certain type of urban dweller.[36]

Whether Irish Catholic, Jewish, or Protestant, the gospel of social reform in Boston was genteel, in Mann's telling, never threatening fundamentally the heart or soul of America. The Irish, being the victims of prejudice, expounded the principles of democracy (50). And like them, leading Jewish reformers managed to face outward from their particular communities in order to address the larger needs of America, including especially the need to tame the laissez-faire system (70). Meanwhile, the Protestant Boston pulpit rallied around a Puritan moralism that joined itself to the "optimistic faith of humanitarianism" in order to demand that Christians show their faith by working for social solutions to the problems of the machine age. This "decay of orthodoxy" meant that sin sprang from the environment rather than the individual soul, and Christianity was stripped of its "supernatural clothing" by evolution and higher criticism (73–74).

Moderates wished to Christianize capitalism, and radicals wished to socialize Christianity, but all worked for something that seems not in much tension with the best of the American tradition: "some kind of cooperative society to take the place of predatory individualism" (77, 98). The sons of Puritan stock who inhabited the prosperous Protestant churches tried to absolve both society and themselves of the sin of such individualism, and they carried their guilt to the institutions of higher learning, trying to imbue institutions such as MIT, Harvard, Andover, and the Episcopal Theological School with the sense that the new social sciences could convert ethics into social action and service (100–106). These reformers of the pulpit and university were moderate compared to certain "freelance intellectuals," but even the latter operated "on the farthest edge of the norm" rather than completely outside it (145).

And Mann goes further still. The key to understanding American reform is the norm rather than the edge—and there is so little edginess to the norm that it's impossible to notice anything deeply hostile to the American tradition. Indeed, Protestants, Catholics, and Jews were simply drawing on the three-thousand-year-old religious tradition stretching from Moses to Leo XIII, including the heritage of the Enlightenment. The Puritans refashioned religion to mean promotion of democracy in the here and now rather than preparation of the soul for that which is beyond earth. They devoted themselves to *Homo sapiens* as their forefathers devoted themselves to God. Likewise, Jewish and Catholic reformers gave themselves over to the idea that a more humane social system was the purpose of religion. And they all met on the common ground of "American equalitarianism," and all spoke "the language of the American dream" (235–36). They saw the America that ought to be rather than the one that was, and thereby provided the tension for a secular age that only religion could have supplied in centuries prior: the tension between the "is" and the "ought." Not simply redefining religion, the reform impulse thereby becomes a new religion for a new age, one deeply in harmony with the trend of American and Western civilization. The comparative flabbiness of mid-twentieth-century liberalism is not to be blamed on the dreamers of that golden age (242).

"In a deep sense," writes Mann, "reform movements in America have been an *obiter dictum* on the Declaration of Independence." Seeing the principles of the eighteenth century through the lens of Emerson, the reformers of the late nineteenth century had confidence that society could progress through "reason and will" (230). Thus does Mann echo the language of *The Federalist* that good government must be the product of reflection and choice rather than accident and force. But the reformers shared a very different conception of reason and a very different conception of man compared to the ones proclaimed in *The Federalist* or the Declaration. The nature and significance of that distinction are completely opaque in Mann's book.

Also in 1954, David M. Potter of Yale offered another form of the consensus view of American history, wherein the American consensus was built around economic opportunity and abundance, and progressive reform directed itself only to more efficacious ways to encourage abundance. American democratic institutions were themselves premised on the good life, materially speaking, as the promise of equality can only be cashed out by making economic opportunity more than just a slogan. Democratic nations of necessity promise this desire-stimulating opportunity and must therefore be ever on the move to ensure the possibility of its satisfaction. The principles of democracy, far from being "universal truths," are rather things that come to sight only when economic conditions are ripe.[37] Americans, compared to their Old World counterparts, have long assumed that the amount of wealth in society is dynamic rather than static and are far more interested in cooperative efforts to generate it than they are in confiscatory efforts to redistribute it.[38] Dynamic wealth creation is both the chicken and the egg of the American republican regime.

In this milieu of hostility to class struggle, populists and progressives wither in significance, their thinking appearing as "incredibly muddled, sentimental, and superficial." Their thought enjoyed neither careful articulation nor doctrinal consistency because American problems have proved so transitory, making strictly logical solutions unnecessary.[39] Again, continuity rather than change has characterized American politics from the reform era through the New Deal.[40]

While rather more conservative than radical, Potter's economism misses the significance of the progressive reconfiguration of American politics because it misses the significance of the regime the founders created. Insisting that their regime was an epiphenomenon of material conditions, and that "individualism" depends not on a philosophy of natural rights but on a utilitarian calculus of what will bring continued prosperity, Potter concludes that individualism can be "modified" at will because it is not "basic" to the American project. Abundance safeguards freedom as freedom aids in securing abundance. The fusion of the two, rather than the "metaphysical" and "heavy-handed" distinctions of political thought, has served to constitute America.[41] Constitutional structure and the restraint it imposes—not to mention any other form of restraint—appear to be not even incidental to the American story.

Yet another important work on progressivism hit the bookshelves of America in 1954, this one by Arthur S. Link of Princeton and Northwestern, the twentieth century's leading expert on Woodrow Wilson. From the first page of his *Woodrow Wilson and the Progressive Era*, Link seems to accept the historicist premises of progressivism, claiming that the progressive movement itself "was the natural consummation of historical processes long in the making," and in particular the inexorable erosion of faith in "*laissez faire* individualism" that merely culminated in the election of 1912.[42] Seeing

Teddy Roosevelt as the great publicist of progressivism, Link identified righteous indignation against big business and high finance as the movement's heart, with Herbert Croly's *Promise of American Life* providing the political philosophy to justify broad federal regulation—something later embraced by the more conservative Wilson. Link does not raise the obvious questions about the idea of "Hamiltonian means to achieve Jeffersonian, or democratic, ends." Would either Hamilton or Jefferson have thought that the rejection by Wilson of certain constitutional limits—not to mention his rejection of the very idea of limited constitutionalism—was a good idea? Are the ends of the American system simply "democratic," even according to Jefferson? In Link's telling, Wilson the "state rights Democrat" was merely battling for "economic democracy" that was essential to "political democracy."[43] The important question was not constitutional but "whether the New Freedom philosophy was sufficiently dynamic to accommodate the advanced progressive concepts."[44] Eventually it did prove sufficiently dynamic—as evidenced by actions such as the appointment of Louis D. Brandeis to the Supreme Court in 1916, and the president's leadership on a legislative agenda that enacted the major points of the Progressive Party's platform of 1912. The more advanced progressives rallied to Wilson's cause.[45]

At the end of the decade, Link was asking, "What Happened to the Progressive Movement in the 1920's?"[46] He sought to challenge the "governing hypothesis" that the 1920s were a period of retrenchment and reaction to reform, guided by crass materialism rather than continued idealism. Link argues that rather than a conscious rejection of reform, the 1920s can be seen as the inevitable result of progressivism's lack of cohesion as a recognizable organization with common goals. Furthermore, the largely middle-class nature of progressivism meant that many of its goals—particularly those related to clean government—were in fact supported by the business community. Whether it was antimonopoly legislation or the Federal Reserve Act, business sensibilities coalesced around what was thought to be good for business.[47] Successful coalition politics allowed idealistic progressives to have political influence but never really to secure control of the national political agenda or of a political party. Furthermore, as progressives fought each other—nativists versus internationalists, farmers versus labor, rural versus urban—they could not recapture the unity they found in the Democratic platform of 1916.[48] Lack of effective leadership also hampered progressive efforts to be a political force. Meanwhile, the urban middle class was defecting from progressive ranks by the 1920s, finding new "social status" and contentment in the booming '20s.[49] In the end, although suffering declined in the 1920s, progressive forces did not disappear. They instead suffered the natural disunity and decay incident to any movement "caught up in the swirl of social and economic change."[50] And they retained enough vigor to re-emerge in 1932.

In 1955, Harvard political scientist Louis Hartz published his classic work on American exceptionalism, which found considerable favor on both the left and right of the American political spectrum. *The Liberal Tradition in America* was an attempt to define the consensus that defined America and that was responsible for the unique contours of American history.[51] The lack of a feudal tradition in America, Hartz asserted, led to an easy and comprehensive embrace of a Lockean liberalism that has lain at the center of the American political tradition since the founding. This liberalism has acted as a kind of intellectual straitjacket and defines the overarching narrative of American history and political development—the pale beyond which American thought and practice cannot go, the "absolute mind of the nation" (260).

Recognizing that mid-twentieth-century Americans still lived in the shadow of the Progressive Era, Hartz brands progressivism as a fundamentally American school of thought, one that operates well inside the defining liberal, nationalistic, and nativist tradition. It had only Whiggery to fight—not feudalism, Toryism, or socialism. Even though the leading progressives like Beard and Smith treated the Constitution without "piety," theirs were interpretations as American as apple pie, and certainly as American as those of any other historians. This was so partly because of their American hero worship—they would rely on a Jefferson, or Hamilton, to suit their mood and emphasis, and failed to see Lockean liberalism itself as a villain. Progressives did not attempt to tamper with the American regime but to reassure it.

Modern scholars of liberal society, by contrast, do not go out of their way to reassure or engage in idle hero worship. They are therefore more radical than the progressives, seeking ways to transcend the American past. "The analyst of American liberalism," according to Hartz, is in a unique position to see the shallowness of all previous quarrels in American history (27–32). America rests on "one of the most powerful absolutisms in the world," which is "the sober faith that its norms are self-evident." Lacking contact with opposing ways of life, such absolutism lacked the passion of European liberalism and went on to support a pragmatism that never presented a serious challenge because it "rested on miles of submerged conviction." American liberalism had no arguments and has needed none (58–59). The Revolution itself was not quite "genuine," for it made no real counterclaims (250).

Such ambient Lockean liberalism, in its insistent destruction of intermediate institutions, both elevates the state and seeks to place limits on it (60). The Constitution that enshrined this effort has survived to become the oldest national constitution in the world because of the reality of political and intellectual solidarity surrounding its liberal premises and meaning—there have been no "fundamental value struggles" in American history (85–86). And in this, Hartz makes two very large assumptions: that the "living constitution" that was well in evidence by the time he wrote was in fact the same Constitution that the founders drafted, and that the shared rhetoric of liberalism means there have been no fundamental disagreements about its meaning. As Harry V. Jaffa points out in his critique of Hartz, the acceptance by Americans of Lockeanism has intensified conflicts over the operational meaning of such a shared inheritance. And it does not follow that quarrels over the meaning of equality are mere phantoms unless equality is set off against its feudal opposite.[52] What is lacking in Hartz is a sense that there is a moral principle underlying Lockean equality that goes beyond popular or individual sovereignty: that equality properly understood is self-limiting and that differences in practice point to different understandings of the principle—not all of which can be correct. Put another way, Hartz misses the moral philosophy of the Constitution—the fact that it enshrines a particular moral view that goes beyond an ill-defined but seemingly grubby democratic capitalism.

In Hartz's estimation, the "great conservative reaction" in American history died without a whimper, its expositors lost from history books. After all, the faux-feudal southerner of the 1860s had, only a short time before, been a Jeffersonian democrat, and thereby put himself in the unenviable position whereby he "slaughters himself with the traditionalist logic he tries to use" (148) so that "anyone who dared to use conservatism in order to refute liberalism would discover instead that he had merely refuted himself" (151). But even if this were true as a matter of logic, it has not proved true as a matter of practical reason. The greatest continuing controversy in American history has always been over the meaning—and nowadays the very existence—of "the Laws of Nature and of Nature's God." The legacy of the conflicted southerner whom Hartz describes was a denial of natural equality. The longer-term legacy, different in emphasis but not in kind, is seen in the denial of the possibility of any natural limits embedded in our constitutional politics. However put, the express denial of the Laws of Nature and of Nature's God has always amounted to fighting words in American history.

The cast of Hartz's argument leads him inevitably to conclude that the progressives merely sought new ways of "running the Lockian race" (223). They could do no real violence to a constitutional tradition in which nature does not appear. Neither natural rights nor community was transformed by the progressive mind. The American progressive merely advanced a program of "trust-busting and boss-busting, which sounded as if he were smashing the national idols but which actually meant that he was bowing before them." Woodrow Wilson showed the "pathetic enslavement" of the progressive tradition to mainstream American Whiggery. "The 'Alger formula' would work if only given a chance," said the progressives "in the irrational grip of 'Americanism.'" They had no language in which to express class conflict and the fundamental inequities of the capitalist system." Croly's view that there was a fundamental difference between the New Freedom and the New Nationalism is indefensible, according to Hartz, when both owed allegiance only to democratic capitalism—and all reformers lived in a "unanimous age" (230–39). Their allegiance to the founders' Constitution was a matter of scant concern for Hartz. He appears not to see the progressives, or the founders, as they saw themselves. The progressives are, in his account, mere ciphers within—or at most channelers on the edges of—the great river of American liberal sentiment:

> In the political arena did not Progressivism actually challenge "Americanism"? What about the attack on Constitution worship and the Courts? Do we not find here the very spirit of iconoclasm, the moving into forbidden areas, the shattering of what Croly called the "sacred character" of the fundamental law? One might reply that even the wildest Progressive revision of the Constitution would not have changed it much. But that is not the real point, which is this: the purpose of blasting legal "Americanism" was to attain Progressive "Americanism," so that the taboo involved was shattered on the surface only to reappear at the bottom. (242)

The idea of an overarching liberal consensus and a corrupting individualism that cuts across American history and across superficially competing political ideologies is a theme that would be picked up a decade later by New Left historian William Appleman Williams, albeit with a different purpose in mind. Hartz, like a kindly British bobby who doesn't want to disturb the tranquility of passersby, merely counsels everyone to move along, for there really is nothing to see. But Hartz lacks the self-awareness of the bobby, not knowing that if the scene of the crime were fully revealed to ordinary citizens they might feel a certain revulsion.

In 1956, historian Robert E. Brown offered a trenchant critique of Beard's *Economic Interpretation*. He notes, with Hofstadter, that Beard's thesis is no longer considered shocking.[53] Indeed, by midcentury it had in large measure been accepted as tame, mainstream, and bland—becoming elevator music for writers of American history. Beard's method—relying on empirical data to demonstrate the economic interests of the founders—was played up by Hofstadter as a signal contribution to American history, yet it is this very method that comes under scrutiny from Brown, in light of Beard's enduring influence. Brown offers a convincing, albeit highly concentrated, critique of Beard: the Constitution was adopted "in a society which was fundamentally democratic, not undemocratic; and it was adopted by a people who were primarily middle class property owners, especially farmers who owned realty, not just by the owners of personalty." The Constitution was not simply an economic document, though of course economic considerations played a role insofar as everyone in such a society was interested in the protection of property, and the document would not have been ratified were they not. But personal rights were equally important to the founding generation.[54] Such observations put both the empirical veracity and salience of Beard's work into question. But such a limited revisionism only indirectly addresses the central objection raised by Beard, and other progressives, to the Constitution: that it has no claim to be grounded in rationally accessible natural truths.

Hard on the heels of Brown's study, Forrest McDonald took up the critique of Beard in *We the People: The Economic Origins of the Constitution*, a sprawling account of the economic interests at play in the framing and ratification of the Constitution.[55] McDonald undercuts Beard's account of landed versus mercantile interests by documenting literally dozens of interests that must be considered. Given the significance of those interests, McDonald insists that matters were far more complex than Beard had allowed and that the "economic interpretation of the Constitution does not work."[56] Cross-cutting cleavages, bargaining, and political compromise, at the national, state, and local levels, do not lend themselves to simple accounts.

Hofstadter, in turn, offers a telling critique of McDonald: "Where Beard had presented, at bottom, two opposing coalitions, business and populism, personalty and realty, creditors and debtors, McDonald emerges with a complex, often overwhelming, variety of political factions and economic groups. . . . Using much finer brush strokes. . . . his palette retains the same somber quality, and he is on one count closer to Beard than he cares to admit: he apparently agrees that the making of the Constitution will conform to a severely economic interpretation, once we get our economics right."[57] While it is too much to say that McDonald gives himself over completely to economics, his book does suggest that the right social-scientific model will get us far down the road to explaining our constitutional origins.

In 1957, Arthur Schlesinger Jr. published the first volume of his *Age of Roosevelt* series, titled *The Crisis of the Old Order: 1919–1933*, which borrowed from and restated much of the earlier scholarship and offered what has become a standard account of the precursors to the Roosevelt administration. By 1919, the "democratic revolution" had been gaining strength for three decades, Schlesinger asserts. It stemmed from the populist challenge to business and generated a host of reforms that relied for their implementation on expanded government power. Progressivism grew out of this populism, but it was a much more staid, moralistic, middle-class ideology, held by established leaders who felt threatened by the nouveaux riches.[58] Herbert Croly was the thinker who saw that the promise of American life was not self-fulfilling and that "automatic processes" would not ensure a brighter future (*Crisis*, 20). (One is tempted, idly, to think that Lincoln might have beaten him to that insight.)

The social gospel of Gladden and Rauschenbusch predisposed Protestant America to vigorous state activity and support for organized labor and gave moral sustenance to Teddy Roosevelt's New Nationalism, which promised mastery of big business and a helping hand "for the individual cast adrift in the great society" (*Crisis*, 21–22). By contrast, the more conservative Wilson rejected Hamiltonianism, opting instead for equal rights for all and privileges for none—a Jeffersonianism of state interference but not paternalism (28). Leaving aside whether such a distinction makes sense, it is clear that Schlesinger does not see any constitutional tensions embedded in either the New Nationalism or the New Freedom. In fact, the Constitution never seems to divert, even momentarily, the

vast flood of historical detail that Schlesinger unleashes in his nearly
five-hundred-page book. The main division in the election of 1912,
according to Schlesinger, was over the meaning of the New Nationalism versus the New Freedom, and particularly the relationship of
those concepts to trust-busting. Schlesinger mentions nothing that
would rise to the level of constitutional significance (32). For example, while Wilson's Jeffersonianism is portrayed as opposing the
"bigness" taken for granted by the New Nationalists—as evidenced
by its insistence on the regulation or breakup of monopoly—it apparently did not oppose bigness in government. But Schlesinger
sees no need to pause over the assumption that Wilson's purportedly Jeffersonian "government regulation" would occur at the national rather than state level (30–31).

Schlesinger concludes his book with the observation that Franklin D. Roosevelt "spoke the spirit that animated both the New Nationalism and the New Freedom" when, in the course of the 1932
campaign, he said that the objective of America was "to put at the
head of the nation someone whose interests are not special but general, someone who can understand and treat with the country as a
whole. For as much as anything it needs to be reaffirmed at this junc-
ture that the United States is one organic entity, that no interest, no
class, no section, is either separate or supreme above the interests of
all" (484). Furthermore, Schlesinger notes approvingly Felix Frank-
furter's characterization of Roosevelt as "the comprehending expression of the diverse interests, feelings, hopes and thought of the mul-
tiple forces which are unified into the nation" (484). And none of
that seems to strike Schlesinger as out of alignment with the American constitutional tradition, including the notion of the president
as a limited constitutional officer. In fact, by the time Schlesinger
penned the second volume in the *Age of Roosevelt* series, he was confidently proclaiming that a president stands or falls on the richness,
plasticity, and capaciousness of his "vision of the future"—the most
distinguishing characteristic of FDR.[59] Forward motion toward a
new world order is a fitting summary of the progressive impulse, but
it is one that Schlesinger reports with a tone of celebration that belies
the depth of its hostility to American founding principles.

Also in 1957, as part of the University of Chicago's History of American Civilization series, political and social historian Samuel P. Hays published *The Response to Industrialism: 1885–1914*.[60] As series editor Daniel J. Boorstin noted in his introduction to the second edition, published almost forty years later, the book has become one of the most widely accepted interpretations of that period in American history—a difficult feat in light of the amount of scholarly interest in the period and the plethora of books available. Intended as a kind of general summary of the period rather than a work of original scholarship, the book is remarkable for its guardedness, even blandness. Hays opens his analysis by placing the rise of industrialism in both economic and psychological contexts: the growth of impersonal forces at the expense of personal contacts, the standardization of life that went along with the standardization of products and production, the specialization of labor that was necessary to support such production, the widespread insecurity that went along with such changes, and the growth of material acquisitiveness among a populace less interested in nonmaterial goals. All of these factors together resulted in a more nationalized, less sectional economy—one in which there would be a popular demand for control and predictability (chap. 1). Culturally, traditional values were weakening, and individuals "sought license to make their own choices" as churches attempted to keep up with the times through social and political action (chap. 2). The "organizational revolution" continued apace, and eventually the ability of citizens to cope with problems through collective action cemented Americans' attachment to the new industrial order (91). Reform activity usually reflected the values and ideals deeply embedded in American society and simply applied them to the conditions of industrial change. Liberty, justice, and equality "took on new forms and meaning with new conditions" (93), but didn't stray too far from the center of gravity of the American experience.

As the civil service expanded and the confidence in technocracy grew, progressives were able to glimpse "what could be done if both private and public decisions were made by professional experts solely concerned with efficiency" (197). The range of human inquiry was

expanded by Darwinism and pragmatism, and intellectuals wor-
ried about the conflict between material and human values. But, it
should be noted, constitutional "values" never come to the surface
in Hays's account. He understands social Darwinism as a right-
wing economic doctrine rather than as a dagger aimed at the heart
of American constitutionalism. He portrays the social gospel and
Christian socialist movements as antidotes to competitive striving.
While he allows that the religious language of the Progressive Party
betrayed a "moral fervor," he passes on evaluating the legitimacy or
long-term significance of such an atmosphere. Likewise, he notes
only in passing that the Supreme Court nullified needed regulation and that progressives attacked it for being a third branch of
the legislature (181).

The next volume in the same Chicago series was from the University of North Carolina's William E. Leuchtenberg and was titled,
appropriately, *The Perils of Prosperity: 1914–1932*.[61] Far punchier
and more opinionated than Hays, Leuchtenberg dealt with his
topic in moral terms, claiming that America wrestled, fundamentally, not only with economic questions but with the moral climate
arising out of them. Constitutional questions were not in the mix.
Progressivism, in Leuchtenberg's telling, had begun to peter out before the irrational exuberance of the 1920s could stomp it into the
dust. Teddy Roosevelt and the Progressive Party, in the name of nationalism, had adopted the views of the "Old Guard" after the election of 1912. While in 1913 progressive intellectuals "were giving
the United States its first intelligent analysis of modern society and
blueprinting an ebullient, buoyantly hopeful program of reform,"
by the end of World War I they had become "tired radicals," convinced, with Croly, of the eclipse of liberalism or progressivism
(123–24). "Having lost faith in progress, in the rationality and dis-
interestedness of man, and in the malleability of society, the intellectuals could no longer retain faith in the prewar political solutions" (125). Progressivism became part of the "orthodoxy" against
which postwar intellectuals felt the need to rebel (149).

In addition to the intellectuals, the "middle-class" progressive
movement also began to withdraw in the face of labor militancy.

The 1920s was a period in which "the country yearned for release from the attacks of the reformers and the demands they made for al-truism and self-sacrifice" (84). The liberalism of the 1920s would lose the evangelical, moral fervor of earlier progressivism and would concentrate its energies on urban problems (137). With the old-time religion snuffed out in the charnel house of war, the bubble of high-minded Wilsonian moralism was destined to be popped, and with it the mighty efforts of the progressives to effect enduring reform.

Calvin Coolidge "served the needs of big business" even more effectively than Warren Harding because he was an "ideologue" rather than a mere politician. He possessed a "seventeenth-century belief in frugality" that was used to justify tax cuts, and his "inac-tivity in office served to demonstrate the insignificance of govern-ment." Leuchtenberg makes no mention of the fact that Coolidge's "ideology" might be interpreted as a reflection on the political philosophy of the American founders and the Constitution they created—as Coolidge himself said it was—or that his "inactivity" might be interpreted as a reflection on the constitutionally limited role of the national as opposed to state governments. Rather, it was all a form of cult worship: "Political fundamentalism was an attempt to deny real divisions in American society by imposing a patriotic cult and coercing a sense of oneness. Admiration for the Constitu-tion became a tribal rite; in the 1920's, Americans, as one English writer noted, were 'a people who, of all the world, craved most for new things, yet were all but Chinese in their worship of their Con-stitution and their ancestors who devised it.' Constitution-worship was a kind of magical nativism" (205).

As the 1950s drew to a close, American scholars were hard at work trying to describe a progressivism that was well within the mainstream of American thought and practice, reflecting a popular reaction against concentrated business interests. UCLA's George Mowry developed this theme in his survey entitled *The Era of The-odore Roosevelt: 1900–1912*, which was more insightful than most when it came to the reach of progressivism. Mowry portrayed the era as marked by rapid material change not only in technology but in larger ways of life, including the decline in provincialism brought about by the large manufacturer and merchant.[62] In the intellectual realm, there was a growing confidence that what had been seen as the ironclad laws of political economy could be overcome by human intelligence and creative activity. Even sin itself came to be seen as an outcome of social forces rather than a theological absolute. Denying original sin went along with the even more remarkable feat of secularizing salvation and bringing heaven down to earth. "Religion had joined scholarship and science in giving sanction to reform" (30). Political conservatism also fell out of favor as the science of society was no longer understood to be mechanistic, and appeals to natural law were overwhelmed by the demand for change.

Mowry rightly notes that so-called "reform" Darwinism had much in common with the rejected "social" Darwinism of Spencer and Sumner, as they both shared a deep belief in evolutionary change. Their main disagreement was over the status and morality of competition, and the possibility of human ingenuity channeling environmental inputs. Progressive reformers, whether favoring decentralization and fair competition or a paternalistic state, embraced moral language because of the necessity for good men to direct the change (chap. 3). Mainstream progressivism was defined by fervent ethical demands, faith in leadership and the ability of man to order the future, and an admixture of belief in democracy and centralization. Despite its potential for radicalism, it was checked by the "comfortable" background of its exponents and their fear of "loss of group status," which helped ensure that it concentrated on "benign social ends" (chap. 5).

Mowry even shows a fleeting appreciation for the constitutional implications of progressivism. He notes, for example, Taft's 1910 pledge to "stand with the Constitution" in the face of the progressives' attacks on the Supreme Court and the rule of law, and their advocacy of direct government, overregulation of business, and the widespread expansion of federal power called for by the New Nationalism (271–72). He also points out Teddy Roosevelt's rejection of Midwest populist progressivism as nothing more than "rural toryism." He describes Roosevelt in terms that at least adumbrate the depth of the progressive assault on the founders' Constitution: "An admirer of organization, a seeker of power, and a glorifier of strength, Roosevelt was really devoted to the New Nationalism. In the interstices of that bundle of doctrines first expounded in Osawatomie and later in the campaign of 1912 lay the seeds of much of the promise and most of the peril of the next fifty years" (295).

In 1958, David Noble offered his most comprehensive take on progressivism entitled *The Paradox of Progressive Thought*, which was an effort to track the climate of opinion shared by leading figures of progressivism. According to Noble, each shared aspects of a "common faith, a common set of assumptions about man and the world," that was "part of the liberal tradition of America." This liberal tradition claims as one of its centerpieces the Hartzian understanding of liberty as the absence of institutional constraint. Because of the unanimity of American opinion on this Lockean ideal, such absolute liberty runs the risk of becoming absolute conformity. In embracing both complete freedom and complete uniformity, the progressives were doing nothing more than embracing, and rearticulating, the central paradox of the American experience.[63]

At the high-water mark of the progressive intellectual movement, men like Croly had settled on the "exhilarating affirmation" that individual effort could change the material environment, which was not of itself destined to reach the ideal. A "religion of progress" resting on the "joyous declaration of man's responsibility and creativity" animated the progressive project.[64] Evangelical reassurances of harmony and earthly salvation were offered to a troubled world, if only the individual were free to create the future, upending the forms of power through social science. Croly and fellow travelers like James Mark Baldwin, Charles H. Cooley, Lloyd, and Ely "had taken historicism, relativism, pragmatism, scientific naturalism, and absolute freedom and underwritten them with a guarantee of inevitable progress. They were Darwinians because they believed the scientific method could be used to demonstrate an ultimate spiritual purpose to the universe."[65] Progress would be a return to "primitive human qualities," which were, paradoxically, set free by an industrialism that brought prosperity, physical proximity, and cooperation as it destroyed traditions and institutions and imbued men with a confidence in their ability to shape the material universe.[66]

As a point of contrast, Noble observes the "theoretical dislocation" of mid-twentieth-century liberalism, identified by writers such
as White, Aaron, and Goldman. These historians recognized that
while the scientism and evolutionary relativism that defined progressivism could be counted on to destroy conservative absolutes, it
could not be counted on to deliver reliably liberal principles. The
anomie that went along with such a realization was anticipated by
the progressive historian Carl Becker two generations earlier, as he
simply lost his faith in rational progress for reasons that were not
rooted in Darwinian evolution.[67] The "disintegration of the myth
of absolute progress" leaves progressivism, and its cozy relationship
to the liberal tradition in America, in tatters. In an age that can
no longer live with paradox, nothing seems available to cement a
national identity or stabilize the American regime. Of course, had
Noble considered the essence and foundation of America to be the
founders' republican constitutionalism, rather than liberal paradox, he might have found another voice in which to express the
American prospect.

In 1959, Russell B. Nye, a Pulitzer Prize–winning cultural historian, published perhaps the most influential regional account of
progressivism, entitled *Midwestern Progressive Politics*.[68] The book
is in essence an account of progressivism in microcosm, one that
echoes the national studies that preceded it, albeit with a good measure of Turner's frontier thesis overlaying the analysis. The Midwest, according to Nye, was defined by a tradition of independence
and contentiousness, exacerbated by the rapid transition from for-
est clearings to modern industrialism. Midwestern farmers were
plagued by problems of transportation, money, credit, and tariffs,
all of which seemed to favor Eastern interests. The old ideals of
agrarian democracy came quickly into direct conflict with the new
industrialism.

Meanwhile, at the intellectual level, laissez-faire theory was "in-
grained in the American tradition" and was "used as a weapon to
silence opposition," as was the new social Darwinism's "survival of
the fittest" paradigm. "The problem, as the Midwest conceived it,
was to reaffirm eighteenth-century democratic faith and to preserve
it against the rising tide of skepticism, cynicism, and, as they called

it, 'plutocracy.'" The political theory of Jefferson and Jackson competed rather straightforwardly with that of "Spencer, Darwin, and Rockefeller," with the aim that "Jeffersonian ends might be accomplished by Hamiltonian means" (chap. 1). Nye therefore sets up the problem in by now familiar, even formulaic, tropes. The regional context and purposes of progressivism seem to differ little from the conventional accounts of its national context and purposes. He seems at a loss to explain how his claim that the "natural-rights concepts" of the Declaration of Independence were "buttressed" by Spencerian doctrines of natural selection, even as Jeffersonianism was held up as model for agrarian reform. He even claims that traditional American doctrines of "self-help and self-attainment reinforced the defense of wealth" (128).

There are many moving parts in this account, but they don't mesh into a seamless whole. One thing is clear to Nye: from 1892 to 1900, there was "a shift, a marked shift, from the old frontier philosophy of self-reliance and laissez faire to a new one of social co-operation—a shift, as Turner phrased it, 'from the ideal of individualism to the ideal of social control through the regulation by law.' Government became on the one hand a policeman to restrain those who would repress or victimize the people, and on the other an instrument controlled by the people's will and responsive to their needs" (124). The state could become, in the words of Lester Frank Ward, a medium for "social engineering." This understanding, according to Nye, "cut away the very foundations of social Darwinism" (138). However, one might also say that it reinforced them, albeit for different purposes: rebel economists and sociologists were but two sides of the same coin, each equally hostile to the founders' natural rights constitutionalism.

For Nye, America is not a constitutional republic but a democracy whose "basic beliefs" include cooperation, equality, and social and economic justice. And these beliefs were reinforced not only by progressive social science but also by religion, in the form of the social gospel. "Social Gospel's basis was theological; Bryan and La Follette's was political. Both were different paths to the same goal"— that democracy might be made "something more than a dream" (159). Neither socialist, nor constitutionalist, nor truly radical, the midwestern progressive was above all a democrat, believing in the power of government to express the will of the majority for social and economic regulation. The shift toward "social control" seems, for Nye, about as controversial as motherhood itself (182–85). Nye's casual use of the phrase "the state" illustrates the point. For him, as for the progressives he is describing, there is little or no distinction between the states individually and the national state. It is, rather, simply "the state" that can be a "positive factor" in society. While midwestern progressives might tactically have favored state-level reforms, at least in the early phases, "governmental do-nothingism" was the real enemy of progressivism and of its ultimate purpose: democracy (187). Darwin and Adam Smith could be overcome with a new "settlement" enforced by state power unmoored from constitutional limits (242). National progressives like Woodrow Wilson differed from the midwesterners not in aim but in "spirit and method," with Wilson concentrating more on economic reforms rather than on broader social and political ones. In addition, Wilson was imbued more with "cold and emotionless" idealism than with the "frontier spirit." But the more nationally minded Wilson nonetheless provided intellectual leadership for the midwestern progressives (284–85).

It was World War I, in Nye's telling, that dispersed the progressive movement and left it unable to regroup. Not only was it dead, it would quickly lie down. Coolidge, said La Follette, represented the "standpat, reactionary theory of government" (298). Although FDR would restate the same problems perceived by midwesterners since the 1870s, the New Dealers lacked the "insurgent heart," replacing it with administrative and social science technique (341–42). Midwestern progressivism was gone, though not quite forgotten. With its passing passed the moral energy that had been single-mindedly concentrated on the creation of an agrarian commonwealth—one that the original Jeffersonians might have loved, at least to the extent they were not devotees of inherently corrupting natural rights doctrines.

Three remaining works served as telling bookends to the 1950s. In 1959, political scientist Andrew M. Scott of the University of

North Carolina put forth an argument that remained unusual in mid-twentieth-century historiography.⁶⁹ He rejected the rather modest role that historians assigned to progressivism and argued for its enduring constitutional and political significance from the New Deal and beyond. Complaining that postwar scholarship on progressivism lacked a sense of the significance of the age, Scott took to task Hofstadter in particular, and especially his reductionist argument, explicated earlier in this chapter, that the middle-class origins of progressives made the movement essentially conservative. Scott rejects Hofstadter's determinism and his claim that he could understand the progressives better than they understood themselves. Scott is more willing than Hofstadter to take the progressives' accounts of their own motivations seriously. The progressives therefore emerge as fully volitional actors, rather than as caricatures or expressions of "the Mugwump type." And Scott notes that Hofstadter commits the same error as the leading scholars and inventors of the Progressive Era did. Like Beard, Smith, or Seligman, Hofstadter oversimplifies diverse motives (687). Such an approach to history seems to place the historians outside or above the inexorable forces that purportedly determine the views and actions of their subjects.

And Scott offers an insight into Hofstadter's writing style that might well be applied to many other scholars of progressivism: "The careful reader of Hofstadter's work can scarcely avoid the question of technique since he will find that results are sometimes achieved by the author's talent in the art of suggestion rather than by explicit argument and supporting fact. Individuals are hung, drawn, and quartered but in such an innocent and disarming way that no unfriendliness seems intended. The skillful imputation of faintly discreditable motives; the artful selection of illustrative materials; damning with the faintest of praise; these and other techniques are used to belittle, patronize and ridicule without striking a direct blow" (688).

The result, for Scott, is that Hofstadter makes progressivism far more tame and conservative, and far more Jeffersonian, than it in fact was. He vastly understates the extent to which leading progressives were willing to use national power in unprecedented ways. Yet the 1912 platform of the Progressive Party was chock-a-block with calls for state (and especially federal) action, and it called for constitutional amendment in the event national reform efforts ran afoul of constitutional limits. As Scott notes, it is a "curious" reading of the times to find the indignant enthusiasms of the progressives to be marked by "gentility and conservatism." When the audience to TR's address at the Bull Moose Convention responded with unrestrained passion to his charge that they "stood at Armageddon and battled for the Lord it was hardly a festival in celebration of capitalism." Nor should the political tallies of the day be ignored: Taft, the closest to a constitutional conservative candidate, ran third to Wilson and TR, and the socialist candidate Eugene Debs received nearly a million votes (691).

Scott also notes that Hofstadter's understanding of the New Deal is distorted by his gloss on progressivism. In Hofstadter's account, there is a radical discontinuity between the politics and ideology of the Progressive Era and the New Deal. While the Depression increased the magnitude of the problems with which reformers had to grapple, they had in their tool kit a variety of extant progressive reforms and ideas, such as a national income tax and the notion of the national government as regulator and even provider of certain works projects. If anything, the Progressive Era was radical on a broader front than the New Deal. Even by Hofstadter's own admission, the New Deal failed to produce a body of political writing comparable to the Progressive Era (695–96).

In the end, "The Progressive Era demonstrated that political power was capable of curbing economic power and that an uncontrolled capitalism would, by easy stages, be replaced by reform capitalism" (699). Whether Scott looks on this eventuality with hope or disdain is unclear from his tone, but it is clear that he attributes to the progressive movement an "inner coherence" and radical quality at odds with Hofstadter's reinterpretation along conservative lines. This coherence is marked by several key features including confidence in man's ability to shape the social environment through democratic politics and expanded executive power, and a new role for religion as harbinger of social change. The progressives blazed the trail for the New Deal (699). And the reader might surmise that

Scott, were he writing today, would say that the progressives blazed the trail for the Great Society and even the cultural revolution that followed it. But it is worth noting that even Scott's volitional account, with its emphasis on the enduring historical significance of the progressives, doesn't quite get to the nature or extent of their historicism and their concomitant attack on the founders' Constitution—a notable lacuna in light of the fact that Scott wrote as a political scientist in a leading political science journal.

John Higham also took on "The Cult of the 'American Consensus'" in a 1959 essay.[70] He notes that through the 1940s and '50s scholars came around to the view that progressive historians such as Turner, Beard, and Parrington got it wrong insofar as they emphasized fundamental tensions and conflict in American history. The story of western democracy versus eastern entrenched interests no longer captivated the imaginations of historians by the mid-twentieth century. They were looking for something newfangled, and as avatars of intellectual trends are wont to do, they found it. For the new breed of historians, American history was not painted in "bold hues of conflict" or torn by "jagged and discontinuous" developments. Instead, a happy homogeneity lay across the fruited plain from the Revolution onward.

Higham observes that the new historical interpretations emphasized continuity and even monism—with a few notable exceptions such as Woodward's *Origins of the New South*. Hofstadter's *Age of Reform* neatly reversed the older views, with populism and progressivism being reconfigured as essentially conservative efforts to recapture and preserve the past.[71] In Hofstadter's account, the New Deal lacked any real intellectual progenitor. Potter's *People of Plenty* emphasized economic similarities rather than differences, reducing claims of difference to the mere *perception* of difference. "A psychological approach to conflict enables historians to substitute a schism in the soul for a schism in society."[72] Hays's *The Response to Industrialism* synthesized the scholarship on the Gilded Age and concluded that one group projected onto another responsibility for changes into which all were thrown. Meanwhile, scholars such as Hartz attacked rather than celebrated uniformity, but it was

uniformity he found. For Hartz, the liberal consensus was stulti-
fying, while for Boorstin the nonideological, pragmatic consensus
was salvific—a mindless lack of ideological commitment that bred
stability. Higham claims that this consensus history, with its lack
of emphasis on divisive principles, amounts to an "anti-progressive
interpretation."[73]

But the limitation of Higham's account is clear: as it rightly
brings to the surface the failure of his contemporaries to recognize
the clash of ideas that defined the progressive age, it never quite
gets to what those ideas were, beyond the ones most commonly
laid out by the progressive historians themselves. Their emphasis
on "conflict" did not often translate into open acknowledgment of
hostility to the founders' Constitution, or to their radical attempt
to reconfigure the Christian religion—and Higham never mentions their attacks on these fronts. In this sense, he seems too close
to the progressivism he describes, and he commits an error similar
in kind to those of the consensus historians he criticizes. Still, he
rightly identifies an enduring consequence of the consensus historians' efforts: they caused a "fog of complacency" to settle over a
history profession that could no longer take ideas seriously.[74] As he
observed a few years later:

> The emphasis on consensus and continuity has softened
> the outlines and flattened the crises of American history.
> A certain tameness and amiability have crept into our view of
> things; perhaps the widespread interest in myths comes partly
> from a feeling that the realities are simply not as interesting.
> The conservative frame of reference is giving us a bland his-
> tory, in which conflict is muted, in which the classic lines of
> social justice are underplayed, in which the elements of spon-
> taneity, effervescence, and violence in American life get little
> sympathy or attention. Now that the progressive impulse is
> subsiding, scholarship is threatened with a moral vacuum.[75]

Alas, Higham's proclamation of the death of the progressive impulse was premature, and his inability to identify the fundamental

thrusts of progressivism marks him as perhaps more sympathetic to consensus history than he recognizes.

Finally, Berkeley historian Henry F. May published his influential *The End of American Innocence* at the very end of the decade. The book traces the role of ideas in the formation of twentieth-century America, with a salutary de-emphasis of socioeconomic causation. According to May, a belief in progress was widely shared by Americans of varying ideological pedigree and was not owned by those who were identified as progressives. But it was progressives who believed they could "speed up" the inevitable; it was they who had the faith that historical forces could and should be stimulated, managed, and directed, and it was this disposition that separated them from their opponents.[76] But even while recognizing this disposition, May concurs with Hofstadter that there was an "actual conservatism" to the progressive project, along with a confident moralism. The social gospel called for a return to the Bible, and "some purpose of restoration" of the "sacred institutions" of American government was stated in most secular progressive rhetoric.[77] The Progressive Era was "the time when eternal morality and progress seemed to be joined together."[78] May does not make clear that the progressives' eternal morality bore almost no relation to that of the founders, or to the Constitution they designed to enshrine it. May portrays Woodrow Wilson as a conservative realist, always seeking to link the present with the organic past. Even Wilson's writings on the problems of committee governance and the prospects for administration as a method and a political principle mark him out, in May's account, as a realist more than a radical.[79]

May does identify thoroughgoing relativism in philosophers such as James and Dewey and in social scientists such as Ward, Sumner, Ross, Ely, and Beard. He does not, however, link their thought directly to that of the great progressive political actors of the day, and in some respects he sets the two groups in opposition to each other. He notes that the intellectuals' relativism played itself out in hostility toward—though not necessarily a repudiation of—"the greatest symbol of American fixity, the Constitution."[80] A decade earlier, he had pointed to the influence of the social gospel on political progressivism and had even suggested that "later in the de-velopment of American liberalism, when direct contact with the early Social Gospel is not provable, its influence is still apparent. The moral, ethical, optimistic and fundamental religious strain that runs through a great deal of twentieth-century progressivism could hardly have been developed without the change in religious opinion."[81]

This guarded recognition of the depth of the progressive cri-tique of America—something that one finds in Scott as well as May—was stillborn. For the times they were a changin'. As the 1950s gave way to the '60s, American scholarship was increasingly defined by the concerns of the "New Left." The deep sympathy of that intellectual coterie with the aspirations as well as the histori-cal orientation of progressivism helped ensure that a full account-ing of progressivism's nature and purposes would be put off for another two generations.

FOUR Progressive Historiography in a Countercultural Age

By the beginning of the 1960s, leading scholars were laying the groundwork for a sustained reaction against what they saw as the political and intellectual conservatism of the previous decades. They set the stage for the rise of the New Left, which would come to prominence in the social sciences and humanities disciplines of American universities. One of the most important players in this movement was William Appleman Williams of the University of Wisconsin, Madison—long a trusty redoubt of intellectual progressivism. Williams published *The Contours of American History* in 1961. His central thesis—in that book and others—was that the story of America is the story of empire. It was a thesis that had a profound influence on a generation of graduate students. It led him and others to consider progressivism as but one manifestation of empire building, and therefore the status quo.

Williams approached the problem from a position that was in many—but not all—respects to the left of leading historians such as Hofstadter and Schlesinger Jr. Williams rejected the psychologism of both and insisted on a return to ideology and interest as central ordering concepts of historical analysis. He offered a gloss on Frederick Jackson Turner's frontier thesis, maintaining that imperial expansion, domestically and internationally, allowed Americans to dodge and elide the pressing problems of race and class injustice. His interest was more in undermining than correcting the dominant liberalism of the day, and he hoped to replace it with something that was more cognizant of the reality of economic expansion through imperial hegemony—but also was more sympathetic to decentralization and localism. He saw deep continuities in the thought of American theorists and political actors across the ideological spectrum, most of whom shared, in Williams's estimation, commitments to individualism and private property rather than the general welfare, and a belief that in light of those commitments expansionism, rather than social democracy or social action, was the best means to achieve social stability. Liberalism was therefore a heresy, not objecting to the idea of the general welfare but falsely grounding it in individual supremacy.[1]

All of this led Williams to see the progressives, including leading figures such as Woodrow Wilson, as Christian capitalists merely trying to harmonize private (including corporate) interests, rather than to challenge the system. Twentieth-century reform efforts amounted to little more than benevolent despotism, adapting "the mercantilism of the Founding Fathers to contemporary circumstances."[2] Tracing the roots of this reality back to Lockean individualism, Williams sees Locke as having rejected Shaftesbury's notion of the importance of conscience and responsibility in favor of individualism, utilitarianism, and pragmatism as "natural" outlooks and behaviors (61–65). Mercantilism, not a new order of the ages based on natural rights, was behind the American founding (115, 147). As mercantilism gave way to the allied philosophy of laissez-faire, most everyone, including so-called reformers, tried to buttress the American commitment to economic aggrandizement and private property. Populists and progressives alike attempted to use the rhetoric of liberty and private property in support of reform that would have placed limits on both—a quixotic pursuit. Williams sees both social gospelers and Roman Catholics as being influenced by Leo XIII's *Rerum Novarum* in 1891, which stressed cooperation and equity between employers and laborers. But this led labor leaders to attempt to improve labor's relative position and to favor economic expansion rather than attacks on private property: to embrace Christian capitalism rather than Christian socialism. Christian capitalist leaders in turn embraced imperial expansion through the missionary movement. Group consciousness rather than individual consciousness came to the fore, but the main contours of American history had not changed (357–58). While Williams allows that one or another version of progressivism has guided American policy throughout the twentieth century, he sees it as having been handicapped by its Babbittry, devotion to efficiency, and ethnocentrism. Even the thought of Christian capitalists such as Ely tended to converge with the interests of corporate leaders (390–401).

Williams insists that the progressives sought to nationalize and Americanize, but it is striking the extent to which he does not attempt to define Americanization—other than in materialist terms. He is willing to allow that John Dewey was the most powerful influence on progressives in the decades after 1910. Dewey developed a philosophy of all-around growth that, in William's account, was weak because of a lack of definition and inherent relativism and encouraged only "ameliorative adjustment to things-as-they-are" and assimilation to corporate interests (405). But Williams does not allow that the "weakness" of such evolutionary pragmatism was in fact a strength insofar as it continuously undermined moral and constitutional norms and expectations. In fine, economic questions loom large in Williams's account, and constitutional questions are all but invisible, as he insists that a fundamental conservatism characterizes even progressive thought:

> Despite all the assertions about old and new orders, and about various fundamental changes that are claimed to have occurred, the essence of American history throughout the twentieth century has been the continuing attempt to resolve the dichotomy between a set of ideas developed in the 1890s and a reality to which they have proved ill-adapted. American leaders have been grappling with one central issue: how to transform a political economy created and dominated by the large corporation into a true social system—a community— without undercutting private property, without destroying

> the large corporation, and while further handicapped by the
> anti-intellectual consequences of the frontier experience . . .
> which offered a surplus of property as a substitute for
> thought about society. (374)

Progressivism, and the New Deal that consolidated it, each failed because neither provided "a class-conscious industrial gentry" looking out for the public welfare, or "a fundamental reorganization of the constitutional and political framework" along syndicalist rather than geographic lines (449).

Michigan State University's Norman Pollack, by contrast, added to the outpouring of scholarship in the early 1960s a quasi-Marxist defense of the populist strain of progressivism, effectively separating himself from the treatment of Hofstadter and others. For Pollack, the populists were far more interested in the structure and consequences of economic power than with the individual personalities or morality of the capitalists. Systemic critiques concentrating on alienation, domination, class struggle, and dialectical development were central concerns.[3] In Pollack's rendering, the populists' language was very much akin to the academic language of the 1960s.

Populism was a radical, forward-looking movement that did not seek to roll back the tide to a preindustrial America. Even William Jennings Bryan's nomination in 1896 served the cause of theoretical radicalism insofar as enough radicals saw tactical advantage in it. Populism in general sought to encourage the full development of human potentiality and "divinity," given the changed circumstances of the industrial age.[4] It was concerned with human freedom and dignity in all their manifestations. Accepting the idea and inevitability of progress, populism longed for its realization.[5]

But perhaps the most pathbreaking book on progressivism to emerge in the early part of the decade was Gabriel Kolko's *The Triumph of Conservatism*.[6] Kolko was a New Left historian who attempted—in the mold of Williams—to construct a grand narrative of American history that revealed the true forces under the surface of epiphenomenal events. For Kolko, the "Progressive" Era was really an era of conservatism, serving the needs of particular classes of men and institutions—especially the business classes. It was "an effort to preserve the basic social and economic relations essential to a capitalist society, an effort that was frequently consciously as well as functionally conservative." Largely about rationalization in service of business, the Progressive Era preserved the major economic interests of the nation and saw business in control of politics rather than vice versa. *Political capitalism* is the term applied by Kolko to describe the dominance of politics by business interests in order to achieve stability, predictability, and security for those interests (2–3). The "Hamiltonian unity" of politics and economics at the federal level provided a bulwark against haphazard state regulations and more genuinely democratic and progressive aspirations (4–6). Kolko claims that in the early years of the twentieth century large corporations failed to stabilize their businesses through consolidation, monopoly, and voluntary agreement and so turned their attention from economics to politics. "The dominant fact of American political life at the beginning of this century was that big business led the struggle for the federal regulation of the economy." Kolko therefore warns—rather presciently, it turns out—that it is wrongheaded to assume that government regulation is "automatically progressive" in the "commonly understood sense of that term" (57–58).

Teddy Roosevelt's fundamental conservatism came down to a defense of business interests and a call for charity in the face of inequality (77). Robert La Follette recognized Roosevelt for what he was and condemned his dismissal of true reformers as demagogues, thus confusing the lines of battle (112). William Howard Taft, meanwhile, simply rededicated himself to "those noble conservative virtues, Reason and Moderation," in order to stifle change. However conservative that change was, Taft was not its harbinger and could not effectively speak the language of his times (190). Wilson too was a conservative, an anti-Bryan Democrat who showed remarkable ideological consistency (205). "Certainly it must be concluded that historians have overemphasized the basic differences between the Presidents of the Progressive Era, and ignored their much more important similarities. In 1912 the specific utterances and programs of all three were identical on fundamentals, and party platforms reflected this common agreement" (281). As for liberal intellectuals such as Lester Ward, Richard T. Ely, and Herbert Croly, their embrace—even divinization—of the state ignored questions of formal and direct democratic control and thus helped make political capitalism possible, whether under the banner of New Nationalism or New Freedom (214–16). "Business supremacy over the control of wealth" continued to be the defining feature of the American economy before, during, and after the Progressive Era (279–80).

In the end, Kolko seems to be describing a kind of crony capitalism. The problem with his analysis is that cronyism is by no means "conservative" as that term would be understood by classical liberals and by no means constitutional as constitutionalism would be understood by the founders. In his single-minded devotion to demystifying the essence of a co-opted progressive movement, he points, albeit indirectly, to its incompatibility with the founders' Constitution of limited and enumerated powers. Kolko's attempt at grand synthesis, while upending traditional understandings of the motives and goals of progressive reformers, nonetheless continues to insist that the story of progressivism is in fact the story of changed economic conditions and the responses to those conditions. It is emphatically not the story of changed constitutionalism, or at least not intentionally. Democratic control over wealth— rather than a return to constitutionalism—is the solution for what ails America (305).

Like Williams's and Kolko's sprawling and influential books and Pollack's more concentrated treatise, Hofstadter's 1962 *Anti-intellectualism in American Life* was written as a reaction against the "political and intellectual conditions of the 1950's."[7] But Hofstadter, as we have seen, was more sympathetic to the Progressive Era than Williams. He was willing to offer something of a celebration of its bringing together of intellect and power, which he saw as an unusual interlude in the history of a country that had repeatedly exhibited "disdain for intellectuals"—another theme that would be at the forefront of American academic thought in the 1960s and '70s.

It was the progressives who saw the need for "humanizing and controlling the large aggregates of power," and it is them we can credit for our move away, at least for a time, from the old Jacksonian suspicion of expertise. In the Progressive Era, "Intellect was reinstalled" in America in the service of change and in "the interests of democracy itself." In this time, a new "moral atmosphere" was created—though not a new regime—by men interested in ideas. Finally, the reins of power were available to the likes of Roosevelt, Wilson, Lodge, La Follette, and others. Among the outstanding political leaders of the age, it was only William Jennings Bryan who kept alive anti-intellectualism. The rest created the brain trusts and offered the moral inspiration that went along with respect for intellect (197–99).

In a familiar story, Hofstadter sees anti-intellectualism, driven by the distaste of "business interests" for intellect, rising from the ashes of the reform movement and from the corpses of ousted reformers. Wisconsin offered a glimpse of this process in microcosm: discontent led to a call for expertise, expertise was realized at the University of Wisconsin under the leadership of Ely, and reaction came in the form of "anti-intellectualist denunciations of university experts" (199–203). Hofstadter does not allow for the possibility that the reasons for reaction might have transcended anti-intellectualism.

Hofstadter suggests that the progressive achievements were limited in the realm of actual political power but that they left America with a powerful uplift in the realm of tone and style, animating intellectuals like Croly, Lippmann, Dewey, and Beard to believe in—and proselytize for—the idea that social control and mastery were finally possible on a large scale (205). The comfort level that politicians like TR and Wilson exhibited in the company of intellectuals seemed grounds for hope, even though they could quickly turn on expertise when it suited them, and even though Wilson was "a creature of the past" when it came to the world of ideas, not nearly sympathetic enough to liberal expertise for the tastes of some of his intellectual contemporaries, or for Hofstadter (207–9).

The political estrangement between intellectuals and the public would continue until the Depression once again created enough discontent that expertise seemed the only solution. In fact, the New Deal was the high-water mark of rapprochement between intellectuals and the public. In Hofstadter's straightforward morality play, just as intellectuals rode high, reactionaries plotted against them (213–14). Though the brain-trusters served the public well, they did not govern it, even as the public persisted in claiming they did. Though experts wielding "pervasive and vital influence" over constitutional officers represented something new in the American regime, Hofstadter can only allow that there was at most "some kernel" of truth in their critics' jeremiads. It is hard to overstate Hofstadter's dismissiveness—sometimes explicit, sometimes implied—when he examines those critics. "The critics of the New Deal exaggerated the power of the intellectuals and also portrayed them as impractical, irresponsible, conspiratorial experimentalists, grown arrogant and publicity conscious because of their sudden rise from obscurity to prominence." The critics were "right wingers" with "cranky" conceptions of power, wielding weapons of "popular prejudice" (217–18).

Hard on the heels of *Anti-intellectualism*, Hofstadter assembled an anthology of progressive writings, consisting of thirty-six documents in total.[8] Yet they did not quite cover the gamut of progressive thinking. They failed—by design, it is reasonable to assume—to convey the radical core of the progressive synthesis. The emphasis of the collection was overwhelmingly on corporate misdeeds and the need for corporate and labor regulation and reform. Only a handful of documents dealt squarely with what might be called the constitutional dimensions of progressivism. Arranged artfully, the first three were excerpts from Justice Holmes's dissent in *Lochner v. New York*, Louis Brandeis's original "Brandeis Brief," and Justice Brewer's majority opinion in *Muller v. Oregon*—the case for which the Brandeis Brief had been prepared, and which in turn cited it. Read together, the selections paint the picture of a formerly "conservative," even social Darwinist, Court finally coming to its senses under the force of progressive argumentation and putting its stamp of approval on a Constitution with a newfound capaciousness for accommodating the regulatory state.[9] Only one document deals squarely with the religious dimensions of progressive thought—selections from Rauschenbusch's *Christianity and the Social Crisis*. And it is embedded in a section of the book otherwise dealing with social and moral issues arising from industrialization. Christianity and the Constitution, when properly interpreted, become useful adjuncts to the progressive project of reforming the material world through regulation.

Hofstadter introduces the volume by noting that those who lived in and held positions of leadership in the Progressive Era were very much aware of its distinctiveness—but only because it differed from the preceding era's "materialism and corruption" in which people's "moral and political capacities" had been exhausted (1). In the face of a land plundered, power concentrated, and values crushed, the progressive movement offered "to develop the moral will, the intellectual insight, and the political and administrative agencies to remedy the accumulated evils" (2–3). The progressives, it turned out, were the original change that everyone had been waiting for: they were characterized by "great heterogeneity"—diversity, in today's parlance—yet they were morally confident, as they were intellectual yet committed to social activism, and deliberate yet impatient with the slow pace of reform.

Continuing his argument that the progressive movement was a function of middle-class angst and dissent, Hofstadter notes that it flourished during a period of comparative prosperity, very unlike the New Deal that followed it (6). With the backbone of American society purportedly clamoring for reform, the movement was less a response to crisis than an optimistic assertion of the possibilities inherent in unleashing real energy in government—an energy strangely divorced from the constitutional limits that frame the discussion of energy in *The Federalist*. In fact, Hofstadter never once mentions the Constitution in his introduction, although the threats to "democracy" appear legion.

Hofstadter suggests that agrarian reformers and the urban middle class came together to oppose crass materialism and found expression in the voices of political actors like La Follette, Wilson, and Roosevelt, intellectuals like Croly and Upton Sinclair, and scholars like Beard, J. Allen Smith, Ely, John Commons, Veblen, Dewey, Ward, and Holmes, all bent on making a "disinterested contribution" to reform (7). All were concerned with the uses to which thought and action could be put. Even churches recognized that Christianity had to make "a contribution" to solving "new moral problems" and therefore become not simply a "religious creed" but a "social force." The "voice of Christian conscience" could be heard in progressive political and economic schemes (8).

Progressivism comes down to a "reformist enthusiasm" with longevity, something that provided the "moral inspiration" as well as some of the "administrative devices" for the New Deal. The magnitude of the progressive reconfiguration of American politics, and the profound organic and theoretical connections between progressivism and the New Deal, completely disappear in Hofstadter's account.

Through his editorial choices—selections and arrangement—Hofstadter keeps alive a central conceit of the progressive self-understanding: "The opening debate of the modern era was between antigovernment ideologues who lacked a sense of humanity . . . and warm-hearted pragmatists keen to use science to alleviate human misery." But this conceals more than it reveals: "Shoved out of the picture was the mainstream of the American political tradition . . . of natural rights and republican self-rule."[10]

In 1964, Samuel P. Hays continued the work he began eight years earlier in his *Response to Industrialism*, with a significant article on progressive reform movements in municipal government.[11] Hays rejects the Mowry-Hofstadter analysis that suggests the movement for "good government" over "machine politics" sprang largely from middle-class reformers. Since the opponents of reform were also often middle class, "one cannot describe Progressive reform as a phenomenon, the special nature of which can be explained in terms of middle-class characteristics" (158). Rather than concentrating on the ideology of reformers, Hays looks at their political practice, that is, who did what and when (157–58). The ideology of "democratization" was used to mask the reality of centralization modeled on "efficient business enterprise" (168). In fact, the "model of efficient business enterprise . . . rather than the New England town meeting, provided the positive inspiration for the municipal reformer" (168).

Hays finds that the source of support for municipal reform came from the upper rather than lower or middle classes. Echoing Kolko, he argues that the "business, professional, and upper-class groups who dominated municipal reform movements were all involved in the rationalization and systematization of modern life" over a "broad and city-wide" range of activities (161). Reform amounted to an attempt by the upper class to take political power from the lower and middle classes, as evidenced by the fact that small businessmen and artisans lacked representation in reform organizations (162). "Reformers, therefore, wished not simply to replace bad men with good; they proposed to change the occupational and class origins of decision-makers" (163)—partly by centralizing representation through a shift from ward to citywide elections, thereby undermining representative government that allowed for the expression of "grass-roots impulses" (168–69). Centralization, rather than broadening, of political control was a consistent goal of the urban reformers in the early twentieth century (167).

Although he does not extend himself in the direction of a full-blown constitutional argument, Hays does note that municipal reform, like other incidents of progressivism, amounted to reliance on experts in "business, in government, and in the professions" who "measured, studied, analyzed, and manipulated ever wider realms of human life" (168). It thus was oriented, not toward restoring a previous order, but toward ushering in a wholly new one: "The Progressive Era witnessed rapid strides toward a more centralized system and a relative decline for a more decentralized system. This development constituted an accommodation of forces outside the business community to the political trends within business and professional life rather than vice versa. It involved a tendency for decision-making processes inherent in science and technology to prevail over those inherent in representative government" (169).

Synthetic accounts of earlier progressive scholarship also began to emerge in the 1960s, including anthologies like *The Progressive Era*, by the University of Chicago's Arthur Mann.[12] For Mann, the roots of progressivism lie in paradox—maldistribution of wealth and power in the context of an egalitarian political tradition. In the face of this paradox, progressives felt the need not simply to sit but to do something—something that would solve "The Social Question." This involved tackling government corruption while simultaneously expanding the power of government (a paradox not mentioned by Mann). The populists of John Hicks's account alike with the city gentry of George Mowry's were animated by interest group politics—further animated, in the case of the gentry, by the disquiet implied in Hofstadter's idea of "status revolution." Whether through New Freedom or New Nationalism, progressives were concerned at the policy level with economic and social security.[13]

In 1966, historian Charles Crowe of the University of Georgia attempted to chronicle the emergence of progressive history.[14] He notes that the discipline of history "came to maturity in America during the golden age of Pragmatism and Progressivism" (109). He might have said the same of other key humanities or social science disciplines.[15] Across the intellectual world, "experience" was supplanting logical reasoning, and belief in "change" was supplanting attachment to the permanent things. As Crowe argues, "Intellectuals and publicists in virtually every field of thought strove mightily to 'bust' the intellectual trusts, to establish an 'open shop' of ideas" (109).

According to Crowe, progressive historians like Turner, Beard, and Parrington shared not so much a scrupulously delineated or precisely shared interpretation of American history but more a sensibility—"a set of related impressions" (112) including a belief in the primacy of process and evolution, pragmatism, economic determinism, relativism, and utilitarianism. The progressive cast to history came to the fore "at a time when professional historians were emerging from the university seminars to capture control of historical writing from the gifted and patriotic amateurs of the XIXth century" (110n5). This theme of professionalization and professional capture was picked up two decades later by University of Chicago historian Peter Novick in *That Noble Dream*—a theme to which we will return in the final chapter of this work.[16]

Crowe notes that by the turn of the century it was virtually impossible to escape the dominance of an evolutionary framework and that the progressive historians extended its reach to the fundamental currents of American history, as evidenced by Beard in both *The Rise of American Civilization* and *An Economic Interpretation of the Constitution* (112). As Parrington said of Beard: "From a critical study of the Constitution came a discovery that struck home like a submarine torpedo. . . . The drift toward plutocracy was not a drift away from the spirit of the Constitution but an inevitable unfolding from its premises. . . . It is not easy to understand today why since Civil War days intelligent Americans should so strangely have confused the Declaration of Independence and the Constitution, and have come to accept them as complementary statements of the democratic purpose of America."[17] Parrington made this observation in what Crowe refers to as the "Summa Theologica" of progressive history, *Main Currents of American Thought*, "a book which thrust a systematic and formalized account of Progressive notions into all the major aspects of American thought and into every corner of national life" (121). After this, progressive history was triumphant, "the inspiration for hundreds of textbooks and possibly thousands of scholarly articles" (122).

Nevertheless, Crowe concludes that progressive history is on the wane, in part because scholars have been "put off by the tale of American history as an orderly march of events toward a 'solution' or near solution to one 'problem' after another" (123). Crowe thus reduces the progressive synthesis to a kind of pragmatic problem solving. There is little to generalize about when it comes to progressivism, at least in Crowe's account of it—an attitude that had become common among certain scholars by the midsixties. For them, progressivism becomes a kind of historical curiosity, a footnote to a dead past.

In 1967, University of California, Santa Barbara historian Otis L. Graham Jr. published a detailed empirical study entitled *An Encore for Reform*.[18] Despite—or perhaps because of—his insistent empiricism, Graham manages to blur the differences between the progressives and the founders by portraying both as simply suspicious of power. Beyond that, he claims the progressives exhibited too much variety to justify generalization. The book traces the opinions of the New Deal that were held by some four hundred "old progressive" reformers, grouping them into "supporters," "opponents," and several other categories. These were individuals who first struggled with the full range of modern social problems and sought to limit economic power "as the Founders had limited political power." They sought not to damage American capitalism or conceptions of justice (5).

According to Graham, the main legacy of the movement was a body of ideas, in the form of values and the techniques to realize them, that laid the groundwork for considerable continuities between the progressive and New Deal periods, the latter borrowing freely from both the New Freedom and New Nationalism (7). But the old progressives did not uniformly endorse the New Deal and instead reflected the "vexatious variety" of a movement that spanned several decades and several political parties, all levels of government, and many professions (9). In Graham's view, "Progressivism was sufficiently fragmented so that it remains inaccessible to those easy generalizations with which we long to make it manageable. The truth about it comes in small assertions, in the limited, the qualified, the discrete statement" (14). It existed for so long, and encompassed so much variety in its goals, reforms efforts, and geographic origins, that even its outlines cannot be made clear (187). The New Deal ultimately found many of its intellectual sources in events and figures more recent than those associated with the progressive movement (178).

Eschewing reductionism, Graham maintains that progressivism accomplished much political good that cannot be reduced to the New Left's caricature of it as a "defensive movement" by a "moralistic middle class" out to preserve its own interests (22). The movement itself, however, was in its death throes by the 1920s, existing only as a remnant (161–66). Along with conservatives, some erstwhile progressives accented "the parade of imaginary horribles" associated with the New Deal (25). Walter Lippman grew suspicious of central planning, and many others rejected paternalism in favor of a level playing field, partly reflecting the differences between the New Nationalism and the New Freedom.

But in all this, the constitutional case against the New Deal rarely comes to the surface. When Graham does mention it, he does not credit it. Old progressive reformers who rejected the coercion of the New Deal's apparently permanent planning mechanisms eschewed "the outraged constitutionalism of the James M. Becks and Herbert Hoovers of the era," instead embracing "the principles of true progressive reform"—a reform that released rather than bound (66–68, chap. 2). Constitutionalism comes across as something that existed only in the perfervid imaginations of the Old Right. As the Constitution sinks beneath the surface of a great ocean of thought, Graham limits himself to carefully categorizing those who attached the cement overshoes.

Also in 1967, Northwestern political and social historian Robert H. Wiebe published *The Search for Order*, a book chronicling shifting American values from the last two decades of the nineteenth century through the first two decades of the twentieth, and in the course of so doing rejecting the status theory of reform. Americans, according to Wiebe, began to move away from the attachments of small town life and local autonomy in favor of newfound sympathy for impersonal bureaucratic norms. They were involved in "a search for order" within a society "distended" by "nationalization, industrialization, mechanization, urbanization," that in turn led to "dislocation and bewilderment."[19] This search for order was driven by those who saw the need for regularity and the rational management of social problems. Neither millenarian reformers nor clingers to the wreckage of the sinking ship of social status, the drivers of progressive reform were members of a confident new middle class that had in many ways created the very problems they now confronted. Torn between the desire to preserve local sovereignty and traditional community life on the one hand and the need to confront massive corporate power on the other, these Americans searched for an elusive political and economic balance, one that found expression in antimonopoly sentiment (44–45, 52). The impulse of many reformers, whether Christian capitalist or Christian socialist, was directed toward the preservation of local communities, not the creation of "a huge apparatus for centralized direction" (74).

But as local communities continued to disintegrate under the pressures of modernization, various social anxieties prevented a unified approach to reform. As the "new middle class" began to emerge, it struggled to find common ground. Professional self-consciousness, aided and abetted by the emergence of the modern university graduate school, bestowed increasingly cohesive identities on the members of the new middle class—identities that transcended the traditional sense of place (121–23). Business and professional associations multiplied, all oriented toward bringing order and stability to a rapidly evolving social environment.

And a funny thing happened as this new middle class came face to face with the "revolution in values" that had been brought about by the theological and philosophical idealists and reformers: "The ideas that filtered through and eventually took the fort were bureaucratic ones, peculiarly suited to the fluidity and impersonality of an urban-industrial world . . . [stressing] techniques of constant watchfulness and mechanisms of continuous management" (145). Wiebe suggests that bureaucratic norms began to replace the organic and historical analogies of the intellectual classes, though it is hardly clear that the bureaucratic orientation he describes was anything other than the logical outgrowth of historical and organic thinking—the means by which History could most efficiently progress (148). In any event, "The new middle class supplied the largest body of adherents to bureaucratic thought" (153). The point was to mesh the many moving parts of the new industrial society as seamlessly as possible, without explicit recourse to some source of social cohesion apart from the nitty-gritty of men's lives. Expertise, rather than idealism, became the point of practical engagement and the object of the new progressive science of politics (161–95). Nowhere in his elaborate rejection of the status theory of progressive reform does Wiebe allow a constitutional consideration to enter.

Also in 1967, cultural historian Allen F. Davis tapped into the "Great Society" rhetoric of his time to tell the story of progressive idealists who spearheaded the "social settlements" movement in immigrant and black areas of Boston, Chicago, and New York in order to tackle the problems of urban poverty head on, including those of working women and children. "The settlement house became one of the principal instruments in this first war on poverty. Located in the middle of the worst neighborhoods and manned by middle-class volunteers, it provided a center of sympathy, help, and hope to nearby slum dwellers."[20] The volunteers were "practical idealists," workers for "social justice," who were, in the mold of those described by Henry May, optimistic and confident that things could be set aright. They were genuinely sympathetic to the concerns of organized labor and the city and were far from the paternalists described by Samuel Hays or George Mowry. Nor could their actions be accounted for by the "status revolution" of Richard Hofstadter.[21] Inspired by a similar settlement movement in England, pioneers like Jane Addams sought to spread education and opportunity, including lectures, artistic programs, and even university education to the working classes (40–41). "The settlement movement and progressive education intertwined at many points," with John Dewey being a member of the first board of directors of Chicago's Hull House and a frequent visitor there (58). Progressive economists such as Richard Ely were also frequent visitors to several settlements (171). Settlement workers and their allies helped draft the new Progressive Party's platform in 1912 and ensured that it was committed to social reform, not just an abstract New Nationalism or the personality of a Theodore Roosevelt (195). They were among those who turned the party's 1912 convention into something of a religious revival meeting (201).

The reformers felt not so much alienated from American life as rationally dedicated to solving the problems of urban America and applying the Christian idea of service, broadly conceived, to the city (27–29). Many if not most were convinced of the economic roots of social problems. Psychologically reductionist accounts rooted in "anxiety, alienation, and guilt" are inadequate to account for the idealism of settlement residents, an idealism buttressed by a certain confidence—perhaps overconfidence—in the power of social science analysis (39).

Writing at about the same time as Davis, and embodying the spirit of the age, Hofstadter discounted the enduring influence of "the progressive historians" in his book-length study of Turner, Beard, and Parrington.[22] Although each of these men produced "central works of twentieth-century American historical writing," Hoftstadter emphasizes less their influence than the context in which they wrote and the sources from which their writing sprang (xi). He therefore offers a history of progressive history in the passive voice. In his contextualized account, differences rather than similarities, and diffusion rather than cohesion, take center stage. The historians don't represent a unified school of thought, largely because of their different experiences and temperaments. They rather represent a style of historical writing that, finally, was not aloof from "popular aspirations" but was instead critical and democratic (3–43).

For Hofstadter, Turner made clear the importance of adaptation and growth in American history and the individualism, mobility, and sense of opportunity produced by the frontier experience rather than by the regime writ large. American democracy came organically from American forests, not from the minds of men (47–83). Turner's importance lay not so much in being the first to see clearly the significance of the West to American political development as in being the first to eschew "old narrative history" and to insist on taking full account of "repetitive sociological processes" (152). Hofstadter notes that New Dealers accepted the importance of the frontier by noting that its end pointed to the necessity of new devices of command and control to ensure continued adaptation and change. When Americans can no longer run away to open land, they must confront the problems of industrial society—and carve out their freedom—through politics. Quoting from FDR's Commonwealth Club speech, with its emphasis on a reappraisal of values and the need for "enlightened" administration of resources, Hofstadter nowhere mentions the tension between FDR's new vision of politics and the founders' Constitution. In his generous quotes from the speech, he edits out the premise on which FDR's vision of enlightened administration rests: the overturning, indeed the reversal, of the founders' theory of natural rights (90). Roosevelt claimed that "the Declaration of Independence discusses the problem of Government in terms of a contract. . . . Under such a contract rulers were accorded power, and the people consented to that power on consideration that they be accorded certain rights. The task of statesmanship has always been the re-definition of these rights in terms of a changing and growing social order." On this view, rights are not natural but conventional, the product of a quid pro quo that depends on an initial grant from the government, and whose meaning is ever-changing, depending on the determinations of politicians and the administrative classes.

According to Hofstadter, Beard, like Turner, turned his back on "the abstract and conservative style of thought" that had dominated America for generations. He too revolted against formalism at a time that was ripe for such revolt (182–83). He was an academic counterpart to muckraking journalists, interested in "reality in the course of change." But "reality" in the sense Hofstadter uses it has to do not with moral realism but with economic and sociological theory. Sharing the functionalist and group interest model of politics put forth by Arthur Bentley a few years prior, along with the arguments of J. Allen Smith as to the undemocratic character of the Constitution, Beard was interested in how ideas and political constitutions served the interests of the groups that designed them (186–87). Under the weight of this emphasis, purposiveness in the old sense was crushed. The Constitution could be seen as having no ends higher than the purportedly grubby materialism of its framers. To the extent that Hofstadter criticizes Beard's overemphasis on motives, it is not to reveal purposes but to complain that "he shifted historical attention away from what was more vital still: the consequences, intended or otherwise, of what was done" (230). Beard's realism was not quite real enough for Hofstadter—though it did rest on the right instincts. "Reality was the opposite of everything the genteel tradition had stood for in literature and the formalistic thinkers in social philosophy. Reality was the inside story. It was rough and sordid, hidden and neglected, and being hard and material and inexorable, was somehow more important than mere ideas and theories." Not content with description, Hofstadter concludes that this conception of reality was a sign that "a modern critical intelligentsia was emerging in the United States" (184).

Beard's book, according to Hofstadter, was "an innovation in form" and a "new historical genre," stripping out as it did narrative history in favor of the "essential facts" of an undemocratic Constitution (211). Yet this innovation in form serves to bury a larger substance in an avalanche of detail, and Hofstadter elides very important facets of the progressive worldview by adopting it as his own. Using his own version of realism to suggest that Beard's economic account of the founders might be too simplistic, Hofstadter suggests the founders were not democrats but first and foremost "nationalists" who only incidentally furthered democracy on a national scale.

This too-clever-by-half version of events destroys the sense that the founding had anything to do with natural rights. That the Constitution was not "democratic" in the modern sense would have been obvious to the founders, and to the extent that they were "nationalists"—better still, Federalists—their federalism served the purpose of enshrining the Laws of Nature and of Nature's God. Further, it was not the Constitution's lack of democracy that was the main object of progressive ire. That was but a means to an intellectual end. Rather, it was the Constitution's effort to recognize certain fixed moral truths, and concomitantly to put some political purposes and processes beyond the reach of change, that animated progressives. Progressives were devotees of democracy in a rather radical sense: to the extent that it could be understood, in principle, to mean "Anything goes," and therefore to be incompatible with constitutional limits rooted in a theory of human equality that transcends time, place, and circumstance.

Meanwhile, by Hofstadter's account, for Parrington the story of America was a great morality play of democratic thought recurrently in opposition to antidemocratic thought. *The Progressive Historians* conjures up each biographical portrait in the first two volumes of Parrington's *Main Currents* to tell the same tale of progress, with Parrington himself taking the side of the dissenters, protesters, and democrats (398, 428). And this retrospective unfolding captures the most important notion of the progressive historians, according to Hofstadter: economic and political conflict as a vitalizing idea.

However, the significance of this "conflict" model, beyond being a historiographical category to which the works of progressive historians can be assigned for filing purposes, is not made clear. It was replaced, according to Hofstadter, by a more consensus-oriented understanding of American history, or one attuned to "complexity" and the "multiplicity of forces" that have driven American history (437–42). But contrary to Hofstadter, it's not quite possible to study the American regime within the frameworks of dualistic conflict, consensus, or the complex interplay of forces. Neither Hofstadter nor the progressive historians he chronicles make it possible to locate a primus inter pares in the world of ideas or men. The rational system of ordered liberty based on equal natural rights, bequeathed to posterity by the founders—of which Lincoln said the task of gratitude to our fathers, justice to ourselves, duty to posterity, and love for our species in general requires us to preserve—is nowhere visible in Hofstadter's account.

Picking up New Left themes at the end of the decade, and eschewing Hofstadter's more mainstream account, historian and journalist James Weinstein casts his avowedly radical gaze on the "false consciousness of the nature of American liberalism," which he claims has been the primary ideology of American business groups and corporate leaders and an important tool in their efforts at social control.[23] To some extent echoing Kolko's account of corporate America's interest in government intervention, Weinstein concentrates more heavily on the shifting understanding of liberalism itself and the consistent, if strategic, embrace of it by business elites. Contrary to Arthur Schlesinger Jr.'s assertion in *The Age of Jackson*, American liberalism has never been antibusiness (xii). From the laissez-faire liberalism of the nineteenth century to the liberalism of state intervention and social control, business leaders have always seen that the business of America is business and have adapted their views accordingly: "To achieve conditions suitable for free competition during the Age of Jackson, the rising entrepreneurs and their political representatives had to believe in, and promote, ideals of equality of opportunity, class mobility, and noninterference. . . . At the turn of the century the new trust magnates also pressed for reform in accordance with their new political, economic, and legal needs. . . . Cooperation and *social* efficiency were increasingly important. . . . In both instances, business leaders sponsored institutional adjustment to their needs, and supported political ideologies . . . in order to gain, and retain, popular support for their entrepreneurial activity" (xiii).

In the Progressive Era, radical critics of centralized command and control were easily co-opted by corporate liberals as the language of social engineering and efficiency overtook the language of localism and individualism (xiv). The liberalism of that era, like the liberalisms that are its direct descendants (including the New Deal and the Great Society), came into existence to serve giant corporations (ix, xv). The New Nationalism and the New Freedom were simply the names attached to the new liberalism, dominated by corporate elites and directed ultimately toward stability for business activity, arriving at this destination via "social concern and social responsibility" (3). An alliance between political leaders such as Theodore Roosevelt, William Howard Taft, and Woodrow Wilson and financial and corporate leaders was effected via the National Civic Federation, which opposed itself to radical politics and various middle-class reform efforts (6–7). "From 1908 until the United States entered World War I, the NCF played a major role in educating businessmen, professionals, and conservative farm leaders in the principles of modern liberalism" (39). With Roosevelt, these groups came to see social reform as an essentially conservative activity (61). From workmen's compensation to the Federal Trade Commission Act of 1914, leaders of large corporations championed progressive reforms that were seen to benefit corporate interests.

Small businessmen got in on the act by favoring the city commission and manager movements, displaying their "broader vision" by removing municipal decision making from mere "politics" (92). With such reforms, radical labor and minority candidates could be kept out of municipal decision making, as the costs of local government to corporations could be contained. Chambers of commerce and boards of trade had figured out a means to dominate American municipalities through new principles of scientific management (116).

Meanwhile, political opposition to corporate control was being overcome:

> In the middle of 1911 a serious threat to big business hegemony in the major political parties appeared to be shaping up; by the summer of 1912 that challenge had been dissipated. La Follette had been pushed aside by Roosevelt; the Progressive Party had shifted the focus of debate onto the problem of trust regulation; Wilson, despite the rhetorical device of the New Freedom, had made it plain that he favored and would protect the "natural" developments of the business world. Although Eugene V. Debs achieved his highest vote in 1912 — some 900,000 votes, or six percent of the total — Wilson's victory signaled the beginning of a period of consolidation and stabilization of the new liberal state. (139–40)

Of those business leaders who rallied to Roosevelt, newspaper publisher Frank Munsey summed up the tenor of the times: "The United States, he wrote, must move from excessive democracy toward a more 'parental guardianship of the people,' who needed 'the sustaining and guiding hand of the State'" (155). World War I served only to confirm the possibilities of long-standing governmental-business partnerships (251).

Great scale — whether of business or state — was essential to this new liberalism, which, in Weinstein's telling, amounts to a version of crony capitalism. In the shell game of twentieth-century American politics, liberal defenders of the corporate order have remained the dominant force, without serious competition. "The right has been sustained as a minor political force by its appeals to the individualism of the free market, but lacking major corporate support has never been a potent challenger to the new liberals. . . . The new liberals, both in the Progressive Era and later in the New

Deal, the New Frontier, and the Great Society, have demonstrated that when faced with immediate threats they can make the necessary adjustments to restore at least a façade of social harmony" (254).

In an attempt to bring some order to the chaos of the historical profession, the *New York Times Book Review* marked the end of the 1960s with a survey of the work of the "radical historians" who had come to prominence during the decade.[24] This meditation on the turmoil within the profession, penned by Johns Hopkins historian David Donald, began with the tumultuous 1969 meeting of the American Historical Association, which was marked by conflict between the "Radical Caucus" and the "Establishment." The radicals aimed their fire at the "consensus" historians who were seen to dominate the field and who minimized conflict as they emphasized the beliefs that most Americans were said to share. Despite the diversity of consensus history's practitioners—ranging from Hofstadter to Boorstin—Donald notes that "the new generation of historians sweepingly condemns all Consensus scholars for accepting, and even eulogizing, a society where poverty is tolerated because it is presumed to be transient; where racial discrimination is permissible because it too will pass away; where political conflict is muted, since everybody agrees upon everything."

Donald's account pays particular attention to Kolko's argument that the progressive period really marked the triumph of big business at the expense of populist interests. Donald takes Kolko's argument to task for being too simplified and schematic, slighting "those Progressive programs designed to promote social justice." And he argues too that Kolko's progressivism is largely compatible with Hofstadter's insofar as "both men view the differences between Wilson and T. R. as superficial, and both hold that neither Democrats nor Republicans seriously challenged the dominance of business."

Donald also takes note of Norman Pollack's depiction of discontented farmers in the 1890s as sophisticated critics of capitalism and Weinstein's identification of Eugene V. Debs as a prophet of present-day discontent but finds them unconvincing. Donald allows that the radicals have reinvigorated the field of American intellectual history and have shown, in the tradition of William Appleman Williams, that even foreign policy must be related to the whole of the American experience rather than individual actors and actions. Donald makes clear that progressive history had become a self-conscious part of the new radicalism within the historical profession. However, "taken as a whole, the work of these Radical scholars fails to carry conviction; these books leave unshaken the Consensus historian's argument that most Americans throughout our history have been contented participants in the capitalist system." Though the radicals have identified "some forgotten corners of our past and rehabilitated some long-neglected men of good will," the only thing left standing in Donald's middlebrow popular account is a safe and relatively bland consensus history.

RUMORS OF DEATH

In light of the competing scholarly accounts of the nature and significance of the Progressive Era, written over three decades and culminating in furious battles within the historical profession, it was perhaps only a matter of time before someone would attempt to put the whole matter to bed once and for all—for the profession and ultimately for the American people. And how better to do it than to claim there was no "there" there to begin with? As the 1970s began, the radicalism of the New Left gave way to a hint of postmodernism.

It was time for "An Obituary for 'the Progressive Movement.' "[25] This death notice was written by cultural historian Peter Filene of the University of North Carolina, and he offered no eulogy. The scare quotes in the article's title betray the author's purpose: to write not so much an obituary for the movement as a denial that it ever existed. In fact, Filene sees significantly less to progressivism than even Hofstadter, who at least allows for some measure of psychological unity among progressives or "temperamental traits" that they shared (24). These traits of optimism and activism are, for Filene, overinclusive and serve to define little. And Hofstadter's "status revolution" theory of the origins of progressive reform is not supported by the mixed historical record of which classes led the charge for progressive reforms (29–30).

Filene accepts the consensus among historians that progressivism was aimed at undermining privilege and expanding both democracy and government power (21). But he claims that much more divided the progressives than united them: for example, Teddy Roosevelt's belief in big government to offset the power of big business, versus what Roosevelt denigrated as the "rural toryism" of the more populist wings of the movement. Additionally, progressives alternately emphasized either democracy or paternalism (26). Such splits point not to a cohesive movement but to various incompatible visions of reform. "In each of its aspects—goals, values, membership and supporters—the movement displays a puzzling and irreducible incoherence" (31). Without a "common identity" felt by its members, a movement is not possible. There are only "shifting coalitions around different issues" (33). For Filene, the idea of a progressive movement is but sound and fury, signifying nothing.

He does not mention the central and enduring thrusts of progressivism: its indifference or hostility to the founders' Constitution, its faith in the power of expertise to solve social problems, and its millenarian, quasi-religious aspirations—each rooted in a strong, relatively unified sense of historical unfolding and thus pointing to deep theoretical unity rather than division. This is perhaps understandable in light of Filene's characterization of the American Revolution as an example of an earlier movement that amounted to little more than "political factionalism and ideological improvisation," forced into coherence only by outside pressures of the British— the "unifying crucible of a crisis" (34). There was, it turns out, not only nothing for progressives to rebel against but no crucible in which progressivism could be formed as a distinct phenomenon in its own right.

In Filene's account of progressivism, there is not only no "there" there but no "there" anywhere. Political phenomena are not political in the sense of resting on coherent arguments about the common good. They are rather epiphenomena of deterministic and

minute historical forces—without identity outside the minutiae.
"It is time," Filene warns us, "to tear off the familiar label and, thus
liberated from its prejudice, see the history between 1890 and 1920
for what it was—ambiguous, inconsistent, moved by agents and
forces more complex than a progressive movement" (34). It is time,
in other words, to accept much of the historicism that animated
progressive thought, in our denial of that very thought.

By contrast, shortly after Filene wrote, business historian Albro
Martin insisted that the report of progressivism's nonexistence was
an exaggeration. Offering a rare, fundamentally conservative account of the deleterious effects of progressive policy, Martin shows
how the railway industry was starved for investment capital in the
Progressive Era and was therefore unable to modernize and expand
to meet the burgeoning demands of American industry in the two
decades leading up to World War I.[26] Concentrating on the Hep-
burn Act of 1906 and the Mann-Elkins Act of 1910, Martin explicitly rejects the mainstream of American historical scholarship,
which portrays the acts as "outstanding achievements of the age of
reform." In Martin's account, they in fact imposed significant costs
on the American economy and represented "intense frustration
of the human spirit." His is a story of "brutal substitution of petty
consistency for sensible pragmatism; of the unconscionable eleva-
tion, by the government of a republic, of one set of interests over
another and over the general welfare; and of a self-serving and all
but cowardly refusal to face public duty." The story he tells "demol-
ishes once and for all the traditional concept of the just and wise
commissioner, that paragon of public service who, for a salary of
$10,000 a year, was to have adjudicated the nation's great economic
problems under the New Nationalism of Theodore Roosevelt and
Herbert Croly. It casts even more doubt on our present-day faith in
the commission management of economic affairs."[27]

Martin's words are harsh—especially given the spirit of American historical scholarship at the beginning of the 1970s. He is un-
sparing in his criticism of the unintended consequences of businesses being deprived, at the behest of clever progressive lawyers
like Louis Brandeis, of the freedom to charge what they would for

goods and services.[28] As a result of this new regulatory climate in the railroad industry, not only economic growth but passenger safety and even national security were put needlessly at risk. Martin reminds us that even at the height of progressive regulatory fervor voices occasionally cried out in the wilderness (albeit to little avail). One such voice belonged to economist Hugo Richard Meyer:

> Meyer's position (and this is what made him so unacceptable to the Progressives) was that the government was simply incapable of devising a rate structure that would ensure the most efficient economic growth of the nation. It was not merely that government officials obviously lacked the practical, day-to-day knowledge of business conditions. . . . Public regulators, in fact, would be unable to resist the complaints of those who were losing out to "progress." . . . When he said flatly, "It is impossible for the State to conserve and promote the public welfare by intervening in the regulation of railway rates," he was, to most people, still back in the nineteenth century with Herbert Spencer.[29]

But however countercultural Martin's account was for its time, his arguments were economic in nature and were concentrated on a single industry. He therefore only hinted at the more fundamental constitutional questions raised by the progressive regulatory state and the loss of freedom that went along with it.

Through the 1970s, the studies of progressivism piled up. Intellectual historian Arthur A. Ekirch of the State University of New York at Albany offered his *Progressivism in America* as a broad summary of the intellectual currents that defined progressivism. In it, he makes passing mention of the progressive movement's embrace of Christian moralism and its rejection of constitutional formalism. Darwinian thought in particular undermined "faith in a fixed law and stable Constitution."[30] But these observations are overwhelmed by Ekirch's insistence that progressives viewed progress less as a creed or philosophic doctrine and more as a concerted effort at cooperation, suffused with moral overtones. Seeing society as an organism, they stressed collective, state action. He presents The-odore Roosevelt as "the superman with the muckrake" rather than as the leader of a party fundamentally hostile to the old Constitu-tion.[31] Wilson, by contrast, was the man who, in TR's words, was "not a nationalist" and was far more conservative than TR in his re-luctance to use government power.[32]

Rare indeed was the scholar of the 1970s who saw anything in progressivism that was fundamentally discordant with the nature of the American regime. One such was R. Laurence Moore, who noted Herbert Croly's claim that "democracy must stand or fall on a platform of human perfectibility." This, according to Moore, would have "startled the Founding Fathers who had tried to frame a government that paid special attention to the permanent flaws in human nature."[33] But his was an outlying observation. The sus-tained effort to reveal the startling nature of progressivism would have to await another generation.

As overlapping and competing histories of progressivism fol-lowed one on the other, the midseventies seemed a good time to offer an assessment of the various scholarly accounts generated over the previous two decades. Stanford's David M. Kennedy delivered such an assessment in the form of a brief but useful historiogra-phy.[34] Kennedy notes that after the publication of Hofstadter's *Age of Reform* in 1955 there was a "babble" of disagreement as to the definition of progressivism. Notwithstanding the rise of this babble to a "discordant crescendo," Kennedy argues that most scholars con-tinue to assume the reality and importance of the subject. Few seem convinced by Filene's conclusion that the progressive movement "never existed" (453). Continuing efforts to make sense of things were therefore necessary.

According to Kennedy's typology, interpretations of progressiv-ism have gone through five major paradigms, each roughly follow-ing on, but not necessarily supplanting or even supplementing, the one that preceded it. These "interpretive modes" are "progressive," "consensual," "new left," "organizational," and "neo-progressive." The first, originating in the early years of the twentieth century in the works of Beard and Parrington, explicitly shared the spirit of its object of study, including broad sympathy for reform. But this interpretive mode had its liabilities: "By postulating that history was made to move by a process of cyclical confrontation between the people and the interests, the progressive historians never bothered to inquire too rigorously about the identity of reformers or about the timing of reform. Moreover . . . few serious questions were raised about the purposes or results of reform; it was simply assumed to have been democratic in intention and to have been largely successful" (455).

According to Kennedy, it was Hofstadter who launched a major assault on the progressive paradigm by raising questions of "identity, timing, motive, and outcome." His "consensual" view, like that of the progressive historians to whom he was reacting, accepted the importance of reform itself as a dominant characteristic of twentieth-century America. But it rejected the centrality of economic and class conflict as driver of democratic history. Instead, it emphasized the commonalities and durability of the American experience, including its commitment to capitalism (455).

The identity question also came to the fore in Hofstadter's analysis. By noting that the Progressive Era had been marked by general prosperity, unlike the Populist Era, Hofstadter emphasized "the discontinuous character of the reform impulse," thus picking up on the work of Mowry and Alfred D. Chandler, who had purported to show that progressives tended to be urban and middle class (456). The New Deal represented the coming to fruition of the "modern" progressive impulse. Furthermore, the concept of "status anxiety" that Hofstadter applied to progressive leadership "shifted the axis of inquiry from an economic to a psychological plane." Hofstadter had "opened the door" to the notion that progressive reform might not be that "progressive" or "liberal" after all (457).

In contrast to Hofstadter, "new left" historians like Kolko and Weinstein accepted the basic progressive framework "while turning it squarely on its head" (458). Conflict—between "the people" and "the interests"—was once again front and center, but in this conflict the people had no champions. Progressives were in fact conservatives, promoting, in Kolko's phrase, "political capitalism" for the purpose of stabilizing the economic and social order in a way that private enterprise alone could not (458). Although Kolko's *Triumph of Conservatism* and Weinstein's *Corporate Ideal* found a sympathetic audience among the younger generation of the '60s and early '70s, the authors' narrowing of the field and period of inquiry and their lack of attention to influences other than those emanating from business limited their scholarly appeal.

Furthermore, Kolko was only repeating "in stronger language" that to which the consensus historians of the post–World War II period had already been pointing: "the intramural and essentially capitalist character of almost all American political debate" (458–59). Whatever the weaknesses of Kolko's account, he has been successful in debunking Arthur Schlesinger Jr.'s famous dictum that the story of American liberalism is little more than the story of efforts to restrain the business community (459). For Kolko, government regulation is far from automatically "progressive" in intent or effect, and Kolko "has helped more than nearly any other writer to demythologize the concept of the state that had inhered in a great deal of liberal historiography" (460).

The first three interpretive paradigms shared an important characteristic, according to Kennedy: they were preoccupied with dualism, that is to say, the tension between the people and the interests, the reformers and the established institutions and modes of political and economic life. By contrast, the "organizational" approach of Hays and Wiebe attempted to transcend dualism, showing the compatibility of reform with new interests, institutions, and ways of life (460). Books such as Hays's *Response to Industrialism* and Wiebe's *Search for Order* show reform not as the consequence of democratic uprising or psychological crisis but as "the confident, purposeful, and successful effort of a new middle class of ambitious professionals and scientific experts to bring system and rationality to . . . disorder, inefficiency, and localism" (460). These books emphasize the emergence of a *new* class, deriving power not from privilege but from knowledge, especially knowledge of the new social sciences. This new class consists of a sort of elite very different from that depicted by the New Left historians.

Hays and Wiebe also repudiate the middle-class/status anxiety thesis developed by Hofstadter and continued by Mowry and others by showing that the biographical profiles of the "reformers" were not systematically different from those of the reactionaries. Far from rebelling against the new orders of industrial society, those that Hays and Wiebe identify as progressives embraced them. Thus does the "organizational" paradigm, while showing a certain indebtedness to Hofstadter in its reliance on the psychological and social as opposed to purely economic realms, ultimately reject the central thrust of Hofstadter's approach root and branch: "Hofstadter had not been unaware of the existence of a new middle class and its association with progressivism, but he did not pursue the point, and despite some confusion . . . he clearly believed the 'typical' progressive—or at least the typical progressive leader—to be a member of a displaced older elite, yearning for the restoration of the moral verities of the nineteenth century. . . . One looks in vain in his pages for any sustained recognition of regulationists like Theodore Roosevelt and Herbert Croly and Walter Lippmann as authentic progressives" (462).

But Kennedy offers a caution: Hays and Wiebe "have embraced a contrary error" by accepting as "progressive" only those people who found the new corporate structures congenial. Wiebe goes so far in identifying "progressivism" with the processes of bureaucratization that it loses any distinct character beyond those processes, and he seems to have moved in the direction of Filene in denying the existence of the progressive movement as a distinct phenomenon (464). Like Hofstadter, the exponents of the organizational paradigm overlook the reality of division among the progressives, and "in Wiebe's case, the argument that his progressives looked confidently to the future and indeed charted the path to modernity is open to strong doubt in light of Otis Graham's findings that only 40 percent of surviving progressives supported the New Deal" (463).

Perhaps all that is left for the chroniclers of progressivism is to recognize that progressives shared "a diffuse sense of engagement with a larger community," a unity in "shared experience with different implications in different cases" (465). And so Kennedy, in the end, is unwilling to see progressives as laying the groundwork for what was to come in their wake. He concurs with Hofstadter and his student Otis Graham that there is a "gulf that separates the progressives from us." We must recapture the "historicity" of the progressive period—the fact that it has become, like all periods of human history, a past that is dead and gone (467). Progressives are neither the "heroes" nor "scapegoats" for the triumphs and failures of the rest of the century. They were simply at the forefront of a liberal tradition that was transitioning "from a defense against state power to a justification for it" (468). Thus does Kennedy's otherwise balanced historiography end on a note of progressive inevitability, not to mention Deweyan confidence in the possibilities of a liberalism transformed.

In contrast to the insularity of so many American chroniclers of progressivism, British historian and Labour Party stalwart Kenneth O. Morgan—in a scholarly volume celebrating America's bicentennial—instructs his readers that American progressivism shared much in common with its British counterpart, as each pointed toward a better, and seemingly inevitable, future.[35] Understanding progressivism as a transatlantic phenomenon, Morgan points to the common goals of reducing privilege, overcoming special interests, and replacing competitiveness with cooperation, while furthering democratization, labor reform, efficiency, and humanity. American progressivism can thus be seen as one facet of a worldwide quest to deal with urbanization and industrialization (246–47). Indeed, "Roosevelt's penchant for commissions of experts to examine questions like the trusts and the tariffs in a scientific and detached way followed closely Lloyd George's own proposals. . . . Like T. R., Lloyd George believed in executives rather than in legislatures" (249).

Noting the continuous influence on Americans of British reform liberalism, Morgan points to the importance of Carlyle, Ruskin, and Darwin to American progressives. In fact, the intellectual and practical debts of the latter to Britain mark the supersession of nativist populism by progressivism proper (251–53). The settlement

house movement, in particular, inspired American middle-class social justice and civic reformers, as did European examples of legis-
lated labor reform. "Scores of American social reformers made the
pilgrimage to London's East End and to other British cities at this
period. Amongst the most notable was the historian, Charles Beard"
(256). Likewise, the ideal of the dispassionate British municipal
civil service inspired American civic reformers who favored city
managers and commission government.

But British influence had its limits. Some American progressives, such as Croly and Steffens, viewed British institutions as too
democratic—and therefore too resistant to centralized paternalism—
while others felt they were not democratic enough, rooted too much
in class segregation (265–66). Notwithstanding these limits, the
picture Morgan paints purports to demonstrate that the connection between American and British progressivism was an intimate
one. "Radical reform" was made possible in America because so
many Americans could see its success overseas: "It was rooted in
basic American ideals dating from the founding fathers and beyond. But, above all, it flourished 'over there,' in Britain in the here
and now. In the Old World, [Americans] beheld a vision of the future, and it worked" (269). In Morgan's analysis, the unique character of American progressivism and its vexed relationship with the
American founding all but disappears from sight.

By the mid-1970s, the attempt to recapture a distinctly American progressivism seemed an increasingly tall order. But three historians were willing to give it a try. Contributing to a single volume
published in 1977, John D. Buenker, John C. Burnham, and Robert M. Crunden responded jointly to Filene's denial of the progressive movement's existence. While admitting a certain amount of
"chaos" in the field, they attempt to create "new syntheses" of progressivism.[36] In the end, however, the main point of contact among
their various syntheses seems to be their shared, if meager, view
"that a Progressive Era did occur, and that it made significant contributions to American history."[37]

Burnham finds a temporally concentrated unity in multiplicity:
"A number of streams in American reform coalesced for a few years,

reinforcing each other so as to cumulate in what contemporaries recognized as progressivism."[38] Together, these streams amounted to a "progressive ethos" and "quasi-religious vision" more than a political program (5). In fact, reformers in general had an "aversion" to government and party politics (16). The streams consisted of "environmental determinists" who believed experts should manipulate the environment for the sake of national, even romantic, goals (10). The uniting of the "idealistic and the efficient" resulted in "as pure an unselfishness as has been seen in history, operating through voluntary associations to bring about widespread and significant changes in American life" (23). Burnham discounts the overemphasis on both politics and psychology, respectively, in the analyses of his colleagues Buenker and Crunden (126–29).

Buenker emphasizes shifting coalitions as a "comprehensive explanation" of the progressive period, rather than questioning the very existence of a movement, as Filene does, or describing it merely as an ethos, as Burnham does.[39] He thus sees himself as "refining" rather than rejecting Filene's conception, a move that ends up "freeing historians from a self-imposed ideological straight jacket" and preventing them from falling prey to what he sees as Burnham's and Crunden's efforts to reinvigorate the "WASP middle class interpretations," which falsely unify progressivism once again as a singular concept (112–13, 122). In his view, loose "shifting coalitions suffer from few of the conceptualizing disabilities associated with a coherent movement. Coalitions are, by definition, temporary. They are not limited to any single social type. They require no fundamental agreement upon values or motives" (35). The "forces" of the Progressive Era simply pushed and pulled individuals in too many directions to expect enduring coherence (43). Coalitions developed around broad categories of issues (49). For example, while labor codes tended to be supported by middle-class professionals, organized labor, and urban workers, tax reform and business regulations were supported by other coalitions (49–53). The Progressive Era came to an end because of the very thing that defined it: "fragile and transitory coalition politics" (59). Not particularly radical because of the compromises needed in coalition politics, progressivism dealt with urbanization and industrialism on a more or less ad hoc basis until the coalitions simply outlived the capacity of their members to pursue common ends (62–63).

Crunden offers yet another analytical framework: progressivism as a cultural, rather than social or political, term. Progressivism simply denotes the "tone" of life around the turn of the century, as "Victorianism" had denoted the tone of the prior century. "Moral tone of voice" serves as the key identifier of the progressives, making progressivism not amenable to the usual methodologies, which rely on traditional tools of quantification and political analysis.[40] The sociological analyses of Hofstadter and Mowry lacked control groups, while the economic analysis of Kolko failed to mention those figures most commonly identified as progressives. Crunden explicitly rejects Buenker's emphasis on "shifting coalitions" because it assumes that the political realm was central to progressivism.[41] Instead, psychology must help us understand the overall cultural milieu of the progressive age.[42] Progressivism was essentially moralistic and religious in tone, as illustrated by Jane Addams's involvement in the settlement movement and even John Dewey's ethical theories as they developed in the context of the progressive educational movement. "Most progressive movements add up to a progressivism that was essentially religious, a public enactment of the Protestant morals that dominated in so many households of the later nineteenth century. The climax came when Theodore Roosevelt so emotionally addressed the delegates of the 1912 convention of the Progressive Party, and exhorted them to stand Armaggedon and battle for the Lord."[43]

Several years later, Crunden made an extended case for progressivism as a "climate of creativity" in which progressives shared no political platform.[44] While he underestimates the political character of progressivism, he does recognize the power and potential of its religious commitment. Protestantism provided the initial energy and direction for the progressives, but their missionary zeal soon became secularized, and the "real legacies of progressivism were in the arts, philosophy, diplomacy, and cultural empathy" (xi). Progressives sought opportunities for "preaching without pulpits" in jobs ranging from settlement work to higher education to law and journalism. Progressivism was more an outlook and a psychology dictated by circumstance than a program to alter the American moral and political universe. John Dewey was a philosopher shaped by, rather than shaping, the climate of creativity, and even Woodrow Wilson was a mere preacher (64, 273). An educated democracy would be a moral democracy, and "the place for Christianity was in this world" (15).

The nature of this cultural milieu was captured in the atmosphere of the very progressive Oberlin College of the late nineteenth century. There, in a world turned upside down, Crunden reports that students pursued careers in ministry at disproportionate rates; that scarcely a soul would admit to voting anything other than Republican; and that, as a visitor noted, "if anyone walking along the sidewalks of Oberlin catches his foot and stumbles, nine chances out of ten, he stumbles into a prayer meeting" (7). And indeed, the very progressive Oberlin of today continues to be a rather spiritual place, with students still routinely gathering to worship the gods.

In 1977, Morton Keller published a sweeping study of public life in late nineteenth-century America, surveying the "character of the nation's public experience from the Civil War to the end of the 19th century."[45] Keller's long book barely hints at the roots and direction of the progressive synthesis. Indeed, debates over the status and meaning of the founders' Constitution don't rate a mention. At best, Keller deals obliquely with some of the central phenomena that laid the foundation for progressivism. He allows that "science, system, organization" were key concepts in American thought after the Civil War and were buttressed by new professional organizations, including the American Social Science Association (122–23). But social reform was the product of a "mix" of "conflicting" desires, including building a new society, preserving the old one, and recapturing a utopian past (126). Even the founders of the American Economic Association, including Ely, adopted an essentially conservative Christian rhetoric and morality in order to attack the problems of industrialism, according to Keller (375).

The idea of a unified, egalitarian nation arising out of the Civil War was overcome by reactionary forces of laissez-faire individualism, racism, and sexism (161). By the 1870s, ideological

appeals were dead, replaced by a "politics of organization" in a society hostile to "large and purposeful public policies" (283). Keller
notes that the idea of a technically trained administration separate from politics was promoted by the likes of Wilson and Frank
Goodnow, but he does not suggest any constitutional or philosophical implications of such an idea (296–97). He quickly passes
over even Holmes's embrace of the notion that law should be a
"prime instrument of public policy-making" without delving into
the depths of Holmes's critique of limited constitutionalism (346).
The early twentieth-century polity was like its late nineteenth-
century predecessor in the "social anxieties and aspirations" with
which it wrestled. But it was a polity that never wrestled with much
more than those (600).

By the end of the decade, Swarthmore's Roger C. Bannister attempted to separate the myth from the reality of social Darwinism.
In his 1979 book *Social Darwinism: Science and Myth in Anglo-
American Social Thought*, he points to the fact that the reform or
Left social Darwinists routinely prefaced their works by falsely
claiming that "Darwinism was widely and wantonly abused by the
forces of reaction." It was in fact the reformers who were the Darwinists, emphasizing an evolutionary framework that "demanded
measures to control an increasingly chaotic 'natural' order. This
perception of disorder was a common thread in the otherwise apparently disparate reforms of the Progressive Era—from the regulation of monopoly, to eugenics, to Jim Crow. Pre-Darwinian evo-
lutionists, cherishing the Enlightenment faith in beneficent laws of
nature, continued to argue that society ought best be left to develop without central direction or controls."[46]

According to Bannister, it was the reformers who, stressing
the importance of "intellect" and "culture" to evolution, demanded
regulation and social control (11). Oliver Wendell Holmes, Lester Frank Ward, and Richard Ely "placed Darwin and evolution
squarely at the service of government intervention and social welfare" (79). Using Darwinism to "condemn competition while defending combination" became the new intellectual status quo, a sort
of "conservatism" of the self-proclaimed reformers (88). Even "racial
Darwinism" was a variety of reform Darwinism, as white progres-

sives viewed disenfranchisement and Jim Crow as being a part of the rational progressive program—just as much a means to good government as municipal reform. Segregation was but one more scientific measure aimed at ensuring cooperation and eliminating conflict in society. In "the complex history of myth-making," the racial Darwinists were rarely called "social Darwinists" (181).

Bannister notes that the critiques of social Darwinism that burgeoned through the 1940s and '50s, including especially those of Hofstadter, culminated in a call for an end to ideology, including the "metaphysics" of discredited doctrines (251). Alas, neither the ideology nor the metaphysics they singled out were what they seemed to be, and only the doctrine of progress marched on. And even Bannister only tangentially raises the fundamental hostility of the doctrines of social Darwinism to the founders' Constitution and the American regime.

The most revealing encapsulations of the scholarship of the 1970s were studies published early in the 1980s. The first was by Princeton historian Daniel T. Rodgers, who dug deep "In Search of Progressivism."[47] Like Peter Filene a decade before him, he came up empty-handed. Rodgers begins his historiographical article by noting that the idea of progressivism as a coherent doctrine fell on hard times in the 1970s. Filene and others tried to dig its grave, but it was a sick man who wouldn't lie down (113). Rodgers's interest lies mainly in identifying the gravediggers and helping them ensure that the improbably quick should become dead.

From his perch at Princeton, and before that at Wisconsin, Rodgers was in an excellent position to note mainstream disciplinary trends and teaching postures when it came to the study of progressivism. He notes that by the mid-1970s teaching had largely devolved into the assertion—deriving from professional disagreement among historians—that the Progressive Era was at most "confusing" and "elusive" (113–14). By the end of the decade, historians searched no longer for the "essence" of progressivism but rather for the "context" in which progressives operated (114).

Of course, one of the hallmarks of progressivism as a philosophical system is its denial of essences, and many historians had for decades accepted that denial as a truism. With context as king, progressivism could be deconstructed into a variety of interest groups, operating in the vacuum created by receding traditional loyalties. In Rodgers's account, Buenker and Filene each furthered this deconstruction by emphasizing the politics of difference and denying that anything like a cohesive movement existed. The only thing that progressivism could be said to manifest consistently was an "ideologically fluid" desire to reshape American society (114). This era without essence presaged "the rise of modern, weak-party, issue-focused politics" (117).

Scholars such Wiebe and Hays searched for context in the organizational revolution at the beginning of the twentieth century, with bureaucracy and professional organization gaining ascendance. This was in effect a denial of Hofstadter's claim that progressivism amounted to a reaction against the consequences of mass organization (118). As Rodgers notes, human intentionality remains elusive in such accounts (119). But some things remain more elusive still in Rodgers's account: there is nary an essence to be seen or a constitutional question to be pondered.

Meanwhile, studies from the Left—such as those by Weinstein and Kolko—emphasized how corporate capitalism captured dissent and tamed the dangers to the hegemony of "the new corporate phase of capitalism" (120). Progressivism in this understanding becomes a species of conservatism.

In this sea of coalition building, concentration of power, and co-optation, Rodgers asks, where was progressivism to be found? Core progressive values receded ever further under the weight of study after study that suggested difference and division. The progressives were at most "users rather than shapers of ideas," possessing no distinct intellectual system or ideology of their own (127). "If the contradictory lists prove anything it is that those who called themselves progressives did not share a common creed or a string of common values. . . . Rather what they seem to have possessed was an ability to draw on three distinct clusters of ideas. . . . The first was the rhetoric of antimonopolism, the second was an emphasis on social bonds and the social nature of human beings, and the third was the language of social efficiency" (123). Rodgers concludes by exhorting historians to "abandon the hunt for *essence* [emphasis in original]" in favor of the ever-shifting contexts in which progressives operated (127). And in this, he offers a very progressive exhortation indeed.

Finally, in 1983, Princeton historian and Woodrow Wilson scholar Arthur S. Link, together with Rutgers historian Richard L. McCormick, wrote a popular summary of the phenomenon of progressivism—but only as it was interpreted by American historians.[48] They maintain that progressivism was not a unified movement but was nonetheless a real and important phenomenon, centering on how Americans defined themselves in terms of responding to social problems at the turn of the century (2–3). The authors dutifully note competing trends in the historical literature. The earliest historians of progressivism saw progressives as common people engaged in an effort to recapture power from corporate titans and party bosses. Beard, Parrington, and Faulkner fall into this mold of insisting on dichotomy and conflict between ordinary Americans and men of wealth and privilege (4). Others, from Hicks in the 1930s to Woodward and Nye in the 1950s, emphasized the agrarian roots of progressivism (4). But by the 1950s, as Link and McCormick recount, historians started to pay more critical attention to the "who" question. George Mowry found progressive reformers to hail from the well-educated urban professional classes, who felt threatened by corporate and union power (4–5). Richard Hofstadter built on this analysis to develop his full-blown social psychology of status anxiety (5). The middle-class foundation of progressivism was maintained by Hays and Wiebe, minus the anxiety. Instead, these latter historians emphasized the farsightedness and confidence of the new middle class, whose members, in the context of modernization, sought to pursue their own ambitions through bureaucratic organization. Meanwhile, for New Left historians like Kolko, progressivism was a triumph of the corporate elites (6).

Link and McCormick therefore approach the problem in a familiar way: by dismissing "an imaginary unified progressive movement" in favor of a study of individual reforms and the goals, rationales, and results of the reformers (11). In general, they find progressivism characterized by distinctive attitudes toward industrialism as well as a faith in progress, that is to say, in the human ability to control the conditions of social life (21). Progressives believed—along the lines suggested by Ward, Ely, and Dewey—in an evolutionary process that man could control. They were inspired by evangelical Protestantism and the perceived power of the natural and social sciences in the service of administrative action (22). They were also inspired by those who could inspire public opinion, including especially Theodore Roosevelt (36). Throughout, this history of progressive history seems to repeat an old mistake: conflating the historians with the history because the authors cannot bring themselves to see the thing in itself.

But the tide was about to turn, and this type of analysis was to be swept aside as a new generation of political scientists joined the fray.

FIVE Intellectual Consolidation and Counterattack

Conservatism and Revisionism from the 1980s to the Present

By the early 1980s, it seemed that the history of progressivism was running out of steam. In a discipline thoroughly dominated by progressives, the conservative drift of the nation, along with new fads and fashions in the academy, diverted scholarly attention away from traditional intellectual and political history. Furthermore, what most historians thought to be the main positions on progressivism had already been staked out, often repeatedly. As we have seen, for some, progressivism represented little more than the cautious efforts of popular—or at least nonelite—interests to check elite dominance. This was, broadly speaking, the view shared by the early liberal historians—Hofstadter, Schlesinger Jr., Link, Mowry, and many more. For others, populism had little to do with progressivism. The New Left historians, such as Kolko and Williams, attempted to upend the liberal or consensus narrative by insisting that corporate elites either drove or co-opted progressive reforms in order to exercise ideological and political control over an otherwise unruly economic order. Those historians enjoyed some success, though liberals did occasionally push back or at least engage in passive resistance in the form of avoidance of the radicals' arguments. For most everyone, progressivism was bound up with the desire for efficiency and expertise rather than the messiness of republican politics, and with a faith in expanded state (especially national) power as opposed to decentralized market forces or the spontaneous workings of civil society. Almost no one saw progressivism as being a fundamental rejection of the founders' Constitution and as embodying a new form of secular millenarianism with enduring regime-level implications.

The dominant positions were occupied by various members of what might be called an academic and cultural establishment. By the 1980s, even the "radical historians" were not so much on the move as tenured and sedentary. Few if any who operated comfortably within the establishment could imagine—and none as yet has answered—the revisionist scholarship that was to come. This failure of imagination is linked to two salient facts: the revisionist accounts of progressivism as a coherent force—one both constitutionally and culturally destructive—have come from the Right more than the Left, and more from the discipline of political science (especially the subfield of political theory) than from history.[1]

COUNTERATTACK: REVISIONISTS TAKE THE FIELD

As I suggested in the introduction to this volume, in recent years there has been a flood of revisionist scholarship on the nature and intellectual origins of progressivism, including the unique challenges it poses to the American constitutional order. Much of this scholarship has been connected to the "Claremont school" of political science, which has long been associated with efforts to clarify the meaning of the founders' Constitution and show its enduring importance for contemporary politics.[2]

The Claremont school originated in the work of scholars associated with Claremont McKenna College, Claremont Graduate

University, and the Claremont Institute for the Study of States-manship and Political Philosophy, the Institute being an independent think tank established in the late 1970s. The Claremont school is deeply influenced by the work of the German American scholar Leo Strauss, who sojourned briefly in Claremont in the late 1960s. Strauss placed the problem of historicism at the front and center of his political and philosophic inquiry. That is to say, he did not simply assume that moral-political understandings cannot be true simply, or that they are epiphenomena of their time and place. In the face of a twentieth-century political science establishment committed to empiricism, positivism, and relativism, Strauss held open the possibility of moral realism.[3]

Overlapping in Claremont in the middle decades of the twentieth century were several of Strauss's earliest and most influential students, including Martin Diamond, Paul Eidelberg, and Harry V. Jaffa. Diamond turned his attention to the American political tradition, taking Charles Beard and the progressive historical consensus Beard helped establish to task for their insistence on the reactionary, antidemocratic character of the founders' Constitution.[4] Eidelberg wrote the first identifiably Straussian book that was critical of Woodrow Wilson for the revolutionary progressivism he articulated.[5] Jaffa, who spent the bulk of his exceptionally long career in Claremont and had the profoundest influence on the development of the Claremont school, spent decades applying the insights and methodological dispositions of Strauss to the American founding, to the political thought of Abraham Lincoln, and to contemporary American politics. He dilated in particular on the failure of both progressives and conservatives to appreciate the nature and depth of Lincoln's effort to preserve the natural rights foundations of America.[6] For Jaffa, America is premised on an understanding of natural rights that stem from the self-evident truth of political equality: the fact that no human being is so naturally superior to another as to be entitled to rule without consent. Consent is therefore the foundation on which legitimate government rests, as well as a moral-political conclusion derivable from a fact of nature.

Together, the prodigious ruminations of these scholars provided the foundation on which subsequent generations of Claremont faculty, graduate students, and sympathetic fellow travelers commenced their scholarly pushback against the progressive synthesis. These scholars came to see American progressivism and its intellectual antecedents—as well as the flowering of these doctrines in contemporary liberalism—as root-and-branch rejections of the idea that there are truths that do not vary with time and place and, as such, rejections of the American constitutional order dedicated to such truths.

Revisionists within, or influenced by, the Claremont school have offered guidance on what they see as the nature of the American republic and the manner in which progressives of various stripes have sought to challenge it. In the course of doing so, they have given insights into the place of the idea of progress in American thought and public life and the enduring impact of the Progressive Era—including the pivotal election of 1912—on contemporary political ideas and practices. As a result of this scholarship, there is new opposition to the progressive vision of America. In general, this scholarship attempts to clarify the nature and extent of progressive claims by laying them out in the concrete circumstances of American politics. When Woodrow Wilson, on the campaign trail, deemed government a "living thing . . . accountable to Darwin, not to Newton," he was encapsulating for political purposes a complex set of philosophical arguments and presuppositions. They are arguments and presuppositions that continue to inform our understanding of the nature, purpose, and scope of government. And they present challenges to the American constitutional order that are indeed very much alive in the twenty-first century.

One of the earliest scholarly arguments that laid important groundwork for later assaults on established positions came in 1984 from the pen of political theorist Charles R. Kesler of Claremont McKenna College and Claremont Graduate University.[7] According to Kesler, Woodrow Wilson offered a comprehensive articulation of a new, historically situated conception of being itself. In Wilson's thought, and to some extent his practice, organic progressive growth replaces nature as the central category and aspiration of the American political order. For Wilson sovereign authority would reside in the people, albeit the people properly understood: that is to say, the people in historical context, the only context in which their wishes could be made manifest. No eighteenth-century anachronism like separation of powers could be allowed to stand in the way of popular sovereignty. Tyranny of the majority being permanently foreclosed by the progress of history, the job of statesmen is to keep the ship of state moving ever forward down the river of history by intelligently reading and then guiding popular will. Such piloting is a job for the one—or at most the few—rather than the many. Statesmanship devolves to leadership informed by ever-shifting historical consciousness and consensus, understood as the products and the working out of the tensions between social organism and environment. It always requires a sympathetic insight into the heart of the people. For Kesler, the unchanging natural order put forth in the Declaration of Independence is Wilson's real enemy: the Constitution is merely the place where the battle is joined.

As Kesler would write decades later, liberalism is the first political movement to seek endless reform rather than something in particular.[8] The shifting sand, rather than the rock of salvation, is liberalism's alpha and omega. The progressives, as progenitors of modern liberalism, claimed that new conceptions of the nature, role, and limits (or lack thereof) on the national government were needed for problems perceived to be wholly new—especially, in the beginning at least, economic problems.[9] For liberalism, as for progressivism, a confidence in (if not full-blown philosophy of) History makes the future rather than the past the only worthy object of contemplation for the serious political thinker.[10]

Perhaps the most comprehensive development of Kesler's insights on Wilson has come from his student, Ronald J. Pestritto, in his 2005 study *Woodrow Wilson and the Roots of Modern Liberalism*.[11] Pestritto sees clearly the role of political theorists such as Kesler in revealing Wilson's thought as a dangerous departure from the sound political principles of the Founding.[12] Pestritto rejects the historical scholarship that understands Wilson as a "conservative" figure in a progressive age. He sees him rather as a radical critic of the founders' Constitution and the social contractarian natural rights conservatism on which it rests, while sharing at least some elements of the more organic conservatism of Edmund Burke and other traditionalists—a "conservatism" of incremental change and growth, without principled limits on government power. Ultimately, however, Wilson must be understood as a thoroughgoing historicist and Hegelian.[13]

Late in the 1980s, political theorist John Lugton Safford undertook an extended if largely overlooked study of the relationship of pragmatism to progressivism that directly engaged the debate between John Hicks and his student George Mowry over whether populism and progressivism were distinct movements, with populism rooted in lowbrow agrarianism, and progressivism in the values of the educated urban classes.[14] Safford sides squarely with Mowry, arguing that the thing that most distinguished progressives was their education and their belief in a new, pragmatic "science of society" combining elements of pragmatism and Darwinism. William James's nominalism was reflected in Herbert Croly's effort to destroy the old individualism of natural rights embedded in the Constitution along with the moral realism that undergirded it.[15] In Croly's understanding, law is always subordinate to the government rather than vice versa. Fundamental law like that of the Constitution derives its force from its congruity with the national will—a view echoed by Woodrow Wilson (54–55). A good deal of pragmatic experimentation is required to maintain such congruity: the nation, for Croly, is a school in need of a schoolmaster. Unlike most of the historians, Safford clearly understands the far-reaching constitutional critique embedded in such a view: "Croly claims that the Populist reformers could not make the transition to Progressivism because the Populists were but reformers of the system, where the Progressives understood the necessity of changing the system itself" (62).

Croly's dismissal of William Jennings Bryan, according to Safford, was based on his view that "he could never accomplish lasting reform because he distrusted the means necessary to the end:

a strong national government, the guidance of various experts, and trust in 'the exceptional man' as political leader" (65). Croly's colleague at the *New Republic*, Walter Lippman, also attacked Bryan as he drew on James and Nietzsche. For Lippman the task of the human mind was not to understand nature as a given but to manipulate it for progressive purposes. Bryan was too unscientific, too habitual, too conventional, to comprehend his own message (74–75).

Safford sees Theodore Roosevelt and Woodrow Wilson as cut from the same theoretical, pragmatist cloth and therefore not being at different poles of a diffuse progressivism. He explicitly rejects the view of Robert Wiebe that Roosevelt was motivated simply by the desire for power and glory. Instead, Roosevelt accepted the pragmatic method, rejecting "most formal philosophical systems," in favor of being "a compassionate Darwinian." Virtue must, according to Roosevelt, "take a tangible and efficient shape" (126–27). For TR, economic efficiency took precedence over moral reform because of his fundamentally pragmatic insight that "immediate betterment always will persuade the average voter before the seemingly non-Pragmatic question of the general good" (131). Wilson, like Croly—but unlike TR—was a believer in human perfectibility. But what united them was their hostility to constitutional formalism based on the view that endless experimental change would promote necessary, and inevitable, organic evolution.

And Safford notes that historians of progressivism rarely make explicit the connections between progressivism and the philosophic ideas that underlie it. Typically, "the family resemblance is taken for granted, influences are hinted at, but little is made explicit and no causal relations are established" (155). The invisible elephant in the room is that which

> produced the family resemblance among historians,
> sociologists, economists, anthropologists, educators and
> philosophers of the Progressive Era. . . . It was the materialist-
> functionalist view of the human mind based on the theory
> of evolution, combined with a disguised Hegelian theory
> of progress. The philosophy of man—what it is to be

> human—is primarily a theory of mind. Virtually all of
> the new social sciences and philosophy had converted from
> the view of mind as a changeless spirit which was capable
> of intuiting eternal truths, to one of mind as a tool of
> adaptation, itself still changing and in the making. (170)

Another important revisionist account, this one from the Left, was political scientist Eldon Eisenach's 1994 study entitled *The Lost Promise of Progressivism*.[16] Like Safford, Eisenach breaks the mold of the historians by concentrating squarely on the intellectual and regime character of progressivism and presenting it as a coherent force. And for him, it is very much a force for good. Eisenach is intent on recapturing progressivism's coherence and promise for very contemporary purposes, including sharpening the effectiveness of the intellectual classes. He argues that the central kernels of earlier progressive thinking can serve as the touchstones of a much-needed national political identity, which can in turn be "constitutive of our personal identities as Americans" (1).

He sees a strong disconnect between the "manipulative, ritualistic, and hollow" public discourse of the nation as a whole and the more "passionate" and "serious" discourse one finds in the contemporary American university (2). As early progressives rejected such things as "the party system, localism, and a rights-based and legalistic constitutional vocabulary" (2), contemporary intellectuals must rally around the essence of progressivism to effect their own changes, beginning—but not ending—in the realm of thought. Americans need common purpose again for the sake of civic responsibility, which, as early progressives saw, is not to be found in "narrow kinds of localism" (5). Only a cosmopolitan nationalism can provide it—one that is rooted in a "social evolutionary framework" of history that can overcome sectarianism and provincialism and link American thought and practice to the broader world, just as it was linked by the early progressives (6).

In this understanding, progressivism can once again be the animating, guiding force of the literati, who can, under the auspices of the common identity it provides, speak with clarity and cultural cohesion on the evils of our day. The problem with contemporary liberal intellectuals, in Eisenach's view, is that they have forgotten their origins and have ignored the potential of early progressivism. As contemporary liberals speak the language of rights and "constitutionalist discourse," America has seen the "euthanasia of articulate and contestable ideas." Contemporary liberalism has, in short, adopted the language of its natural adversaries. The ideas of contemporary liberals, insofar as they rely on the constitutionalist language they share with conservatives, appear to "thoughtful people" as grievous errors (4). If only we could once again—but more completely—throw out constitutional formalism, we could hear the call to a "larger life" and escape the "illusory individualism" that "thwarts civic capacity and democratic purposes." This would allow a new wave of "social justice" to wash over the land (5). In fact, it is "quite clear" to Eisenach that claims voiced in terms of rights need to meet certain tests before they are even accorded a "serious hearing" (5–6).

The conservatives who opposed early progressives spoke "the tough legal language of constitutional powers" and defended things we now understand to be "quaint or dangerously reactionary" (46). And pity today's poor conservatives who, perhaps unaccountably, remain concerned with the age-old tension between individualism and the public good. They are even more ignorant of their debts to progressivism than are today's liberals, "if only because so few of them have their primary home in major American universities" (6). Such ignorance and ingratitude must be overcome. To help us, we can fall back on the many lessons of progressive "academics and intellectuals": "that all social knowledge deserving a hearing must be cosmopolitan in origin and national in import. . . . Specialized knowledge and training is at once a call to examine critically the institutions and practices of our society . . . and a pledge to national service . . . unmediated by party, interest, region, or sectarian religion. . . . The only viable democracy is national democracy. . . . They saw the university as something like a national 'church'—the main repository and protector of common American values, common American meanings, and common American identities" (7).

In Eisenach's church of cosmopolitanism, only the cosmopolitan are welcome at the altar. The social evolutionary framework holds no place for those who have stubbornly refused to evolve toward "new and higher ways of life" (27). In Eisenach's telling, the reconstituted, truly progressive and politically correct American university of the future threatens to be everything it is today—and then some.

Eisenach's full-throated embrace of progressivism has the virtue of getting much right. He demonstrates that he understands the deep roots of the progressive synthesis. He argues that it is a mistake to place too much emphasis on Beard or Croly: they came to the game late. Croly didn't write his first book until 1909, Beard in 1913, "well after most of the serious intellectual innovation had already taken place and had dominated the universities" (39). Both writers were derivative—Croly from such thinkers as Albion Small and Simon Patten, and Beard from Edwin Seligman. And unlike so many chroniclers of the twentieth century, Eisenach understands progressives as they understood themselves, in that he identifies the important and revolutionary character of their ideas. For him, progressivism represented regime change—with concomitant change in "narratives" and "identities"—that hasn't been captured by liberal consensus historians. He offers a telling rebuke to Daniel Rodgers: "The vanquished of the old regime simply disappear without a trace in Rodgers's analysis while the remaining conflict is only *among* the Progressives *who now seem to be almost everyone.* It is no wonder, then, that the beginning of Rodgers's search (and that of most historians of Progressivism) begins at the turn of the century, that is, after most of the larger theoretical and cultural battles had already been long fought and on their way to being won in the dynamic and creative reaches of American society" (23n21).

Eisenach also sees the extent to which secular religiosity was among the core traits of the progressives—the belief that a "national will" must be strong enough "to encourage sacrifice for social justice and the common good" (62). But even as national will becomes a stand-in for God, Eisenach devotes little time to reflecting on what the new dispensation might do to traditional religion or to public policy pursued under the banner of righteousness. He does recognize that Croly's "monarchy of the Constitution" was seen by progressives as "a barrier to democratic national purpose" because of the decentralizing thrust of federalism and, with it, the perpetuation of "constricted lives" (73).

In the progressive understanding, public opinion would become "public conscience" and a means of "social control and transformation" rather than simply an accumulation of individual preferences. A "spiritual elite" consisting of public moralists, social scientists, and charity workers would "reflect the new image of Christ," resulting in progress away from the need for "external coercion." A nation of common values would supplant rule of law (chap. 3). As German idealism and philosophy of history came to inform American theology, older millennial themes were merged into Darwinian social evolution, thereby overcoming doctrinal differences and, indeed, the need for institutional religion. Democratic faith replaced religious faith. Sociology and philosophy were sacralized, thereby guaranteeing that, even in a secular age, religious rhetoric maintained its place in American discourse and national identity (101–2). "Beginning around World War I, members of what later came to be called 'fundamentalist' churches were increasingly consigned to the cultural equivalent of resident alien status. But it was modernized evangelical theology and the new social sciences and not secular liberalism that drew up the expulsion orders" (103).

Eisenach also sees the important constitutional dimensions of progressive thought, much of which treated traditional legal scholarship as a "fossilized" relic. Some progressive thinkers, including Wilson, attempted to mediate the relationship between law and progressive social theory through a new version of realism, informed by evolutionary history, though the gap could never quite be bridged because of progressivism's stress on "inner character, shared values, public opinion, social knowledge, and spiritual progress" as opposed to formal political institutions (111 and chap. 4). The more "conservative" Wilson was therefore seen, by Croly and others, as a threat to progressive ideals because of his "strong defense of the American Constitution" (122). Rooted in party and sectionalism, Wilson appropriated potentially "transformative" ideas for cramped ends and the protection of existing interests. Thus, while recognizing the depth of progressive suspicion of the Constitution, Eisenach comes close to airbrushing Wilson out of the portrait of progressivism he paints. Wilson is at best on the margins, leading the charge toward New Deal liberalism.

Eisenach's ultimate point is to emphasize what progressivism brought to the table that is still useful (and still rejected by both constitutional conservatives and rights-talk liberals). The progressives "articulated an ideal of a national democratic community where equality was achieved more by sharing projects in common and by participating on the basis of equal respect than by being equally protected in one's rights against others. Contemporary liberal public doctrine is deeply distrustful of political democracy defined by shared values. Progressive public doctrine, in contrast, was premised on this definition" (219). Modern liberalism lost the messianic, national vision of progressivism and thus became different in kind from its predecessor. And in this fact lies the provenance of the great mistake made by historians like Rodgers and Filene in denying the coherence or even existence of the progressive movement. Steeped in modern liberalism, disaffected by the wane of New Deal hopes, and unable to pin a vision for the future on a confident expression of progressive nationalism, they could no longer see the heart and soul of the phenomenon they described. "Because it was thought that Progressivism had no future, historians soon decided that it had no coherent and authoritative past either" (257). Our goal, then, should be to reappropriate the best features of progressive public doctrine, recognizing the magnitude of the progressive achievement that once connected national pride to a sense of mutual obligation and social justice (258).

THE GROWTH OF THE CONSTITUTIONALIST CRITIQUE

A flurry of scholarship on progressivism produced over the last two decades has adopted an explicitly revisionist tone and has directly or incidentally pointed to the need for a robust defense of the founders' Constitution. This scholarship recognizes the nature and depth of the progressive rejection of the Constitution and suggests that this rejection was effectively hidden as progressive historians wrote the "official" interpretations.

The end of the twentieth century seemed—at least to a handful of influential political scientists and even a historian or two—the right occasion to reconsider the political thought that had guided America at the turn of that century. In the 1999 anthology *Progressivism and the New Democracy*, University of Virginia political scientist Sidney M. Milkis points to the desire of progressive reformers to "circumvent the constraints of limited constitutional government" by establishing various economic, political, and intellectual organizations that would enable the mass of people to assume direct control over their destinies.[17] Milkis gets to the heart of the uniquely American character of progressivism: "To the extent Progressive democracy was radical, it represented a sui generis American form of radicalism—one conceived to rescue American individualism from an emotive attachment to the Constitution, especially the designated 'high priests' of the Constitution."[18] In the face of much of progressivism's commitment to direct popular rule, conservatives of the day, such as William Howard Taft, "sought terra firma in a defense of the Constitution."

It is precisely this terra firma—constitutional conservatism—that the revisionist scholarship has sought to reinvigorate. Such a reinvigoration is critical in light of the fact that opposition to popular rule, among conservatives as much as liberals, is today often seen as "heretical."[19] But if it be a heresy, it is a heresy only against false orthodoxy. And it is one that has much to teach contemporary populists of all types, whether they be progressives or conservatives, political actors or intellectuals.

Writing in the same volume, other scholars also point to the political character and enduring legacy of progressivism. Ohio University historian Alonzo L. Hamby seeks the "restoration of meaning to the word 'progressivism'" in the self-understandings of progressives.[20] The progressives engaged not only in "practical political action" but in "innovative political theory" committed to nothing less than reformulating the liberal state. The New Deal, and modern liberalism itself, can be seen as evolutionary developments of progressivism, sharing many elements with their predecessor.[21]

Rutgers political theorist Wilson Carey McWilliams also rejects the idea that progressivism was so variegated as to be incoherent and notes that the progressives themselves saw that they were part of a movement.[22] The millenarian aspects of their thought gave them moral energy, even as they denied the old moral science that insisted on the compatibility of faith and reason, and even as they no longer had "the assurance that it is possible to derive morals from nature." As the moral law expired, so too did the Constitution.[23] The point of civilization was to overcome nature so that human beings could transcend what earlier American political science had asserted to be the permanent limits imposed by it.[24] A general relativism and commitment to the pursuit of human perfection—or something close to it—characterized broad swaths of progressive thought.[25] But such notions always existed in an evolutionary framework. Evolution was thought by the progressive "reform Darwinists" to reward "cooperative action" as opposed to earlier forms of American individualism.

Political scientists Martha Derthick and John J. Dinan deal with progressivism's assaults on older understandings of federalism. Progressives were intent on undermining limits on federal power, blaming states' inaction for the necessity of centralization and engaging in innovative political theory.[26] The progressives rejected the Constitution's framework of enumerated powers, as well as the idea that the Constitution was to be a permanent check on public opinion.[27] With these innovations, dual federalism was put on the road to extinction by a new, national federalism that would make the states permanent second-tier players in the American system. The modern administrative state, dedicated to liberal ideals, would thereby ride roughshod over older conceptions of legalistic checks on national sovereignty.

And indeed, as political scientist Jerome Mileur writes, belief in "the positive national state" guided by an informed and activist citizenry marked the "coherent intellectual and political core" of progressivism.[28] Politics for the progressives was no longer the science of government, as it was for the founders. It was instead the science of achieving high national purposes—purposes that would overcome mere low politics. Institutional checks and balances, as well as the horse trading and partisanship of mere politicians, had to give way to elevated desires.[29] Centralized political action, rather than restraint on such action, was the sine qua non of a functioning political democracy.[30] "The Progressives were nationalists, but they were not institutionalists. Indeed, their theory of governance was behavioral, not institutional—one in which . . . education (moral and scientific), not the frame of government, disciplined political actions. In this, they were quite unlike the founding generation of Constitution-makers."[31]

In 2009, Hillsdale College political scientist Will Morrissey drew attention to the dilemma faced by the leading statesmen of the Progressive Era in coming to terms with progressivism's ultimate denial of human nature and natural right in favor of a democratic pantheism and belief in species perfectibility, something especially noticeable in Rauschenbusch's equation of Christian love with social action.[32] Rauschenbusch's theology of progressivism, secularized by Croly and others, comes to sight in American politics as "living constitutionalism" aided by strong executive leadership (30–31). TR emphasized moral reform and a kind of progressive virtue ethics—the self-government of strong uncomplaining citizens and strong leaders confronting the challenges of modernity. But in so doing, he elided the dangers to self-government of an empowered national state (91–93). William Howard Taft, by contrast, paid more attention to the rule of law, though he too downplayed, without denying, the foundation of the American republic in fixed natural right. He was concerned with practical rather than theoretical solutions to maintaining the American constitutional order in a progressive age (128). "Taft agreed with Roosevelt in thinking that the hard realities of modern life . . . required Americans to construct a more administratively centralized state with professional staffing. But whereas Roosevelt would preserve self-government by cultivating an ethos or political culture of strenuous or muscular Christianity and liberalism, culminating in a president who acts as steward of the national welfare, Taft foresaw danger there" (155). But Taft's moderate understanding of governmental power and rule of law lacked electoral appeal, and it would quickly be replaced by Wilson's full-blown rejection of natural rights,

together with the founders' Constitution (156). Wilson's millenarianism, both Christian and Hegelian, purported to channel the heretofore dangerous thumotic passions through the honor of Christian leaders of men (171–73). For him, "God and history, war and
passion drive real men in the real world. The providential rule of
the Creator-God, incarnated in the person of Jesus Christ, makes
of the world a system of transformative power. The leaders who
align themselves with this power are saved from egoism" (213).
He thus sees no danger in finally throwing off the shackles of
constitutionalism.

In the end, by incorporating various elements of the progressive synthesis into their thinking, TR, Taft, and Wilson alike proved
not up to the challenge of preserving self-government. "Progressive-
era presidents began to build the modern state in America, but resisted the regime consequences of statism, particularly its tendency
toward oligarchy and away from both executive control and popular self-government. This proved difficult" (228).

Progressive political rhetoric has also come under sustained
scrutiny in recent years, notably by Saint Vincent College political
scientist Jason R. Jividen. According to Jividen, TR, Wilson, FDR,
Lyndon Johnson, and Barack Obama each offer rhetorical versions
of Abraham Lincoln that fundamentally distort his thought by
downplaying his attachment to natural rights principles and limited constitutional government. That Lincoln's idea of equality is
"rooted in the Laws of Nature and Nature's God, and tempered by
the realities of political practice . . . distinguishes Lincoln's equality
from many variants of modern egalitarianism, which often seek to
secure equality of substantive outcomes or results, sometimes at the
expense of competing political and constitutional goods."[33] TR presents Lincoln as someone who would have "endorsed democratizing
political reforms to address social and economic inequality . . . on
the principle that the people are the rightful masters of their public
servants and the Constitution." In so doing, however, TR rejects
Lincoln's principles, which were rooted with the founders in the
idea of an unchanging human nature, one that would make pure
democracy dangerous (62–63). Wilson meanwhile sought to ap-

propriate Lincoln for purposes of promoting protean understandings of equality, progress, and rhetorical presidential leadership, each of which was hostile to Lincoln's natural rights constitutionalism (64–66). FDR, Johnson, and Obama in turn appropriated Lincoln to buttress their arguments for an expanded state apparatus dedicated to the promotion of positive rights—unlimited by natural rights theory or tempered by moderation—to be vouchsafed by government (132, 152, 164). Absent the standard of nature to which Lincoln adhered, "the ends of government are open to perpetual redefinition, and any principled limits placed upon the means to which we might consent in the pursuit of those ends no longer have any objective basis" (177). Ironically, for more than a century progressives have appropriated Lincoln in a manner that demonstrates they believe him to be "fundamentally wrong in his understanding of the political world" (178).

A notable aspect of the revisionist scholarship is the attention it pays to the progressives' conservative contemporaries—the subject of another more recent anthology edited by historian Johnathan O'Neill of Georgia Southern University and political scientist Joseph Postell of the University of Colorado, Colorado Springs, entitled *Toward an American Conservatism*.[34] A century ago, constitutional conservatives rejected the claim that the American constitutional framework had to be abandoned or radically altered because of changing circumstances, as they rejected the idea of the unlimited evolution or perfection of human beings. These people, including the likes of William Howard Taft, Calvin Coolidge, Herbert Hoover, and various Supreme Court justices, were given, at best, short shrift by twentieth-century historians. Their embrace of, or at least refusal to reject, natural rights philosophy—and the Constitution that they saw as its political expression—were often the subject of caricature rather than astute scholarly analysis, largely because such a position can't be taken seriously once the major premises of progressivism have been adopted *sub silentio* by its scholarly interpreters. But such caricatures can no longer easily be made, as it has been shown that "constitutional conservatives did not retreat to social Darwinism, radical individualism, or any of the other dogmas

with which they are so frequently identified" and in fact were willing to embrace reasonable regulation to deal with new economic
and social challenges, albeit regulation rooted in understandings of
limited constitutionalism.[35] In this account, the first step to recov-
ery of constitutionalism is to understand what constitutional conservatives of the Progressive Era thought they were doing, as opposed to what their progressive critics said they were doing.

As Milkis argues in the same volume, Taft cannot be reduced
to a "symbol of standpattism" but must be understood as someone
who rejected TR's expansive view of executive power rooted in public opinion or "pure democracy," in favor of the view that executive
power is limited to specific constitutional grants.[36] Taft was not
averse to the passage of reform laws but was skeptical of what would
become the overwhelming tendency of the twentieth century: the
passage of myriad laws, without proper deliberation or pause, whose
purpose is to attract votes, leaving the possibility of effective administration as an afterthought.[37]

Meanwhile, William A. Schambra of the Hudson Institute argues that the election of 1912, in which Taft directly confronted
TR, should remind us of the terms on which the Constitution
might still be an object of veneration. For Taft and his allies such as
Elihu Root and Henry Cabot Lodge, progressive legislation was one
thing but TR's attacks on the Constitution were another.[38] Their
concerns were rooted in the skepticism, shared by the founders, of
democracy, given fallen human nature. This is an insight developed
at length in *The Federalist*, and a proper respect for the founders'
Constitution amounts to an acceptance of the primacy of James
Madison's observation that government is the greatest of all reflections on human nature. "If men were angels, no government would
be necessary. If angels were to govern men, neither external nor internal controls on government would be necessary. In framing a
government which is to be administered by men over men, the great
difficulty lies in this: you must first enable the government to control the governed; and in the next place oblige it to control itself. A
dependence on the people is, no doubt, the primary control on the
government; but experience has taught mankind the necessity of

auxiliary precautions." In short, the first principles of American political reasoning led the constitutional conservatives away from TR and toward Taft, as they might lead us back toward the Constitution itself.

Postell argues that Calvin Coolidge, like Taft, was no ideological opponent of progressive reform policies, as evidenced by his embrace of them when he was governor of Massachusetts. However, he also embraced the idea of constitutional limits and believed some matters were inappropriate objects of national responsibility. He drew on both theoretical and traditional foundations in his embrace of the American founding, and in particular the truths expressed in the Declaration of Independence. He was not averse to progress but chose to judge it "on a fixed scale of better and worse," with the natural truths of the Declaration as his touchstone.[39]

Herbert Hoover draws the attention of political scientists Gordon Lloyd and David Davenport, who argue that Hoover's attack on the "New Deal's elaboration of progressivism" marks the beginning of modern American conservatism, rooted as it is in suspicion of federal power. While not opposed to constructive engagement of government with the private sector, Hoover's approach was a middle ground between pure laissez-faire and government by permanent bureaucracy that was articulated and desired by progressives.[40] Hoover was a believer in voluntary associations and collective endeavors not "owned" by the government—as evidenced by his extensive history of involvement in international relief efforts. Rejecting the substance of FDR's Commonwealth Club address, Hoover saw it as proposing to alter the very foundations of American life through redistribution by governmental administration, with government moving from the role of umpire to dictator—a role incompatible with the Declaration's and Constitution's clear assertions of fixed limits to governmental power.

On the legal front, George Mason law professor David Bernstein argues that the hostility to the *Lochner* case, from contemporary conservatives and progressives alike, is rooted more in "mythical morality tales" of the Progressive Era than in dispassionate analysis. Bernstein rejects Richard Hofstadter's claim that the Supreme

Court's pre–New Deal jurisprudence was premised on social Darwinism. Hofstadter cites Oliver Wendell Holmes as his source, though Holmes was, ironically, the only social Darwinist on the Court at the time he leveled his charge.[41] For Bernstein, the Progressive Era Court was witnessing, not a battle between social Darwinists and reformers, or formalists and antiformalists, as much as a battle between justices who believed there were inherent limits on governmental power to infringe prepolitical natural rights, including liberty of contract, and those who did not.[42]

In 2013, Hillsdale College historian Paul D. Moreno published *The American State from the Civil War to the New Deal.*[43] The book's subtitle encapsulates his revisionist view: *The Twilight of Constitutionalism and the Triumph of Progressivism.* The author notes the central conceit of twentieth-century American history: the triumphalist portrayal of an ever-expanding national state, one that would finally offer authentic liberty—freeing individuals not only from inequality but from the reactionary idea that human nature itself imposes permanent constraints. Moreno suggests that it was, ironically, the Obama presidency that brought this progressive narrative squarely before the bar of public opinion. Enduring doubts about the constitutionality of the Patient Protection and Affordable Care Act, commonly known as "Obamacare," conjoined with concerns about unprecedented levels of government spending, have shown that older notions of constitutional limits still animate at least some American citizens.

These are citizens who continue to demand a full hearing for constitutional arguments, long after the political classes have given up on such things. The attitude of the political classes to constitutionalism was nowhere better captured than in then-Speaker of the House Nancy Pelosi's dismissive response to a question about the constitutionality of Obamacare: "Are you *serious?*" she asked her questioner, with an incredulous laugh.

According to Moreno, we now occupy a "twilight zone between constitutional and unlimited government" (1). For him, the political philosophy of the founders is alive, if on life support. The founders were neither laissez-faire libertarians nor statists but constitutionalists, and their arguments are echoed in the voices of many Americans who believe that the Constitution has a fixed meaning that binds political actors and that is in turn informed by a moral and political philosophy anterior to the Constitution. This view allows that a genuine *common* good exists even in the face of considerable individual freedom—and that the government is bound to respect and pursue it. Under this old view, "class legislation" could not be tolerated (1–2).

Moreno opens his argument by considering the "old regime" left by the Civil War Republicans, who embraced the founders' constitutionalism even as they adopted Hamiltonian mercantilist economic policies in the postwar era—an era defined, in the economic realm, by the American industrial revolution. Moreno points to the postwar demobilization of the Union Army as evidence of Republicans' commitment to antebellum constitutional understandings and the founders' commitment to minimalist federal power (7–16). He further argues that the Republican revival of the "American System" of Hamilton and Henry Clay, "based on protective tariffs, banks, and internal improvements," was largely within antebellum constitutional understandings (16). This constitutional consensus started to give way rapidly with the advent of "early progressivism," which came to the fore from 1900 to 1913 under Republican administrations. It was a philosophy that embraced state power and, concomitantly, rejected the idea of a fixed, natural rights constitutionalism that sought to maintain limits on power. "Progressivism shared a belief that the old constitutional system was inadequate, and that a significant empowerment of government (at whatever level) was needed. It shared the organic, evolutionary, and historicist features of post-Enlightenment, Romantic Western thought" (49).

Moreno also notes that the federal judiciary in the late nineteenth century did not, contrary to scholarly caricature, embrace laissez-faire social Darwinism but rather undertook the honest and difficult effort to keep governmental power within constitutional limits in a rapidly industrializing America. Moreno makes clear what is by now the emergent consensus among revisionist scholars:[44]

No Darwinism had any impact on the late nineteenth-century American judiciary. . . . Most judges of that era had

> attended small, denominational colleges untouched by or
> hostile to historicism, utilitarianism, and Darwinism. . . .
> The dominant theory in all major schools in the United
> States . . . reflected a philosophy of "moral realism," a belief
> that moral truths existed, could be known, and that happi-
> ness consisted in living in conformity with them. . . . What
> progressives called "laissez-faire constitutionalism" derived
> from this older tradition of moral philosophy, rather than
> from any nineteenth-century economic theory, and certainly
> not from Darwinism. (53–54)

Moreno further avers that what is usually called laissez-faire constitutionalism "derived from eighteenth-century moral philosophy,
supplemented by antebellum equal rights, anti-monopoly, and anti-
slavery thought" (57). And this constitutionalism generally allowed
the courts to embrace the expansion of state police power for progressive purposes, only occasionally insisting on constitutional limits, as in the *Lochner* case. This observation is again contrary to mainstream history, not to mention the view articulated by the Supreme
Court's first progressive, Oliver Wendell Holmes, in his famous
Lochner dissent, when he claimed that "the Fourteenth Amendment does not enact Mr. Herbert Spencer's Social Statics." Justice
Peckham's majority judgment in that case had in fact rested not
on newfangled evolutionary theory but on the assumption that
"government is limited because free men are capable of governing
themselves" (100). None of this prevented Teddy Roosevelt's call
for a radical "New Nationalism," which came to encompass the demand for popular recall of judicial decisions (119). The rejection
of orthodox constitutionalism was highlighted at the Progressive
Party convention of 1912, when Senator Albert J. Beveridge, in his
keynote speech, rejected the natural rights constitutionalism of
the founders and their idea of equality of opportunity in favor of
equality of result (125).

Moreno argues that "late" or "advanced" progressivism extended from 1913 to 1933. This phase was led by Woodrow Wilson, who, with the election of 1916, became less circumspect and

embraced in practice what his earlier, scholarly critique of the founders' Constitution had suggested in theory. Moreno points out that Wilson's early scholarship was openly critical of the founders' Constitution, arguing against separation of powers as the founders conceived it in favor of a system at once more administratively concentrated and "responsible" to public opinion. He also expressed hostility to the natural rights philosophy of the Declaration of Independence (129).

It was undoubtedly the case that "Wilson presented a more profound critique of the founders' Constitution than anything uttered by Theodore Roosevelt." What was truly remarkable in the political context of the time was that "nobody in the Taft campaign noticed it. Their anti-Roosevelt passion blinded the Taft constitutionalists to the threat of Wilson, particularly as Wilson avoided the courts" (130). Moreno points to Wilson's rejection of Roosevelt's court proposals during the 1912 campaign and suggests that Wilson foresaw the possibilities of a progressive jurisprudence long before such a jurisprudence had become routine. In Wilson's words, "Law has an infinite capacity for adjustment, providing those who administer the law have a capacity for adjustment" (135). Wilson seemed to anticipate that, in the fullness of time, judicial bodies would become the natural allies of progressive forces.[45] Moreno's synoptic account—sweeping across the writings of the "early" and "late" Wilson—is therefore at odds with the lore of so many historians who preceded him. There is no fundamentally "conservative" Wilson to juxtapose against the more radical Roosevelt. Each offered his own thoroughgoing, progressive rejection of the founders' Constitution, albeit with different emphases and intonations. Late progressivism—Wilsonian progressivism—was about power no less than earlier progressivism: "Progressive rhetoric about 'democracy' often obscured profound progressive suspicion of popular government, since progressives were more interested in powerful government than democratic government. Indeed, the successful use of the formal amending process weakened progressive arguments that the Constitution was unworkably inflexible. Perhaps what made the Seventeenth Amendment a 'progressive' measure was its weakening of constitutional limitations, which stood in the way of democratic, monarchical, oligarchical, or technocratic power alike" (137). Wilson's 1916 turn toward a more vigorous progressivism, his move from "New Freedom" to "New National-ism," might well have been opportunistic—an attempt to win over Bull Moose voters—but such opportunism was not inconsistent with an unchanging statist philosophy (150). Wilson understood that his job was to win, but he could only win what History was prepared to accept, and the clearest manifestation of History's judg-ment was public opinion.

Moreno maintains that although there was a certain degree of reaction against statism in the 1920s, there was also a maintenance or expansion of the progressive status quo, even in the face of War-ren Harding's inchoate suspicion of executive power and Calvin Coolidge's more thoughtful and principled constitutionalism—a constitutionalism that accepted the finality of the moral truths expressed in the Declaration of Independence and rejected "prog-ress" away from natural rights. Progressives had won the day by winning intellectual battles and winning Congress to boot. Consti-tutionalism, despite some shallow efforts to reinvigorate it, was dead (177–88). Even the Taft Court—the one to which he appointed five justices and on which he eventually sat—did not roll back the progressive tide (189–209). And it's worth noting in this context that no Supreme Court could long withstand the fact that the legal academy, itself an artifact of progressive ideology, had recognized that progressive judges could make progressive law if they were consistently educated along progressive lines.[46]

For Moreno, the progressive constitutional revolution culmi-nated in the New Deal period, from 1933 to 1940. FDR forcefully embraced Wilson's anticonstitutional ideas, notably in his Com-monwealth Club Address given during the 1932 campaign, which laid the groundwork for twentieth-century liberalism. "Roosevelt rhetorically transvalued the values of the Founding, substituting an entitlement-based ethos for the rights-based one of the Found-ing" (3). He promised a "redefinition" of the rights outlined in the Declaration of Independence, implying government was the provider rather than protector of rights. Meanwhile, Roosevelt's antagonist Herbert Hoover was himself too steeped in progressive ideology and impulses to recognize the depth of Roosevelt's constitutional critique. He offered only objections without reasons (226).

Other voices cried out in the wilderness. Writer and political analyst Walter Lippman, objecting to Roosevelt's court-packing plan, warned of the totalitarian statism that progressivism prefigured. "Nearly everywhere," Lippman remarked, "the mark of the progressive is that he relies at last upon the power of officials to improve the conditions of men. . . . All that now passes for progressivism . . . calls for the increasing ascendancy of the state." Moreno points out that Lippman saw progressives as repudiating "a two-millennia tradition that sought 'to find law which would be superior to arbitrary power'—constitutionalism, in a word" (287). And lest there be any doubt about Roosevelt's earnestness, Moreno notes that the "craftiness of the court-packing plan has obscured the political philosophy that Roosevelt brought to the fight. His repeated stress on the Court's failure to 'pull in tandem' in the 'three-horse team' of the federal government served as a homely metaphor for a deeper, Wilsonian view of the Constitution. Roosevelt rejected the separation-of-powers, checks-and-balances basis of the Constitution for a cooperative, organic one—the Newtonian for the Darwinian basis of politics, as Wilson put it" (297).

The cadre of progressive intellectuals who dominated the 1930s gave plenty of support to this view: natural rights were dead and had to lie down. Father John Ryan, according to Moreno, concerned himself only with purported "economic rights and liberties," rather than with dangers to religious liberty (303). Constitutional scholar Edward S. Corwin chose to see the Constitution as an instrument of popular sovereignty dedicated to progress, rather than a "barrier of custom, magic, fetish, tabu," designed to limit power (301). Believers in the constitutionalism of the founders were at best premodern cultists and mythologizers—at worst psychologically disordered.

Once a chastened Supreme Court saw that resistance to progressive constitutionalism was futile, and a reconstructed Supreme

Court saw that it was wrong-headed, there was free rein (save for only occasionally recalcitrant public opinion) to complete the progressive and New Deal vision of American politics. The defeat of Roosevelt's court-packing plan turned out to be a long-term victory for progressivism by insulating the Court from political pushback. As Moreno notes, no president has ever directly confronted the Court since (327–28). And this observation should cause us to contemplate an important fact: it is judicial rather than executive power that is now at the vanguard of the continuing progressive revolution in politics, as well as the revolt against natural rights constitutionalism.[47]

THE CONSOLIDATION OF THE REVISIONIST CRITIQUE

Another recent volume, referenced earlier, has brought together the leading contemporary critics of the progressive intellectual synthesis: *Progressive Challenges to the American Constitution: A New Republic*.[48] In it, Schambra develops his argument concerning the significance of the election of 1912, claiming that the Tea Party movement is a populism that is constitutional—rather than simply populist.[49] The Tea Partiers are unlike the earlier populists, insofar as they have a genuine concern for proper constitutional constraint on democratic will. Their wrestling with the problem of democracy and its relationship to the Constitution is a first step toward recovering the Constitution from the progressive opprobrium beneath which it has labored for over a century. For Schambra, contemporary debates over the limits of democracy echo the arguments between Taft and Roosevelt in the run-up to the uproarious Republican convention of 1912. That contest saw TR pointing to the democratic deficits of the Constitution. The key shift in TR's rhetoric was his move from a progressive legislative agenda to a progressive constitutional agenda. The radicalism of his proposals to deal with those perceived deficits drove Republicans such as Elihu Root and Henry Cabot Lodge—who had been longtime backers of TR—into the Taft camp. In the end, Root

agreed with Taft that the result of the convention was more important than the election itself because it settled the critical question
of 1912, namely, whether the Republican Party should be seized
by and carried over to populism. For Schambra, both scholarly and
populist constitutionalists can therefore look to 1912 for guidance.

In the same volume, Milkis considers yet another legacy of the
1912 election.[50] He reminds us of the dispute between Madison
and Jefferson over whether the Constitution should be protected
from passionate factionalism and suggests that Jefferson's position
has been vindicated in the progressive notion of a "living Constitution," one that each generation might define. In particular, the
election of 1912 challenged voters to rethink the deepest meaning
of their Constitution, and such rethinking was showcased in the
debate among four impressive candidates: Roosevelt, Taft, Eugene
Debs, and Woodrow Wilson. The election of 1912 was in effect the
rare presidential contest that verged on engaging political philosophy in the full sense. The campaign was in many ways an argument over James Madison and *The Federalist Papers* and whether
the checks and balances of the founders' Constitution would survive. The progressive promise to remake the Constitution from a
lawyer's document, supported by the veneration of the people, into
a living constitution—and a platform for bold and persistent experimentation—resonated widely. In the words of TR in the 1912
campaign, "The people themselves must be the ultimate makers of
their own Constitution." With this election died the conservatism
of Taft, to be supplanted by contemporary conservatives' commitment to a strong executive and mass democracy.

On the political philosophy of progressivism, University of
Virginia political scientist James W. Ceaser offers a nuanced tracing
of the manner and extent of the progressives' rejection of the founders' natural rights doctrine.[51] Ceaser argues that progressives generally condemned efforts to overthrow the government by action outside of established law, favoring instead democratic methods of
social change. Yet at the same time they made clear their plans to
alter the basic character of the political and economic system and
to discard the theoretical foundation of natural rights philosophy

that underlay it. Their immediate target was the Constitution itself. Embracing the Enlightenment's scientific project, they used that project in a new way—as a tool to attack the founders' constitutionalism and its principled grounding.

Also considering matters of political philosophy, University of Oklahoma historian Wilfred M. McClay sketches the philosophical roots of progressivism by examining the thought of one of its greatest exponents, John Dewey.[52] For Dewey, science, education, art, and all other creative human activities find their ultimate meaning when harnessed to the great project of democracy. Dewey argued that there was no tension between scientific expertise and democratic sentiment. Science, in his account, was nothing more than an exemplification of the process by which intelligence might be socialized. It thus becomes the key source of disinterested authority in a democratic society. Education, the central task of civilized life, is properly understood as nothing more than a formal name for the process of adaptation, the process by which experience, in the form of the full findings of science as well as other less systematic forms of human inquiry, is incorporated into the individual's pattern of habits, ideas, perceptions, and emotions. With educational institutions working properly, all the chronic frictions that bedevil modern social life will, in Dewey's scheme, be harmonized so that the interests of the individual, as well as those of the "public," will be fully expressed and realized.

Though Dewey, like other progressives, had high ambitions for social science, he was equally adamant that experts not become a clerisy or self-vaunting aristocracy and that even the most recondite social knowledge must be "indissolubly wedded to the act of full and moving communication." By the time that Dewey published *The Public and Its Problems* in 1925, however, the general notion of a "public interest"—so central to progressive thought— was crumbling under a concentrated assault by younger skeptics and realists; and, as McClay notes, it has never regained the general plausibility that it had a hundred years ago. In our own day, on issue after issue, from climate change to constitutional law, the tension between science and democracy, between accredited experts and *vox populi*, remains. It has proved to be a tension that Dewey's brand of progressivism could not resolve.

Meanwhile, the political theory of the modern administrative state has been scrutinized for several decades by political scientist John Marini of the University of Nevada, Reno.[53] He has shown the origins of the administrative state in progressive political thought and ideology. The argument of progressives, and then contemporary liberals, was that the modern state—and unlimited national power—were the inevitable consequences of the progress of certain economic and social forces unleashed by modernity. That argument disguised the fundamentally political, and consciously anticonstitutional, character of progressive reforms, according to Marini. In the progressive dispensation, all "natural" laws are reduced to physical or biological laws, and government cannot be limited by fixed moral truth.

A recurring theme of the present work has been the importance of progressive Christianity to the growth of the administrative state, not to mention the moralistic tone of contemporary liberalism—and how American historians managed to gloss over this phenomenon. Recently, in the *Progressive Challenges* volume, Pestritto and political scientist James Stoner of Louisiana State University have dilated on these matters. Pestritto argues that a particularly fervent strain of social gospel Christianity helped birth modern progressivism and the administrative state.[54] Pestritto notes that strong attachment to religious faith is associated more with progressivism's contemporary critics than with its friends, so it is not uncommonly assumed that earlier liberalism, including progressivism in particular, was accompanied by atheism or antireligious animus. In the case of America's original progressives, however, that was far from the case. Early progressivism adopted a rhetoric that might seem at home among members of today's Christian Right.

Stoner in turn shows the influence of Catholic social thought on our understanding of the modern state.[55] The harmony of sentiment between Fr. John Ryan—the member of the Catholic clergy who had the most influence on twentieth-century social policy—and Richard Ely—the great progressive economist—provides the intellectual framework through which Catholicism and progressivism came to be united in their mutual quest for social solidarity through economic policy. Like the Protestantism described by Pestritto, Catholicism was turned against democratic capitalism in the quest for a more rational, scientific state. The roots of the modern welfare state can thus be said to predate the middle part of the twentieth century.

The progressive presidency has come under attack from various angles. In addition to Kesler's and Pestritto's explication and critique of Wilson's hostility to the Constitution, Bowdoin College political scientist Jean Yarbrough has spent much time on the origins and implications of Teddy Roosevelt's political thought.[56] She notes that historians have spilled far too much ink on the practical policy positions of the progressives and not nearly enough on their political philosophy. She points to the influence of progressive intellectual Herbert Croly on TR, especially in the latter's summoning of the nation to a "New Nationalism," whose purpose was to move beyond the pursuit of private, materialistic goals. According to both TR and Croly, democracy could be achieved only through the vigorous exercise of national power, whereby the central government would become less the enforcer of neutral rules and more the driver of social growth. Croly offered TR the intellectual framework by which he could better grasp and articulate his own intuitions and inclinations. Croly in effect deepened TR's understanding of himself and emboldened him to further action and argument. TR's "New Nationalism" planted the axiom that government, and not the individual, was the source, and therefore the arbiter, of all property rights. But historians were largely oblivious to this and more, with Hofstadter going so far as to dismiss his thought as "a bundle of philistine conventionalities."[57]

According to Yarbrough's *Theodore Roosevelt*, political scientists too have given TR "a pass" insofar as his rhetoric seems in many ways to place him with the founders and with Lincoln (5). But the ideas he embraced "posed a fundamental challenge to the principles for which his heroes stood" (13). Evolutionary biology and social Darwinism were prime among those ideas (13–19). The young TR was also exposed to smatterings of Hegelianism, with its dismissal of natural rights in favor of liberty being the product of the state (43). Nature itself was, for him, little more than the struggle for survival—a struggle that, in both principle and practice, could be helped by steady governmental expansion. From Frederick Jackson Turner, TR drew the idea that the story of America was not the story of political liberty and the development of institutions conducive to it but the story of progress, in terms of the development of an American race (82). On top of all this, TR distanced himself from the political science of *The Federalist*, with its insistence that men could not separate their opinions, interests, and passions from their political judgments. With a sanguinity characteristic of progressives, TR thought that virtue could and should routinely rise above self-interest and that such virtue would not likely be cultivated in a Hamiltonian, commercial republic (118–19). Along with the social gospelers, TR had confidence in his power—if following his own moral compass—to eradicate earthly evils through altering or denying what the founders had thought was unchanging human nature (133–37).

Yarbrough points to the fact that TR also dismissed Tocqueville's warnings about tyranny of the majority and soft despotism, which was another characteristic tendency of progressives (270). In fact, the battle between TR's New Nationalism and Wilson's New Freedom was little more than "a family quarrel about the direction of progressivism unhinged from the Constitution of the Framers" (247). Both men sought to replace the old constitutional order of individual rights with a new one that would bow more effectively to popular will (246–47).

One historian who hasn't neglected constitutionalism is O'Neill, who, as discussed earlier in this chapter, has helped bring to sight the important but largely forgotten story of the contemporaneous rejection of progressivism's goals, including especially the role of William Howard Taft in maintaining a constitutional presidency.[58] O'Neill argues that Taft viewed with alarm the beginning of the modern presidency in Roosevelt's "stewardship" theory—a kind of routinization of prerogative—holding that the president could legally do whatever the needs of the people demanded. Unsuited though he was for modern mass democracy, Taft robustly exercised executive power while retaining a more constitutionally sound vision of the presidency than that of the progressives. On matters ranging from the party system, to centralized budgeting and cabinet control, to the Ballinger-Pinchot affair, Taft displayed a commitment to executive leadership but also to a sober republican and constitutionalist conception of such leadership that remained rooted in consent and the separation of powers.

And of course, most twentieth-century historians left much to be said on the relationship of progressivism to the judicial and legislative branches. These important lacunas are now being addressed, including the long-term outlook for the progressive synthesis in an age when progressive thinkers and political actors no longer view the presidency as the primary driver of history, largely because of the very real limits imposed by the founders' Constitution. My work on the Supreme Court examines the philosophical and jurisprudential underpinnings that support contemporary understandings of a living Constitution.[59] I trace the origins and implications of those understandings in the social Darwinism and pragmatism that is so visible in early progressive jurisprudence. My claim is that the federal judicial branch—thanks largely to Oliver Wendell Holmes and Louis Brandeis—has adopted, more than any other branch of government, a progressive view of the Constitution. This view holds that the Constitution must be interpreted in light of an outlook that insists on the historically situated, contingent, and organic nature of the state, society, and human person. According to this theory, our place in History determines the meaning of our Constitution more than its text, tradition, logic, or structure, and it is the Court's role to keep updating our fundamental law accordingly.

I have argued that this historicist approach to the Constitution has been embraced by judicial appointees of different presidents from different decades, Democrat and Republican, "liberal" and "conservative." A major revolution in American political thought was necessary to bring such a diverse cast of characters to the same view of the Constitution. It is a revolution that, by its nature, cannot end. The age-old question of "what works" has been divorced from a sense of constitutional restraint, which has been replaced by an organic conception of a state unlimited in principle, whose growth and development must be oriented to buttress contemporary understandings of democracy and the choosing self. Our constitutional jurisprudence therefore seems destined to depart more and more from the constitutional moorings established by the founders and from the ideals of the rule of law, that is, the application of authoritative norms, consensually and publicly adopted, having as their end the protection of fixed natural rights.

Legal scholar Eric Claeys of George Mason University has also entered the fray by noting that even as the scholarship critical of progressive political theorists and actors has grown, political practice has done far less to confront the legacy of progressivism.[60] He suggests that only very recently has the revisionist scholarship been put to good use in the form of concrete efforts to restore the founders' natural rights constitutionalism. In particular, he has concentrated on the "Regulations from the Executive In Need of Scrutiny" Act, and its attempt to revive preprogressive constitutionalism in a practical and prudent manner. The act would reduce the legal power of executive branch agencies to make policy independent from Congress, thus restoring proper authority to constitutionally designated officers and reducing the overall growth of the administrative state. In his analysis of what Congress might do to roll back the progressive tide, Claeys reaches back to the political science of *The Federalist* and its conception of separation of powers in support of natural rights.

Together, this latest revisionist scholarship—coming about a hundred years after the election of 1912—has provided the resources by which informed citizens, scholars, and political actors might be encouraged to reconsider the nature of their constitutional republic, from its natural rights philosophical premises to the competing theories of progressive history that have in many ways supplanted them. As progressive history came to replace nature as the fundamental ordering idea of American politics, so it laid the groundwork for the contemporary embrace of the "living constitution" that replaced the founders' formal, fixed Constitution. The reverberations of this movement are still being felt on matters as diverse as the size and scope of government, fiscal policy, freedom of conscience, constitutional interpretation, and the overall political and cultural drift of the nation. The revisionist scholarship, emanating largely but not exclusively from the discipline of political science, should provide a framework for continued deliberations over such weighty regime questions. And it might it even give us hope that the American academy, after decades of listing portside, is still capable of generating balanced arguments on matters of vital national concern.

SIX The Shades of History

History, said political scientist Thomas B. Silver, can be a weapon, wielded to advance a political cause. And it is a particularly effective weapon in the hands of those public intellectuals who seem to wield it most effortlessly.[1] But weapons are most effective when they are fired in concert. This requires not simply willfulness but unanimity of purpose, or at least a shared perception of common enemies. This raises the critical question, which I have largely begged to this point, of how best to account for the weaponization of American history since the 1940s. Some clues are offered by those who have studied the history and growth of the modern academic disciplines.

Toward the end of the twentieth century, University of Chicago historian Peter Novick wrote *That Noble Dream*, a history of the history profession in America. In it, he offers — almost by accident — insights into how twentieth-century historians developed and maintained positions that both expressed a progressive consensus and became impervious to change or challenge from the outside. The key to understanding the historical profession, for Novick, is the enthroning of the idea of "objectivity." From the very beginnings of the profession, this idea reflected mere consensus rather than truth. Consensus is objectivity's poor relation — the best that historians can do. The "noble dream" of historical objectivity is just that.

The notion of objectivity washed onto American shores from Germany, at about the same time as the founding of the American Historical Association in 1884. The professionalization of history meant there was no longer any room for "gentleman amateurs," and their "literary presentation" gave way to a new form of history that was to be factual, empirical, and value-neutral. "No group was more prone to scientific imagery, and the assumption of the mantle of science, than the historians. The historical seminar, said Herbert Baxter Adams, had 'evolved from a nursery of dogma into a laboratory of scientific truth.'"[2] Within the confines of the AHA, objective "truth" came to be understood in pragmatic terms—the opinion that was agreed to by all or most of the newly professionalized historians and that grew out of standardized techniques of historical investigation. By the turn of the twentieth century, the most important consumer of history was the professional rather than the layman, and insularity went hand in hand with the illusion of objectivity. Criticism was sacrificed for the sake of comity within the profession (52–59).

Professionalization in turn demanded bureaucratization, which occurred within the confines of the German-patterned scholarly university, and bureaucratization bred further demands for homogeneity and comity (63–85). Furthermore, whether emphasizing organism or environment, continuity or discontinuity, conservatism or reform, institutional "germ theory" or the social and economic context in which institutions originated and operated, evolution was the watchword of the profession in the early twentieth century (88).

In other words, professional American historians were, in various ways, thoroughly progressive from the get-go. Though Novick does not say it, such consensus on the evolutionary framework necessarily pointed to a denigration of the American regime of natural rights and introduced a progressive presentism to historical analysis. The ever-shifting interactions between organism and environment determined the contours of the social and political for the evolutionist in a way that a formal constitutional framework could not even aspire to.

Novick maintains that the idea of objectivity came under mild assault in the aftermath of World War I. The war had undermined the optimism and faith in progress that had grounded historians' belief in "objective" truth in any form (111). Comity within the profession also declined as a generation of scholars arose who emphasized conflict and self-interest. But these new historians were not "all that radical" and generally retained a belief in the economic system and the American Revolution (241–49).

Novick claims the post–World War II period saw a reaffirmation of "consensual values" and an embrace of the American experience rather like the period that antedated World War I (320). Postwar American historical writing was dominantly "counter-progressive" in its newfound emphasis on continuity and consensus in American history, beginning with Hofstadter's 1948 effort to find the "common climate of American opinion" and continuing through Hartz's elaborate ideological consensus argument and Boorstin's assertion that Americans were nonideological (332–33). Even the progressives were defanged (but only partially debunked) and assimilated to the common climate. Cultural as well as academic trends reinforced dominant patterns of thought: "Democratization of hiring meant that outrageously inappropriate appointments became rarer, but so, too, did adventurous ones, as the need to satisfy a consensus often favored the bland and uncontroversial" (363). Even the new generation of radical historians remained committed to objectivity—William Appleman Williams prime among them (423). Only from the sixties onward did an increasing number of historians begin to share a mood of "diffuse skepticism" (598).

Novick's account is partly right, although, as I have argued, historians and the ideas with which they dealt were rather more radical than Novick allows. It is nevertheless true that the professionalism and scientism of historical inquiry converged on rationalist evolutionary categories, and in this sense faith in objectivity had a foundation that was at once firm and fluid, impervious to critique and protean in what it could assimilate. But the one thing it could not assimilate, or even relate, was the founders' Constitution. And Novick himself is an example of how this came to be. In rejecting the idealism of purported scientific history, he nevertheless explicitly embraces the historicism that underlies it, severing history from ultimate intelligibility. The historian can never point to *what is*: truth claims are not simply contestable but "essentially confused" and ultimately meaningless. Of the Declaration of Independence's self-evident truths, Novick asserts that "rarely have so many ambiguous terms and dubious propositions been compressed into such a brief passage" (7). Novick appears to believe (though presumably not in his capacity as historian) that certain things are in fact objective: liberty and equality. But in the end, his account suggests there is no professional history capable of dealing with America on its own terms, whether that history be progressive or "counterprogressive," scientific or relativist.

The historical profession can perhaps be forgiven some of its confusion and tendentiousness on regime questions when one reflects on parallel developments in allied disciplines. In the mid-1970s, historian Mary O. Furner of the University of California, Santa Barbara traced the professionalization of American social science. Taking cues from Robert Wiebe, she emphasizes the increasing importance of professional expertise in the rapidly changing social order from the Civil War through the Gilded Age.[3] As natural science gained in prestige throughout the nineteenth century, there was a perceived need for social science to follow suit, and the social science disciplines and professions as we have come to know them were invented to serve this demand (1). Ambitious, professionally trained social scientists—with vocabularies, journals, and disciplines of their own fashioning—replaced the amateurs who attempted to span a wider range of human experience. Large ethical questions receded as objects of professional engagement, in return for job security and immunity from outside pressures, although the tension between neutral scholarship and social reform was never quite overcome (5–8).

Economics in particular was ripe for such specialization as the "social question" came to the fore. Richard Ely, Simon Patten, Henry Carter Adams, and others made the opinions of professional social scientists matter, even as those opinions were very much informed by an ethical content (49–58). The tension between the new socially conscious economics and the older laissez-faire, exemplified by William Graham Sumner, presented a challenge for a discipline in the throes of self-creation. Some sort of "outward unity on basic issues" was required (59).

Compromise became inevitable, although one or another version of Ely's dictum that the state is "an ethical agency whose positive aid is an indispensable condition of human progress" guided much of the professionalization movement (73). The edge was taken off ideological commitment by full-time, disciplinary scholarship as such scholarship found its home within the confines of traditional universities. But it was difficult for careerism to win a decisive victory over social concern in disciplines that by their nature dealt with social and political phenomena. The tensions between advocacy and objectivity were laid bare by Ely's teaching at the Chautauqua summer school between 1887 and 1892, where his efforts to burnish his religious and ethical bona fides were seen to conflict with objective social science (119): "Ely became the symbol of the dubious tie between ethics and economics. New school colleagues gradually came to agree that their former spokesman might be seriously misplaced as head of their professionalization movement. They sought a level of authority which some of his activities undermined. Ely was not toppled by outside pressure. Professionals with training and inclinations similar to his own stripped him of his power in the profession" (124). Ironically, Ely's resignation as secretary of the American Economic Association did not so much destroy the influence of his ideas as simply clear the way for professionals "with training and inclinations similar to his own" to occupy positions of authority not only in the AEA but in what would become the main source of social scientific authority over the next century: the university. And with their greater institutional protection and privilege, not to mention stealth, came greater influence. As Ely and other progressives occasionally ran into trouble at their home institutions—Ely at Wisconsin—the lesson was learned: to put knowledge in the service of society, one had to be careful with "popularization," or overt politicization. But serving society remained the goal, and caution became routine—to the point of image management on the part of academics, including Ely himself (147–62, 204). "When Ely relinquished his claim to activism, he exchanged advocacy for acceptability" (162). By the end of the nineteenth century, professional economists had settled on a policy of defending their peers who operated within disciplinary confines and who did not stray too far from a wider social consensus (228, 259). The new economics became at once more cautious, more insular, and more influential.

By the 1890s, the middle and even upper classes increasingly evinced a concern for social welfare. Many of their members—businessmen, politicians, professionals, humanitarians—threw in their lot with progressives of various stripes, and reformism was rendered respectable. The reform movement directed its energies not at attempting to roll back modernity but at "developing agencies and techniques for continuous and efficient regulation of the complex process involved in urban, industrial life" (265). And this required specialists, particularly specialists from the at least outwardly domesticated social sciences. Furner here reiterates the mainstream scholarship on progressivism:

> Progressives were identified as urban, middle class, business and professional people by George Mowry. . . . Richard Hofstadter . . . emphasized the difference in reform type between Populists and progressives and ascribed the motivation of middle-class progressives to a status revolution. Robert Wiebe . . . explained the role of a new middle class of managerial and professional people who identified strongly with their occupation and endeavored to develop flexible mechanisms for the efficient management of a complex urban society in which their specialties were important. Gabriel Kolko . . . showed how big business used regulatory measures that have been considered "progressive" to consolidate political capitalism. (266n11)

By the turn of the twentieth century, a secure academic social science position could lead to influence on the larger society (277). And this was true of other burgeoning social science disciplines. Political science concerned itself with preparing students for public administration and then for staffing teachers of public administration at colleges (283). In order to continue consideration of the broader, but complementary "social questions," sociology was invented as a discipline (291). And ultimately, "Academic professionals, having retreated to the security of technical expertise, left to journalists and politicians the original mission—the comprehensive assessment of industrial society—that had fostered professionalization in social science" (324). Throughout the twentieth century, this symbiotic relationship was preserved. The American university generated—and gave the patina of scholarly credibility to—various forms of progressive social science, which was then spread by popularizing historians and members of the elite media, who had been educated by the very scholars whose work they now promoted.

Following closely on Furner, historian Thomas L. Haskell of Rice University offers an interpretation of the last generation of "amateur" social scientists, including the cultural reasons for their displacement by disciplinary professionals. Haskell operates, broadly speaking, within the psychological, "crisis of authority" school of interpretation and offers a case study in Wiebe's larger "search for order," which was necessitated by the dissolution of the isolated communities of American life.[4] He concentrates on the essentially amateur American Social Science Association, from its founding in 1865 to its demise in 1909, when it was fully supplanted by the modern disciplines of history, economics, political science, and sociology—disciplines drawing their membership from the universities.

The life and times of the ASSA—the big-tent "mother of associations"—tracks closely the changing conceptions of how best to explain increasingly complex social phenomena and "to institutionalize sound opinion" in the waning decades of the nineteenth century. It was founded with a bold confidence expressed in its organizing documents: "When the laws of Education, of Public Health, and of Social Economy are fully ascertained, the law of the land should recognize and define them all" (106). The ASSA was closely allied with early efforts at civil service reform and the establishment of investigative commissions. Consisting largely of nonacademic professionals who were oriented more to reform than dispassionate analysis, the ASSA was the original clearinghouse for intellectuals attempting to establish authoritative guidance over diverse areas of inquiry and to concentrate this expertise in the hands of the gentry.

The organization was soon viewed as inadequate to its task when the need for full-time specialists became apparent. These were specialists who embraced the concept of "interdependence," which provides what Haskell refers to as the "interpretive keystone" to his approach. With it, he seeks to replace accounts suggesting that American social thought at the turn of the century was largely a product of the convergence of intellectual positivism and idealism, or ideas that could be shared only by intellectuals. The recognition of the interdependence of social phenomena, by contrast, provides a link between social thinkers and everyday people and offers a more comprehensive view of the large-scale transformations in American thought and social practice.

After the Civil War, everyone experienced the shift of life and mind away from family, sect, and village (14–15). Haskell claims that the "main point of cleavage between the rising professional theorists examined by Morton White and the declining amateur [ASSA] theorists studied in these pages is the recognition of, or the failure to recognize, the objective fact of social interdependence and its larger theoretical implications" (15). Terms like *urbanization, industrialization*, and *modernization* fail to capture the breadth and complexity of this intellectual shift. In the notion of interdependence and the "non-formalistic social theory" that at once depended on it and accounted for it, a new "paradigm" of social-scientific investigation was inaugurated (20). It was a paradigm shift that was helped along by the interests of a "genteel class" desirous of rebuilding its claims to authority on a new "functional expertise" (22).

Doubt and uncertainty were "triggered certainly by Darwin and historical criticism of the Bible" but were also pervasively rooted in this growing sense of interdependence and the concomitant difficulty of "easy, unambiguous causal attribution" that characterized the thinking of the earlier generation of amateur, essentially voluntarist social scientists (46–47). Such simple attribution also characterized the thought of early professionals like William Graham Sumner, who was sensitive to historical forces but too conservative in his rejection of reform that might wrestle them into submission. The ASSA's moonlighting amateurs represented the voluntarist strain long after it had gone out of fashion, with its leaders continuing "to attribute to individuals a degree of causal potency that obscured historical, cultural, social, and economic determinants of human behavior" (165). They "imputed independence to variables that were really the dependent, last links in long chains of causation" (205).

By contrast, the social scientists of the progressive period would seldom locate causation "close to the surface" or in the will of individual actors. They wished to enhance individuality and defend the individual against powerful forces, while simultaneously denying human autonomy (251). The decline of the ASSA therefore paralleled the growth of the progressive mind.

Tocqueville noted the tendency of historians in democratic times to downplay the role of great men in favor of general causes, for it is difficult in such times to discern individuals who exert "a very lasting power over the mass." Societies are seen to obey dominating forces rather than human command. Historians thereby "take away from peoples themselves the ability to modify their own fate"—they teach them only how to obey. But such systematization yields benefits to the democratic historians themselves: "It always furnishes them some great reasons that quickly pull them through the most difficult spot in their book and supports the weakness or laziness of their minds, all the while doing honor to their profundity." He goes on to note that "historians who live in democratic times . . . consider a nation has reached a certain place in its history and affirm that it was constrained to follow the path that led it there. That is easier than instructing us on how it could have acted to take a better route."[5]

The first major association to break off from the ASSA—the American Historical Association—set the pattern for those that would follow. Unlike the ASSA, the AHA, according to Haskell, "was the formal expression of a genuine community of inquiry . . . solidaristic enough to insulate its members from public opinion, to submit their idiosyncrasies to communal discipline, and to perform the other authority-enhancing functions" (176). It was, in short, a guild—and one dedicated to a new kind of intellectual orthodoxy.

In the 1990s, Johns Hopkins historian Dorothy Ross argued that American social science from the outset accepted certain orthodoxy, in particular the Enlightenment conception of history as progress and unidirectional advance, informed by varying degrees of positivism and idealism.[6] Francis Lieber, America's first political scientist (or at least the first man to hold that title), exploited "the resonances between German understanding of the state and American Whig culture" (38).[7] There were, to be sure, natural laws or at least recurrent natural processes that informed such a conception, but they served to animate a nature very much in motion, rather than to protect a set of rights in repose. There was no room in such thinking for a key distillation of the modern project—the American founders' distillation—that sought to check the excesses of the Enlightenment: the idea that there exist immutable Laws of Nature and of Nature's God that compel the dispassionate mind and require, as a matter of justice, limited republican government.

Not only the laws of nature but their source—nature's God—came under attack in the wake of the scientific naturalism and positivism that reached a crescendo with the publication of the *Origin of Species*. Most "gentry intellectuals . . . adjusted the basis of their Christian faith to avoid cognitive conflict with natural science. For all of them, however, the influence of positivism forced for the first time in America a divorce between natural knowledge and revealed Christianity and a determination to develop natural knowledge on its own terms" (57).

According to Ross, the idea of historical development in all things sat uneasily with the old idea of American exceptionalism and precipitated a crisis of authority. This created a vacuum that the mugwumps abhorred and attempted to fill with men of character and expertise. Universities were reformed on the basis of their sense of what was required to reestablish order and buttress American principles in the context of the new social sciences (61–64). Class and professional interests pulled in unison—and both pulled

America away from its founding principles. Political scientists like Lieber, Herbert Adams, and John W. Burgess "wanted to protect established institutions from the demos by subordinating individual rights to history and the community" (74). Meanwhile, political economists like Sumner also sought to give "American" principles a firm scientific foundation without ties to traditional ethics or theology (79–97). Others such as Richard Ely tried to harmonize at least the spirit of Christianity with a new economic order. But all were committed to a profound historicism and a concomitant willingness to diminish the idea of ordered liberty resting on unalterable natural rights.

As the Gilded Age gave way to progressivism proper, "social scientists expressed a new trust in the secular forces at work beneath the chaos of change and a new confidence in their ability to understand and shape the future" (149–50). Economists, sociologists, political scientists, and historians could all agree: individual and social interests could be harmonized with the intelligent application of technique. With such a shift in "historical consciousness," it was perhaps inevitable that religious language would eventually become window dressing rather than the motive force for liberal social engineering. Social morality became less grounded in a particular religious dispensation or political philosophy and more a function of what the times required, floating rather freely in the flux of progressive aspirations. The American "exceptionalist ideal" would be realized in the "approaching future" (217). One might say the ever-approaching future: in the fullness of time, this would become a fully secularized millenarianism.

By the 1920s, scientism attempted "to make the achievement of science an end in itself and thereby to find order amid historical flux" (390). Scientism is the "most striking outcome of exceptionalist history," its quantitative techniques "blind to what cannot be measured" and often blinding us "to the human and social consequences of their use. The manipulators of social scientific technique, intent on instrumental rationality, cannot notice the qualitative human world their techniques are constructing and destroying," according to Ross (472).

And in that observation, we can discern a characteristic of contemporary social engineering, whether at the intellectual or policy levels: obliviousness to what it constructs and destroys, includes and excludes, analyzes and advocates. Above all, it is oblivious to the point at which it abandons moderation and slides into hubris.

Also in the 1990s, University of Texas historian Mark C. Smith argued that social science's turn from normative concerns after World War II was part of a broader "end-of-ideology movement" based on relativism and the belief that no important sources of conflict existed in American public life. This, it turns out, was but another way of saying that by the 1940s there was enough consensus around the progressive consensus that social scientists could afford to wear their hearts less obviously on their sleeves, compared to many of their colleagues just a generation earlier. Alternatively, for professional purposes they were oblivious to their heart's desire.

Smith notes that even as Charles Merriam, the progressive behavioral political scientist, supported a "New Bill of Rights" to go along with Roosevelt's Four Freedoms, he seemed not to realize that such a position might be in conflict with his commitment to quantitative analysis. This bill of rights was presented by Roosevelt as something that would supplement the "inalienable political rights" of the Constitution, which were "inadequate to assure us equality in the pursuit of happiness." Rather, government-guaranteed rights, based on "economic truths that have become accepted as self-evident," were necessary to vouchsafe that pursuit. These included such things as the right to a useful and remunerative job, the right to earn enough to provide food, clothing, and recreation, and the right to a good education. Less self-evident than merely desirable, these purported rights were bound to come into conflict in myriad ways with the self-evident truths of the American founders that constrained rather than enabled government power. But no attempt at theoretical reconciliation needed to be made by minds convinced of the practical necessity for policy action. Merriam "simply could not conceive that anyone could not believe in such obvious truths."[8]

Historians went along for the ride. "Historians such as Daniel Boorstin and Arthur Schlesinger, Jr., described America's past as lacking significant conflict and praised American political thought lavishly for its practical orientation. The goal was . . . a non-normative political and social system in which competing elites agreed on basic issues and turned to trained technicians to boost economic production, run the social system smoothly, and assist malcontents in their adjustment and acceptance of the system."[9]

Brandeis historian Morton Keller has noted the American historical profession's "Rip Van Winkle-like slumber" over the course of the twentieth century when it came to writing political and governmental history, with some notable exceptions. And by the latter part of the century, historians awoke to the "race-class-culture Tong wars and the strictures of Marxist and post-Marxist analysis."[10] Neither was conducive to an attempt to reengage American political history and the American regime on their own terms.

The field was left to political scientists—at least those willing to take up the task. With the reconsideration of progressivism by these political scientists, political history and political science are converging again. American historical writing might once again be past politics as political science becomes "political history brought up to date."[11]

However, a funny thing has happened as the reconsideration of the progressive synthesis has begun to spread in mainstream political science circles. Witness *The Progressives' Century*, a sprawling 2016 volume edited by Stephen Skowronek and Bruce Ackerman of Yale and Stephen M. Engel of Bates College.[12] As the editors allow in their introduction, the progressives were insurgents who "pressed a comprehensive critique of the old order," including its constitutional foundations. For progressives, institutional constraints on the national government had to give way to allow for programmatic action, part of an all-out "assault on limits." In this sense, they were unabashedly anticonstitutional.

The editors insist that progressivism is now on the defensive as a result of contemporary conservatives laying siege to it. The twenty-one contributors the editors assemble don't do much to cash out this claim. Dealing with a few central questions and many ancillary ones, this catchall volume has a cumulative effect similar to the historical works that went before it—it makes the progressive synthesis appear more diffuse, and more mainstream, than it is.

Rather than claiming that progressivism is on the defensive, it would perhaps be more accurate to observe that it has merely had to defend itself—for the first time—as a result of the recent siege. As Charles Kesler has suggested, "Progressivism has never been in a fair fight, an equal fight, until now, because its political opponents had largely been educated in the same ideas, had lost touch, like Antaeus, with the ground of the Constitution in natural right, and so tended to offer only Progressivism Lite as an alternative."[13]

Even the need for an intellectual defense would come as news to a lot of contemporary progressives, including many contributors to *The Progressives' Century*, who are under the mistaken impression that their wholesale rejection of the founders' Constitution is as American as apple pie. Just how far should the revisionism go? According to the editors, the revisionist reappraisal of the modern American state and the progressive ideas that underlie it has already "grown more radical" and "polemical." The editors' sympathies, like those of the mid-twentieth-century historians, seem clear enough. While they insist that "conservative revisionism all but compels a broad reconsideration of the rise of Progressivism as the pivot point in the development of modern American government," one cannot help but sense this is largely to provide fodder for the "American political development" subfield of political science with which they are associated. *Déformation professionnelle* is as likely to creep into this subfield as any other, especially when "objectivity" precludes the deep attachment to the Constitution and to the regime that is experienced by the revisionists. And yet it is the revisionists who appear to the editors, and many of the contributors, to be the radicals.

The revisionists—or "rejectionists" in the editors' lingo—are renouncing what "should be familiar to most Americans," including especially faith in government's ability to solve socioeconomic problems. These rejectionists would even go so far as to undermine our purported confidence in enlightened expertise and leadership. In the end, the editors' counsel is that it is best not to "choose sides on the legacy of progressivism." Surely we can build consensus around that.

The chapters that deal most squarely with the rejectionists—those by Ken I. Kersch of Boston College and Steven M. Teles of

Johns Hopkins—convey the tone of the volume, even as they do a commendable job of offering a quick, if incomplete, guide to some of the most trenchant critiques of the progressive synthesis. Kersch notes that progressivism is now central to accounts from the intellectual Right as to how the founders' Constitution was abandoned.[14] This marks a shift from earlier conservative critiques—which tended to concentrate on countermajoritarian "activist" judges—toward a more robust political theory of the American founding that is juxtaposed against the rampant historicism of the progressives. In short, the center of gravity of constitutional conservatism has moved away from the law schools and toward the discipline of political science. It is being articulated by "Straussian political theorists" who are capable of engaging the elaborate theory of progressivism and offering a critique that "cuts much deeper" than the earlier legalist-originalist one.

But Kersch insists that things are complicated when it comes to the progressive synthesis, which was "diverse and often self-contradicting." The insights—or "obsessions," as the author prefers—of the Straussians are tinged with "religious foundationalism" and "dog-whistle implications" demanding "an oathlike allegiance" to natural law. Serving this fundamentalism of the rejectionists are "apocalyptic stories of faith and heresy, salvation and damnation, friends and enemies, loyalty and treason," and "constitutional McCarthyism," revealing "the very egoism they hold damnable in their enemies." Kersch argues that the political theorists' critique of progressivism has been useful in reinforcing conservative identities, overcoming older cleavages, and forging a new conservative political movement at both the intellectual and populist levels.

These "movement" implications are taken up by Teles in his examination of the intellectual and popular channels through which the new critique of progressivism was spread.[15] The political theorists moved their ideas through think tanks like the Claremont Institute and Heritage Foundation and then opinion journalists like Jonah Goldberg and Glenn Beck. The Tea Party movement was given a "coherent account of the fall" by intellectuals who explained and defended the founders' Constitution against progressive assaults.

The Claremont school of political science figures prominently in Teles's account. And indeed, as I have suggested, scholars in the Claremont orbit have long argued that the US Constitution—and indeed any form of limited government—rests on an understanding that there are permanent principles of political right derivable from a proper account of human nature, including the fact that humans are politically equal, and fallen, beings. In other words, it rests on what purports to be truth rather than consensus. In rejecting any account of an unchangeable human nature, the progressives went deep to attack the heart of American constitutionalism. So Teles is right to suggest that this school is responsible for the remarkable resurgence of interest in the founders' political theory, dormant for so long among intellectuals blinded by the progressive synthesis. And along with this resuscitation of the founders, the progressives have indeed come under some popular assault.

In good political science fashion, Teles bases much of his analysis on interviews, especially with scholars in the Claremont orbit. But he is not quite at home with the zoological specimens he is studying, so he sees them as curiosities. To him, they appear unlike earlier and more congenial Straussians who were willing to make a reasonable peace with a progressivism they understood to be a mere response to political necessities. This is a progressivism that can ultimately be squared with constitutional norms, even if it occasionally overreaches.

The thing an attentive reader is most likely to conclude from *The Progressives' Century* is that, far from putting the progressive synthesis on the run, the revisionist scholarship still has a long way to go, among political scientists almost as much as historians.

HISTORY AS PRESENT POLITICS

Like the progressivism that spawned it, contemporary liberalism both benefits and suffers from lack of clarity on the part of its chroniclers. When the story of liberalism is told by liberals, it is usually unfolded as a doctrine without dogma, a merely pragmatic set of political dispositions aimed not at theorizing but at problem solving in an ever-changing world. While it might have "ideals" or "vision," liberalism is presented as but a modest, even conservative, outlook.[16] But in truth, liberalism was all about theory from the very beginning—a theory deeply hostile to America's premises.[17] "Modern liberalism had always been a complex blend of an evolutionary rights doctrine . . . a unified State directed by experts . . . a philosophy of history that assured that rational progress was possible and indeed inevitable . . . and a faith in political leaders who could envision history's next move. . . . The second and third elements depended on hierarchy, education, and authority. . . . The first and fourth were more fluid, open-ended, and relativist."[18] Keeping this complex amalgam politically viable—in both the electoral and policy realms—has always been a difficult task, and one that the most progressive of all presidents, Barack Obama, inherited just as liberals themselves fought over their faith in, and ranking of, its various elements.

Seemingly trying to preempt this conflict within the liberal tradition—not to mention preemptively defend the tradition from outside assaults—twentieth-century historians insisted on the absence of the progressive idea. Its utter strangeness, from the point of view of the founders' Constitution, rarely comes across in their bland consensus accounts that serve more to show the profound disconnect between American historical scholarship and America's constitutional moorings. In many cases the historians had imbibed political orientations—deliberately or through subtle osmosis—from the very movement they were chronicling. These, together with the disciplinary constraints under which they labored, led them to miss, or conceal, the eight-hundred-pound gorilla in the living room of American politics. We may say that collectively they are guilty of a strange complicity of understatement. Only recently have scholars outside the historical profession identified progressivism for what it was and continues to be: a fundamental rupture with the roots of American order.

Notes

Foreword

1. *The Federalist Papers*, ed. Charles R. Kesler (New York: Signet Classic, 2003), No. 49, pp. 311–12.
2. *The Federalist Papers*, No. 51, p. 319.
3. Abraham Lincoln, Letter to Henry L. Pierce and Others, April 6, 1859, in *Selected Speeches and Writings by Abraham Lincoln* (New York: Vintage Books/Library of America, 1992), p. 216.
4. Herbert Croly, *The Promise of American Life* (New York: Macmillan, 1909).

Introduction

1. On the wax and wane of the idea of objectivity among historians, see Peter Novick, *That Noble Dream: The "Objectivity Question" and the American Historical Profession* (New York: Cambridge University Press, 1988). This is a subject to which I shall return in the final chapter.
2. Scholars who have been at the forefront of this reconsideration include James W. Ceaser, *Nature and History in American Political Development* (Cambridge, MA: Harvard University Press, 2008); Charles R. Kesler, *I Am the Change: Barack Obama and the Crisis of Liberalism* (New York: Broadside Books, 2012); John Marini and Ken Masugi, eds., *The Progressive Revolution in Politics and Political Science* (Lanham, MD: Rowman and Littlefield, 2005); Sidney Milkis, *Theodore Roosevelt, the Progressive Party, and the Transformation of American Democracy* (Lawrence:

University Press of Kansas, 2009); Ronald J. Pestritto, *Woodrow Wilson and the Roots of Modern Liberalism* (Lanham, MD: Rowman and Littlefield, 2005); Jean Yarbrough, *Theodore Roosevelt and the American Political Tradition* (Lawrence: University Press of Kansas, 2014); and Bradley C. S. Watson, ed., *Progressive Challenges to the American Constitution: A New Republic* (New York: Cambridge University Press, 2017). The latter volume includes contributions from most of the aforementioned scholars as well as Eric R. Claeys, Wilfred M. McClay, Johnathan O'Neill, William Schambra, and James R. Stoner.

3. Bradley C. S. Watson, *Living Constitution, Dying Faith: Progressivism and the New Science of Jurisprudence* (Wilmington, DE: ISI Books, 2009).

4. See Julian E. Zelizer, *Governing America: The Revival of Political History* (Princeton, NJ: Princeton University Press, 2012), 1–4.

5. Zelizer, *Governing America*, 96.

6. See, for example, Joseph Postell, *Bureaucracy in America: The Administrative State's Challenge to Constitutional Government* (Columbia: University of Missouri Press, 2017).

7. Readers interested in such an account might start with Thomas G. West, *The Political Theory of the American Founding: Natural Rights, Public Policy, and the Moral Conditions of Freedom* (New York: Cambridge University Press, 2017).

ONE The Revolt against the Constitution

1. Charles R. Kesler, *I Am the Change: Barack Obama and the Crisis of Liberalism* (New York: Broadside Books, 2012), 35.

2. Richard Hofstadter, *Social Darwinism in American Thought*, rev. ed. (1944; repr., Boston: Beacon Press, 1955), 125.

3. Morton G. White, *Social Thought in America: The Revolt against Formalism* (New York: Viking Press, 1949), 241–46.

4. Kesler, *I Am the Change*, 33. This argument is central to the recent critical scholarship on progressivism to which I referred in my Introduction. See also Ronald J. Pestritto, *Woodrow Wilson and the Roots of Modern Liberalism* (Lanham, MD: Rowman and Littlefield, 2005).

5. Kesler, *I Am the Change*, 49.

6. Woodrow Wilson, "The Study of Administration," *Political Science Quarterly* 2, no. 2 (June 1887): 215.

7. Herman Belz, "The Constitution in the Gilded Age: The Beginnings of Constitutional Realism in American Scholarship," *American Journal of Legal History* 13, no. 2 (April 1969): 111.

8. Hofstadter, *Social Darwinism*, 4. The phrase *social Darwinism* gained widespread intellectual currency as an appropriate descriptor of an amalgam of ideas only with the publication of the first edition of this book in 1944.

9. John Dewey, "The Influence of Darwinism on Philosophy," in *The Influence of Darwinism on Philosophy and Other Essays in Contemporary Thought* (New York: Henry Holt, 1951). Subsequent page citations to this work are given parenthetically in the text.

10. The only other contender for the throne was the vigorous, pragmatic individualist frontier strain of thought associated with such figures as Frederick Jackson Turner and Mark Twain. But this strain, even in the explicitly progressive iterations of Turner, was never as theoretically unified as social Darwinism, and it never unified the intellectual classes in quite the same manner. Not coincidentally, it could not undermine so directly or consistently the principled understanding of the American founding articulated by Lincoln. Nevertheless, Turner's frontier thesis attracted a good deal of attention from historians of progressivism, as I detail later.

11. There are problems with this Deweyan tendency to identify nature as final cause or form with changelessness. Such an account comes close to capturing the essence of Plato's forms, but for Aristotle there are no fixed, immutable ideas separate from matter. Rather, things develop to their natural perfection, which for human beings is happiness, relying on a combination of intellectual and moral virtue. There is a tension in Aristotle between philosophy (man as knower) and politics (man being a political animal, i.e., a virtuous actor, rather than, or in addition to, a knower). It is far from clear, in either Aristotle or Plato, how these virtues interact at all levels. But what is clear is that there is no simple teleology in Aristotle when it comes to human beings. Simple teleologies are for the lower forms, whereas for humans there are choices involving politics, ethics, and philosophy, and nature many times misses its mark. Furthermore, for Aristotle, essence is not form simply, but activity or what a thing does. In his science, repose does not represent the highest state of being. Although there is a good amount of truth to Dewey's characterization of Western science, or philosophy, as the search for the transcendent, he seems wrong insofar as he puts a Platonic gloss on Aristotle.

12. See, for example, John Dewey, *Reconstruction in Philosophy* (Boston: Beacon Press, 1957).

13. This is why we do not expect great statesmen—exercising practical and theoretical wisdom—to be young, whereas mathematicians might be.

14. William James, "What Pragmatism Means," in William James, *Essays in Pragmatism*, ed. and introd. Alburey Castell (New York: Hafner Press, 1948); originally delivered by James as a lecture in 1906.

15. James, "What Pragmatism Means," 153–54.

16. James, "What Pragmatism Means," 146.

17. One need only compare the constitutional rhetoric of Lincoln to that of virtually any recent president to see this difference in stark relief. See Jeffrey K. Tulis, *The Rhetorical Presidency* (Princeton, NJ: Princeton University Press, 1987).

18. Philip P. Wiener, *Evolution and the Founders of Pragmatism* (Cambridge, MA: Harvard University Press, 1949), 191.

19. Louis Menand, *The Metaphysical Club* (New York: Farrar, Straus and Giroux, 2001), 302.

20. Indeed, Menand notes that the growth of American social science was a consequence of the rejection of the notion that evolutionary laws cannot be improved upon by public policy. See Menand, *Metaphysical Club*, 302.

21. John Dewey, *Liberalism and Social Action* (1935; repr., Amherst, NY: Prometheus Books, 2000), 29. Subsequent page citations to this work are given parenthetically in the text.

22. See especially Frederick Jackson Turner, *The Significance of the Frontier in American History* (New York: Henry Holt, 1921). Turner's "sectional thesis," though less well known, expresses a similar "scientific" approach. See Frederick Jackson Turner, *The Significance of Sections in American History*, introd. Max Farrand (New York: Henry Holt, 1932).

23. Charles A. Beard, *An Economic Interpretation of the Constitution of the United States* (New York: Macmillan, 1913).

24. Beard appeared to revise and soften his stance on both the nature and the extent of the Constitution's vices in his and Mary Beard's wartime book, *The Beards' Basic History of the United States* (New York: Doubleday, 1944).

25. Vernon Parrington, *Main Currents in American Thought*, 2 vols. (New York: Harcourt, Brace, 1927).

26. Kesler, *I Am the Change*, 39.

27. Kesler, *I Am the Change*, 43.

28. Kesler, *I Am the Change*, 55.

29. Kesler, *I Am the Change*, 100.

30. Kesler, *I Am the Change*, 109.

TWO The Real Presence of Christ

1. Johnathan O'Neill, "Constitutional Maintenance and Religious Sensibility in the 1920s: Rethinking the Constitutionalist Response to Progressivism," *Journal of Church and State* 51, no. 1 (Winter 2009): 24.

2. See, for example, Mark Warren Bailey, *Guardians of the Moral Order: The Legal Philosophy of the Supreme Court, 1860–1910* (DeKalb: Northern Illinois University Press, 2004), and Linda Przybyszewski, "Judicial Conservatism and Protestant Faith: The Case of Justice David J. Brewer," *Journal of American History* 91, no. 2 (September 2004): 471–96.

3. See Ronald J. Pestritto, "Making the State into a God: American Progressivism and the Social Gospel," in *Progressive Challenges to the American Constitution: A New Republic*, ed. Bradley C. S. Watson (New York: Cambridge University Press, 2017), 144–59, and James R. Stoner Jr., "Progressivism, Social Science, and Catholic Social Teaching in the Building of the American Welfare State," in Watson, *Progressive Challenges*, 160–70. I will return to these arguments in chapter 5. Compared to Christian progressivism, earlier Christian movements, including even politico-religious movements such as abolitionism and transcendentalism, had at their core concerns for individual sin and salvation, or at least individual purification.

4. Ernst Breisach, *American Progressive History: An Experiment in Modernization* (Chicago: University of Chicago Press, 1993), 108.

5. Daniel T. Rodgers, "In Search of Progressivism," *Reviews in American History* 10, no. 4 (December 1982): 123–24.

6. Rodgers, "In Search of Progressivism," 126.

7. Richard Hofstadter, *The Age of Reform* (New York: Knopf, 1955), 205n9.

8. John A. Ryan, *A Living Wage: Its Ethical and Economic Aspects* (New York: Macmillan, 1906).

9. See Stoner, "Progressivism, Social Science."

10. Luigi Bradizza, *Richard T. Ely's Critique of Capitalism* (New York: Palgrave Macmillan, 2013), 7.

11. Richard T. Ely, *The Social Law of Service* (New York: Eaton and Mains, 1896), preface, n.p. Subsequent page citations to this work, as *Social Law*, are given parenthetically in the text.

12. Richard T. Ely, "Social Aspects of Christianity," in *Social Aspects of Christianity and Other Essays* (New York: Thomas Y. Crowell, 1889), 1–2. Subsequent page citations to this work, as "Social Aspects," are given parenthetically in the text.

13. Richard T. Ely, "The Church and the World," in *Social Aspects of Christianity*, 60. Subsequent page citations to this work, as "Church," are given parenthetically in the text.

14. Richard T. Ely, "The Social Crisis and the Church's Opportunity," in *Social Aspects of Christianity*, 152 (emphasis in original). Subsequent page citations to this work, as "Social Crisis," are given parenthetically in the text. This hardly seems an accurate account of the Psalms, where "I" and "me" appear hundreds of times.

15. Bradizza, *Richard T. Ely's Critique*, 6.

16. Bradizza, *Richard T. Ely's Critique*, 132–33.

17. Richard T. Ely, "Philanthropy," in *Social Aspects of Christianity*, 88.

18. Richard T. Ely, *Socialism: An Examination of Its Nature, Its Strength and Its Weakness, with Suggestions for Social Reform* (New York: Thomas Y. Crowell, 1894), 70–71. Subsequent page citations to this work are given parenthetically in the text.

19. See Bradizza, *Richard T. Ely's Critique*, esp. Introduction.

20. Bradizza, *Richard T. Ely's Critique*, 6. As Bradizza makes clear, scholars of Ely's thought avoid addressing the soundness of his ideas, including his rejection of laissez-faire and a natural rights theory of property, either because they wish to avoid controversy in their academic writings or because they are sympathetic to progressive premises and aims. In Bradizza's formulation, "Scholars have tended to praise or blandly note his reform efforts, or neutrally trace the origin and development of his ideas, or recount his prophetic demands for welfare state apparatuses, or note the influence of his students and textbooks" (16). Actual criticism, including attempts to determine whether his ideas and prescriptions are sound for the American regime, has largely been absent (see 13–16).

21. See Bradizza, *Richard T. Ely's Critique*, esp. chap. 3.

22. See Bradizza, *Richard T. Ely's Critique*, esp. chap. 2.

23. Bradizza, *Richard T. Ely's Critique*, esp. conclusion.

24. Bradizza, *Richard T. Ely's Critique*, esp. chap. 1.

25. Bradizza, *Richard T. Ely's Critique*, 53.

26. Richard T. Ely, "Ethics and Economics," in *Social Aspects of Christianity*, 127–29.

27. Walter Rauschenbusch, "Remarks to the Tenth Annual Session of the Baptist Congress, Philadelphia, May 19, 1892," reprinted in *A Rauschenbusch Reader*, ed. Benson Y. Landis (New York: Harper, 1957), 146.

28. Pestritto, "Making the State," 147.

29. Walter Rauschenbusch, *Christianity and the Social Crisis* (1907; repr., New York: Macmillan, 1913), 42. Subsequent page citations to this work, as *Christianity*, are given parenthetically in the text.

30. Walter Rauschenbusch, *A Theology for the Social Gospel*, in *Rauschenbusch Reader*, 114. Subsequent page citations to this work, as *Theology*, are given parenthetically in the text and are to this excerpted edition.

31. Walter Rauschenbusch, *Christianizing the Social Order* (New York: Macmillan, 1912), 475. Subsequent page citations to this work are given parenthetically in the text.

32. Walter Rauschenbusch, *The Social Principles of Jesus* (Philadelphia: Westminster Press, 1916), 196.

33. Walter Rauschenbusch, *Prayers of the Social Awakening* (Boston: Pilgrim Press, 1910), preface.

34. Walter Rauschenbusch, "The Social Meaning of the Lord's Prayer," in *Rauschenbusch Reader*, 34

35. Rauschenbusch, "Social Meaning," 35.

36. Walter Rauschenbusch, "A Social Litany," in *Rauschenbusch Reader*, 75.

37. Rauschenbusch, *Dare We Be Christians?* (1914), in *Rauschenbusch Reader*, 82.

38. Walter Rauschenbusch, "Remarks Delivered at the Baptist Congress, Augusta, December 5, 1893," in *Rauschenbusch Reader*, 131.

39. Walter Rauschenbusch, "Remarks Delivered at the Baptist Congress, Toronto, May 13, 1889," in *Rauschenbusch Reader*, 145.

40. Francis L. Broderick, *Right Reverend New Dealer: John A. Ryan* (New York: Macmillan, 1963), 82, 85, 216.

41. Broderick, *Right Reverend New Dealer*, 21, 45.

42. John A. Ryan, preface to *A Living Wage: Its Ethical and Economic Aspects*, rev. ed. (New York: Macmillan, 1920), iv.

43. Richard T. Ely, introduction to Ryan, *Living Wage* [1920], vi.

44. Broderick, *Right Reverend New Dealer*, vii.

45. Broderick, *Right Reverend New Dealer*, 108.

46. See Broderick, *Right Reverend New Dealer*, 278. There is little to suggest that the church's voice has shifted in the half century since Broderick made this observation.

47. Ryan, *Living Wage* [1920], 49. Subsequent page citations to this work are to this edition and are given parenthetically in the text.

48. Broderick, *Right Reverend New Dealer*, 20.

49. And this was far from the only paradox of Ryan's life. His service on the board of the American Civil Liberties Union astonished some of his Catholic confreres. See Broderick, *Right Reverend New Dealer*, 142.

50. Broderick, *Right Reverend New Dealer*, 53.

51. Broderick, *Right Reverend New Dealer*, 40.

52. Broderick, *Right Reverend New Dealer*, 38.

53. John A. Ryan, *Distributive Justice: The Right and Wrong of Our Present Distribution of Wealth* (New York: Macmillan, 1916), preface, n.p. Subsequent page citations to this work, as *Distributive Justice*, are given parenthetically in the text.

54. John A. Ryan and Moorhouse F. X. Millar, *The State and the Church* (New York: Macmillan, 1922).

55. John A. Ryan, "The End of the State," in Ryan and Millar, *State and the Church*, 196–98.

56. Ryan, "End of the State," 199.

57. Ryan, "End of the State," 203.

58. Ryan, "End of the State," 215.

59. John A. Ryan, "The Proper Functions of the State," in Ryan and Millar, *State and the Church*, 222.

60. Ryan, "Proper Functions," 225.

61. John A. Ryan, "The Rights of the Citizen," in Ryan and Millar, *State and the Church*, 277.

62. John A. Ryan, "Comments on 'The Christian Constitution of States,'" in Ryan and Millar, *State and the Church*, 28.

63. Ryan, "Comments," 53.

64. Ryan, "Comments," 32, 60.

65. Ryan, "Comments," 55.

66. Charles R. Kesler, *I Am the Change: Barack Obama and the Crisis of Liberalism* (New York: Broadside Books, 2012), 158.

67. For an account of why such an earthly paradise is likely impossible, see Edward C. Banfield, *The Unheavenly City* (Prospect Heights, IL: Waveland Press, 1990).

68. Kesler, *I Am the Change*, 120.

69. See Hillary Rodham Clinton, *It Takes a Village: And Other Lessons Children Teach Us* (New York: Simon and Schuster, 1996).

70. Kesler, *I Am the Change*, 81.

71. Kesler, *I Am the Change*, 120.
72. Kesler, *I Am the Change*, 157.

THREE Gray in Gray

1. Ernst A. Breisach, *American Progressive History: An Experiment in Modernization* (Chicago: University of Chicago Press, 1993), 12–13. Subsequent page citations to this work are given parenthetically in the text.

2. Edward A. Purcell Jr., *The Crisis of Democratic Theory: Scientific Naturalism and the Problem of Value* (Lexington: University Press of Kentucky, 1973), 88. For further discussion of the relationship of legal realism and other legal doctrines to progressive political thought, see Bradley C. S. Watson, *Living Constitution, Dying Faith: Progressivism and the New Science of Jurisprudence* (Wilmington, DE: ISI Books, 2009).

3. John Higham, *History: Professional Scholarship in America* (1965; repr., Baltimore: Johns Hopkins University Press, 1983), 7.

4. See Higham, *History*, esp. sec. II, chap. 1.

5. Higham, *History*, 110.

6. Herman Belz, "Changing Conceptions of Constitutionalism in the Era of World War II and the Cold War," in *A Living Constitution or Fundamental Law? American Constitutionalism in Historical Perspective* (Lanham, MD: Rowman and Littlefield, 1998), 95–127.

7. See Belz, "Changing Conceptions of Constitutionalism," and also Bradley C. S. Watson, *Civil Rights and the Paradox of Liberal Democracy* (Lanham, MD: Lexington Books, 1999), and Watson, *Living Constitution, Dying Faith*.

8. Harold U. Faulkner, *The Quest for Social Justice: 1898–1914* (New York: Macmillan, 1931). Subsequent page citations to this work are given parenthetically in the text.

9. Arthur M. Schlesinger and Dixon Ryan Fox, "Editors' Foreword," in Faulkner, *Quest for Social Justice*, xv.

10. Faulkner, *Quest for Social Justice*, 245–47.

11. Peter Novick, *That Noble Dream: The "Objectivity Question" and the American Historical Profession* (New York: Cambridge University Press, 1988).

12. Richard Hofstadter, *Social Darwinism in American Thought*, rev. ed. (1944; repr., Boston: Beacon Press, 1955), 3–6. Subsequent page citations to this work are given parenthetically in the text.

13. Richard Hofstadter, *The American Political Tradition and the Men Who Made It* (New York: Vintage Books, 1948). Subsequent page citations to this work are given parenthetically in the text.

14. Richard Hofstadter, "Beard and the Constitution: The History of an Idea," *American Quarterly* 2, no. 3 (Autumn 1950): 195–96. Subsequent page citations to this work are given parenthetically in the text.

15. See also J. Allen Smith, *The Spirit of American Government* (New York: Macmillan, 1907).

16. Richard Hofstadter, *The Age of Reform: From Bryan to FDR* (New York: Vintage Books, 1955). Subsequent page citations to this work are given parenthetically in the text.

17. Both essays can be found in Richard Hofstadter, *The Paranoid Style in American Politics and Other Essays* (New York: Alfred A. Knopf, 1965).

18. William G. Anderson, "Progressivism: An Historiographical Essay," *History Teacher* 6, no. 3 (May 1973): 430.

19. Arthur Schlesinger Jr., *The Vital Center* (Cambridge, MA: Riverside Press, 1949), viii. Subsequent page citations to this work are given parenthetically in the text.

20. Henry Steele Commager, *The American Mind: An Interpretation of American Thought and Character since the 1880's* (New Haven, CT: Yale University Press, 1950). Subsequent page citations to this work are given parenthetically in the text.

21. Richard Aaron, *Men of Good Hope: A Story of American Progressives* (New York: Oxford University Press, 1951), xi–xiv. Subsequent citations to this work are given parenthetically in the text.

22. David W. Noble, "The New Republic and the Idea of Progress, 1914–1920," *Mississippi Valley Historical Review* 38, no. 3 (December 1951): 387–402.

23. Noble, "New Republic," 391.

24. Noble, "New Republic," 392–93.

25. Noble, "New Republic," 397.

26. David W. Noble, "Herbert Croly and American Progressive Thought," *Western Political Quarterly* 7, no. 4 (December 1954): 537–53.

27. Noble, "Herbert Croly," 547.

28. Noble, "Herbert Croly," 553.

29. C. Vann Woodward, *Origins of the New South: 1877–1913* (1951; repr., Baton Rouge: Louisiana State University Press, 1964).

30. Woodward, *Origins of the New South*, 371–74.

31. Woodward, *Origins of the New South*, 395.

32. Woodward, *Origins of the New South*, 471–81.

33. Eric F. Goldman, *Rendezvous with Destiny* (1952; repr., New York: Knopf, 1958). Subsequent page citations to this work are given parenthetically in the text.

34. Daniel J. Boorstin, *The Genius of American Politics* (Chicago: University of Chicago Press, 1953), 1. Subsequent page citations to this work are given parenthetically in the text.

35. In some ways, Boorstin's conservatism echoes that of Russell Kirk, whose classic, *The Conservative Mind: From Burke to Eliot*, was released the same year as *The Genius of American Politics*.

36. Arthur Mann, *Yankee Reformers in the Urban Age* (Cambridge, MA: Belknap Press of Harvard University Press, 1954), vii. Subsequent page citations to this work are given parenthetically in the text.

37. David M. Potter, *People of Plenty* (Chicago: University of Chicago Press, 1954), 115–16.

38. Potter, *People of Plenty*, 118.

39. Potter, *People of Plenty*, 121–22.

40. Potter, *People of Plenty*, 122–23.

41. Potter, *People of Plenty*, 126–27.

42. Arthur S. Link, *Woodrow Wilson and the Progressive Era* (1954; repr., New York: Harper Torchbook, 1963).

43. Link, *Woodrow Wilson*, chap. 1.

44. Link, *Woodrow Wilson*, 55.

45. Link, *Woodrow Wilson*, 224–25, 229–30.

46. Arthur S. Link, "What Happened to the Progressive Movement in the 1920's," *American Historical Review* 64, no. 4 (July 1959): 833–51.

47. Link, "What Happened," 836.

48. Link, "What Happened," 840.

49. Link, "What Happened," 843.

50. Link, "What Happened," 851.

51. Louis Hartz, *The Liberal Tradition in America: An Interpretation of American Political Thought since the Revolution* (New York: Harcourt, Brace and World, 1955). Subsequent page citations to this work are given parenthetically in the text. Strikingly, Hartz pays no attention to religious conflict in America or to the Civil War.

52. Harry V. Jaffa, "Conflicts within the Idea of the Liberal Tradition," *Comparative Studies in Society and History* 5, no. 3 (April 1963): 274–78.

53. Robert E. Brown, *Charles Beard and the Constitution: A Critical Analysis of "An Economic Interpretation of the Constitution"* (Princeton, NJ: Princeton University Press, 1956), 17.

54. Brown, *Charles Beard*, 197–200.

55. Forrest McDonald, *We the People: The Economic Origins of the Constitution* (Chicago: University of Chicago Press, 1958).

56. McDonald, *We the People*, vii.

57. Hofstadter, *The Progressive Historians* (New York: Alfred A. Knopf, 1968), 224.

58. Arthur Schlesinger Jr., *The Crisis of the Old Order: 1919–1933*, vol. 1 of *The Age of Roosevelt* (Cambridge, MA: Riverside Press, 1957), 17–18. Subsequent page citations to this work are given parenthetically in the text.

59. Arthur Schlesinger Jr., *The Coming of the New Deal*, vol. 2 of *The Age of Roosevelt* (Cambridge, MA: Riverside Press, 1958), 587–88.

60. Samuel P. Hays, *The Response to Industrialism: 1885–1914*, 2nd ed. (1957; Chicago: University of Chicago Press, 1995). Subsequent page citations to this work are given parenthetically in the text.

61. William E. Leuchtenberg, *The Perils of Prosperity: 1914–1932* (Chicago: University of Chicago Press, 1958). Subsequent page citations to this work are given parenthetically in the text.

62. George Mowry, *The Era of Theodore Roosevelt: 1900–1912* (New York: Harper and Row, 1958), chap. 1. Subsequent page citations to this work are given parenthetically in the text.

63. David W. Noble, *The Paradox of Progressive Thought* (Minneapolis: University of Minnesota Press, 1958), v–viii.

64. Noble, *Paradox*, 76.

65. Noble, *Paradox*, 102, 123–26.

66. Noble, *Paradox*, 227, 244–45, 250.

67. Noble, *Paradox*, 15–32.

68. Russell B. Nye, *Midwestern Progressive Politics: A Historical Study of Its Origins and Development* (East Lansing: Michigan State University Press, 1959). Subsequent page citations to this work are given parenthetically in the text.

69. Andrew M. Scott, "The Progressive Era in Perspective," *Journal of Politics* 21, no. 4 (November 1959): 685–701. Subsequent page citations to this work are given parenthetically in the text.

70. John Higham, "The Cult of the 'American Consensus,'" *Commentary*, February 1959, 93–100.

71. Higham, "Cult," 94–95.

72. Higham, "Cult," 95.

73. Higham, "Cult," 96.

74. Higham, "Cult," 100.

75. John Higham, "Beyond Consensus: The Historian as Moral Critic," *American Historical Review* 67, no. 3 (April 1962): 616.

76. Henry F. May, *The End of American Innocence: A Study of the First Years of Our Own Time, 1912–1917* (New York: Alfred A. Knopf, 1959), 21.

77. May, *End of American Innocence*, 22.

78. May, *End of American Innocence*, 29.

79. May, *End of American Innocence*, 113–14.

80. May, *End of American Innocence*, 162.

81. Henry F. May, *Protestant Churches and Industrial America* (New York: Harper and Brothers, 1948), 229.

FOUR Progressive Historiography in a Countercultural Age

1. Greg Grandin, "Forward to the 2011 Edition," in William Appleman Williams, *The Contours of American History* (1961; repr., London: Verso, 2011), xxvi.

2. William Appleman Williams, "Preface to the 1966 Edition," in Williams, *Contours of American History*, xliv–xlv. Subsequent page citations of this work are given parenthetically in the text.

3. Norman Pollack, *The Populist Response to Industrial America: Midwestern Populist Thought* (Cambridge, MA: Harvard University Press, 1962), 25, 68.

4. Pollack, *Populist Response*, 13.

5. Pollack, *Populist Response*, 23.

6. Gabriel Kolko, *The Triumph of Conservatism: A Reinterpretation of American History, 1900–1916* (New York: Free Press of Glencoe, 1963). Subsequent page citations to this work are given parenthetically in the text.

7. Richard Hofstadter, *Anti-intellectualism in American Life* (New York: Alfred A. Knopf, 1963), 3–23. Subsequent page citations to this work are given parenthetically in the text.

8. Richard Hofstadter, ed., *The Progressive Movement: 1900–1915* (Englewood Cliffs, NJ: Prentice Hall, 1963).

9. The nature of the Court at the time was quite different from what Holmes claimed it to be. Holmes was, ironically, the only Darwinist on the Court when he excoriated the institution for its purported right-wing social Darwinism. Furthermore, the Brandeis Brief helped

usher in a new era of progressive jurisprudence comprehensively hostile to the founders' Constitution. See Bradley C. S. Watson, *Living Constitution, Dying Faith: Progressivism and the New Science of Jurisprudence* (Wilmington, DE: ISI Books, 2009).

10. Charles R. Kesler, *I Am the Change: Barack Obama and the Crisis of Liberalism* (New York: Broadside Books, 2012), 66.

11. Samuel P. Hays, "The Politics of Reform in Municipal Government in the Progressive Era," *Pacific Northwest Quarterly* 55, no. 4 (October 1964): 157–69. Subsequent page citations to this work are given parenthetically in the text.

12. Arthur Mann, *The Progressive Era: Liberal Renaissance or Liberal Failure?* (New York: Holt, Rinehart and Winston, 1963).

13. Mann, *Progressive Era*, 1–5.

14. Charles Crowe, "The Emergence of Progressive History," *Journal of the History of Ideas* 27, no. 1 (1966): 109–24. Subsequent page citations to this work are given parenthetically in the text.

15. For an account of the establishment and growth of the American law schools as well as the discipline of political science in the Progressive Era, see Watson, *Living Constitution, Dying Faith*, esp. chap. 6. For more on the discipline of political science, see Denis J. Mahoney, *Politics and Progress: The Emergence of American Political Science* (Lanham, MD: Lexington Books, 2004).

16. Peter Novick, *That Noble Dream: The "Objectivity Question" and the American Historical Profession* (New York: Cambridge University Press, 1988).

17. Vernon Parrington, *The Beginnings of Critical Realism in America*, vol. 3 of *Main Currents in American Thought* (1927; repr., New Brunswick, NJ: Transaction Publishers, 2013), 410–11.

18. Otis L. Graham Jr., *An Encore for Reform: The Old Progressives and the New Deal* (New York: Oxford University Press, 1967). Subsequent page citations to this work are given parenthetically in the text.

19. Robert H. Wiebe, *The Search for Order: 1877–1920* (New York: Hill and Wang, 1967), 12. Subsequent page citations to this work are given parenthetically in the text.

20. Richard C. Wade, foreword to *Spearheads for Reform: The Social Settlements and the Progressive Movement, 1890–1914*, by Allen F. Davis (New York: Oxford University Press, 1967), vii.

21. Richard C. Wade, foreword to *Spearheads for Reform*, by Allen F. Davis, xiii. Subsequent page citations to this work are given parenthetically in the text.

22. Richard Hofstadter, *The Progressive Historians* (New York: Alfred A. Knopf, 1968). Subsequent page citations to this work are given parenthetically in the text.

23. James Weinstein, *The Corporate Ideal in the Liberal State: 1900–1918* (Boston: Beacon Press, 1968), xi. Subsequent page citations to this work are given parenthetically in the text.

24. David Donald, "Radical Historians on the Move," *New York Times Book Review*, July 19, 1970, https://www.nytimes.com/1970/07/19/archives/radical-historians-on-the-move-radical-historians.html.

25. Peter G. Filenc, "An Obituary for 'the Progressive Movement,'" *American Quarterly* 22, no. 1 (Spring 1970): 20–34. Subsequent page citations to this work are given parenthetically in the text.

26. Albro Martin, *Enterprise Denied: Origins of the Decline of American Railroads, 1897–1917* (New York: Columbia University Press, 1971).

27. Martin, *Enterprise Denied*, xii–xiii.

28. Martin, *Enterprise Denied*, 17.

29. Martin, *Enterprise Denied*, 154.

30. Arthur A. Ekirch, *Progressivism in America: A Study of the Era from Theodore Roosevelt to Woodrow Wilson* (New York: New Viewpoints, 1974), 29.

31. Ekirch, *Progressivism in America*, chaps. 8–9.

32. Ekirch, *Progressivism in America*, 171.

33. R. Laurence Moore, "Directions of Thought in Progressive America," in *The Progressive Era*, ed. Lewis L. Gould (Syracuse, NY: Syracuse University Press, 1974), 38.

34. David M. Kennedy, "Overview: The Progressive Era," *Historian* 37, no. 3 (May 1975): 453–68. Subsequent page citations to this work are given parenthetically in the text.

35. Kenneth O. Morgan, "The Future at Work: Anglo-American Progressivism 1890–1917," in *Contrast and Connection: Bicentennial Essays in Anglo-American History*, ed. H. C. Allen and Roger Thompson (Athens: Ohio University Press, 1976), 245–71. Subsequent page citations to this work are given parenthetically in the text.

36. John D. Buenker, John C. Burnham, and Robert M. Crunden, *Progressivism* (Cambridge, MA: Schenkman, 1977), iv–v.

37. John D. Buenker, John C. Burnham, and Robert M. Crunden, introduction to *Progressivism*, vii.

38. Burnham, "Essay," in Buenker, Burnham, and Crunden, *Progressivism*, 5. Subsequent page citations to this work are given parenthetically in the text.

39. Buenker, "Essay," in Buenker, Burnham, and Crunden, *Progressivism*, 31. Subsequent page citations to this work are given parenthetically in the text.

40. Crunden, "Essay," in Buenker, Burnham, and Crunden, *Progressivism*, 73.

41. Crunden, "Essay," 107.

42. Crunden, "Essay," 75–76.

43. Crunden, "Essay," 98.

44. Robert M. Crunden, *Ministers of Reform: The Progressives' Achievement in American Civilization, 1889–1920* (New York: Basic Books, 1982). Subsequent page citations to this work are given parenthetically in the text.

45. Morton Keller, *Affairs of State: Public Life in Late Nineteenth Century America* (Belknap Press of Harvard University Press, 1977). Subsequent page citations to this work are given parenthetically in the text.

46. Roger C. Bannister, *Social Darwinism: Science and Myth in Anglo-American Social Thought* (Philadelphia: Temple University Press, 1979), 9. Subsequent page citations to this work are given parenthetically in the text.

47. Daniel T. Rodgers, "In Search of Progressivism," *Reviews in American History* 10, no. 4 (December 1982): 113–32. Subsequent page citations to this work are given parenthetically in the text.

48. Arthur S. Link and Richard McCormick, *Progressivism*, The American History Series (Arlington Heights, IL: Harlan Davidson, 1983). Subsequent page citations to this work are given parenthetically in the text.

FIVE Intellectual Consolidation and Counterattack

1. This is not to say that the discipline of political science as a whole has been immune to progressive influences. On the contrary, it is fair to say that American political science was founded on progressive principles, including the central progressive belief in "directed progress." For a full account of the origins of American political science, see Dennis J. Mahoney, *Politics and Progress: The Emergence of American Political Science* (Lanham, MD: Lexington Books, 2004). See also chapter 6 in Bradley C. S. Watson, *Living Constitution, Dying Faith: Progressivism and the New Science of Jurisprudence* (Wilmington, DE: ISI Books, 2009), for an account of progressivism's influence not only on the foundations

of the discipline of political science but on those of modern American law schools.

2. For those interested in a fuller exploration of the "Claremont school" of political thought, two notable collections bring together scholars in the Claremont orbit—mostly political scientists—who articulate various aspects of its critique of progressivism: *Progressive Challenges to the American Constitution: A New Republic*, ed. Bradley C. S. Watson (New York: Cambridge University Press, 2017), and an earlier work, *The Progressive Revolution in Politics and Political Science: Transforming the American Regime*, ed. John Marini and Ken Masugi (Lanham, MD: Rowman and Littlefield/Claremont Institute, 2005). In this chapter, I offer summaries of some of the key arguments that appear in *Progressive Challenges*.

3. For a brief account of Strauss and Straussianism, see Mark C. Henrie, "Straussianism," *First Principles Journal*, May 5, 2011, www.first principlesjournal.com/articles.aspx?article=871.

4. See, for example, Martin Diamond, "Democracy and *The Federalist*: A Reconsideration of the Framers' Intent," *American Political Science Review* 53, no. 1 (March 1959): 52–68.

5. Paul Eidelberg, *A Discourse on Statesmanship: The Design and Transformation of the American Polity* (Urbana: University of Illinois Press, 1974).

6. For Jaffa's most extended meditations on the trajectory of American political thought, see *Crisis of the House Divided: An Interpretation of the Issues in the Lincoln-Douglas Debates* (Chicago: University of Chicago Press, 1959) and *A New Birth of Freedom: Abraham Lincoln and the Coming of the Civil War* (Lanham, MD: Rowman and Littlefield, 2000). For a brief account of Jaffa's political thought and legacy, see Bradley C. S. Watson, "Harry V. Jaffa: 1918–2015," *Modern Age* 57, no. 3 (Summer 2015): 85–88.

7. Charles R. Kesler, "Woodrow Wilson and the Statesmanship of Progress," in *Progressive Challenges to the American Constitution: A New Republic*, ed. Bradley C. S. Watson (New York: Cambridge University Press, 2017), originally published in *Natural Right and Political Right*, ed. Thomas B. Silver and Peter W. Schramm (Durham, NC: Carolina Academic Press, 1984).

8. Charles R. Kesler, *I Am the Change: Barack Obama and the Crisis of Liberalism* (New York: Broadside Books, 2012), 18.

9. Kesler, *I Am the Change*, 36–37.

10. Kesler, *I Am the Change*, 38.

11. Ronald J. Pestritto, *Woodrow Wilson and the Roots of Modern Liberalism* (Lanham, MD: Rowman and Littlefield, 2005).

12. Pestritto, *Woodrow Wilson*, 21.

13. Pestritto, *Woodrow Wilson*, 262.

14. John Lugton Safford, *Pragmatism and the Progressive Movement in the United States* (Lanham, MD: University Press of America, 1987), ix.

15. Safford, *Pragmatism*, chaps. 2–3. Subsequent page citations to this work are given parenthetically in the text.

16. Eldon Eisenach, *The Lost Promise of Progressivism* (Lawrence: University Press of Kansas, 1994). Subsequent page citations to this work are given parenthetically in the text.

17. Sidney M. Milkis and Jerome Mileur, eds., *Progressivism and the New Democracy* (Amherst: University of Massachusetts Press, 1999), 7.

18. Sidney M. Milkis, "Introduction: Progressivism, Then and Now," in Milkis and Mileur, *Progressivism*, 16.

19. Milkis, "Introduction," 25–26.

20. Alonzo L. Hamby, "Progressivism: A Century of Change and Rebirth," in Milkis and Mileur, *Progressivism*, 43.

21. Hamby, "Progressivism," 45, 57, 65.

22. Wilson Carey McWilliams, "Standing at Armageddon: Morality and Religion in Progressive Thought," in Milkis and Mileur, *Progressivism*, 103.

23. McWilliams, "Standing at Armageddon," 107.

24. McWilliams, "Standing at Armageddon," 108–9.

25. McWilliams, "Standing at Armageddon," 112–13.

26. Martha Derthick and John J. Dinan, "Progressivism and Federalism," in Milkis and Mileur, *Progressivism*, 82–83.

27. Derthick and Dinan, "Progressivism and Federalism," 84–85.

28. Jerome M. Mileur, "The Legacy of Reform: Progressive Government, Regressive Politics," in Milkis and Mileur, *Progressivism*, 265.

29. Mileur, "Legacy of Reform," 270–71.

30. Mileur, "Legacy of Reform," 272.

31. Mileur, "Legacy of Reform," 278–79.

32. Will Morrissey, *The Dilemma of Progressivism: How Roosevelt, Taft, and Wilson Reshaped the American Regime of Self-Government* (Lanham, MD: Rowman and Littlefield, 2009), 5–7. Subsequent page citations to this work are given parenthetically in the text.

33. Jason R. Jividen, *Claiming Lincoln: Progressivism, Equality, and the Battle for Lincoln's Legacy in Presidential Rhetoric* (DeKalb: Northern

Illinois University Press, 2011), 9. Subsequent page citations to this work are given parenthetically in the text. For more on the progressive origins and implications of Barack Obama's political rhetoric, see Kesler, *I Am the Change*.

34. Johnathan O'Neill and Joseph Postell, eds., *Toward an American Conservatism: Constitutional Conservatism during the Progressive Era* (New York: Palgrave Macmillan, 2013).

35. Johnathan O'Neill and Joseph Postell, "The Conservative Response to Progressivism," in O'Neill and Postell, *Toward an American Conservatism*, 8.

36. Sidney M. Milkis, "William Howard Taft and the Struggle for the Soul of the Constitution," in O'Neill and Postell, *Toward an American Conservatism*, 64–65.

37. Milkis, "William Howard Taft," 76.

38. William A. Schambra, "The Election of 1912 and the Origins of Constitutional Conservatism," in O'Neill and Postell, *Toward an American Conservatism*, 95–119.

39. See Joseph Postell, "'Roaring' against Progressivism: Calvin Coolidge's Principled Conservatism," in O'Neill and Postell, *Toward an American Conservatism*, 181–208.

40. Gordon Lloyd and David Davenport, "The Two Phases of Herbert Hoover's Constitutional Conservatism," in O'Neill and Postell, *Toward an American Conservatism*, 236–237.

41. See David Bernstein, "The Progressive Origins of Conservative Hostility to *Lochner v. New York*," in O'Neill and Postell, *Toward an American Conservatism*, 35–38. See also David Bernstein, *Rehabilitating Lochner: Defending Individual Rights against Progressive Reform* (Chicago: University of Chicago Press, 2011). I make the same point in *Living Constitution, Dying Faith*.

42. Bernstein, "Progressive Origins," 39–41.

43. Paul D. Moreno, *The American State from the Civil War to the New Deal: The Twilight of Constitutionalism and the Triumph of Progressivism* (New York: Cambridge University Press, 2013). Subsequent page citations to this work are given parenthetically in the text.

44. See also Watson, *Living Constitution, Dying Faith*, and Mark Warren Bailey, *Guardians of the Moral Order: The Legal Philosophy of the Supreme Court, 1860–1910* (DeKalb: Northern Illinois University Press, 2004).

45. For a full account of how this did in fact come to pass, see Watson, *Living Constitution, Dying Faith*.

46. See Watson, *Living Constitution, Dying Faith*, chap. 6. See also Bradley C. S. Watson, "Republics of Conscience: Progressive Law Schools and the Crisis of Constitutionalism," *National Review*, October 29, 2012.

47. See Watson, *Living Constitution, Dying Faith*.

48. Watson, *Progressive Challenges*.

49. William A. Schambra, "The Problem of Democracy: Recovering the Constitution from the Progressives," in Watson, *Progressive Challenges*, 11–30.

50. Sidney M. Milkis, "Theodore Roosevelt, the Progressive Party, and the Ascendance of the Living Constitution," in Watson, *Progressive Challenges*, 31–64.

51. James W. Ceaser, "Progressivism and the Doctrine of Natural Rights," in Watson, *Progressive Challenges*, 67–86.

52. Wilfred M. McClay, "John Dewey and the Dilemma of Progressive Democracy," in Watson, *Progressive Challenges*.

53. For a recent iteration of this scholarship, see John Marini, "Progressivism, the Social Sciences, and the Rational State," in Watson, *Progressive Challenges*, 105–43.

54. Ronald J. Pestritto, "Making the State into a God: American Progressivism and the Social Gospel," in Watson, *Progressive Challenges*, 144–59.

55. James Stoner, "Progressivism, Social Science, and Catholic Social Teaching in the Building of the American Welfare State," in Watson, *Progressive Challenges*, 160–70.

56. Jean M. Yarbrough, "The Promise of the New Nationalism and Its Challenge to the Framers," in Watson, *Progressive Challenges*, 173–95. See also Yarbrough, *Theodore Roosevelt and the American Political Tradition* (Lawrence: University Press of Kansas, 2014). Subsequent page citations to this work are given parenthetially in the text.

57. Yarbrough, *Theodore Roosevelt*, 2.

58. Johnathan O'Neill, "William Howard Taft and the Constitutionalist Presidency in the Progressive Era," in Watson, *Progressive Challenges*, 196–225.

59. Bradley C. S. Watson, "One Supreme Court: Oliver Wendell Holmes, Louis Brandeis, and the Progressive Revolution in Constitutional Jurisprudence," in Watson, *Progressive Challenges*, 257–90. For a fuller version of this argument on the unique role of the Court in promulgating a fundamentally anticonstitutional progressive vision of the future, see Watson, *Living Constitution, Dying Faith*.

60. See Eric Claeys, "Progressive Political Theory, Contemporary Politics, and the REINS Act," in Watson, *Progressive Challenges*, 291–322.

SIX The Shades of History

1. Thomas B. Silver, *Coolidge and the Historians* (Durham, NC: Carolina Academic Press, 1982).

2. Peter Novick, *That Noble Dream: The "Objectivity Question" and the American Historical Profession* (New York: Cambridge University Press, 1988), 33. Subsequent page citations to this work are given parenthetically in the text.

3. Mary O. Furner, *Advocacy and Objectivity: A Crisis in the Professionalization of American Social Science, 1865–1905* (Lexington: University Press of Kentucky, 1975), xi. Subsequent page citations to this work are given parenthetically in the text.

4. Thomas L. Haskell, *The Emergence of Professional Social Science: The American Social Science Association and the Nineteenth-Century Crisis of Authority* (Urbana: University of Illinois Press, 1977), v–viii. Subsequent page citations to this work are given parenthetically in the text.

5. Alexis de Tocqueville, *Democracy in America*, ed. and trans. Harvey Mansfield and Delba Winthrop (Chicago: University of Chicago Press, 2000), vol. 2, pt. 1, chap. 20.

6. Dorothy Ross, *The Origins of American Social Science* (Cambridge: Cambridge University Press, 1991), 8–9. Subsequent page citations to this work are given parenthetically in the text.

7. Ross, *Origins*, 38. See also Bradley C. S. Watson, "Who Was Francis Lieber?," *Modern Age* 43, no. 4 (Fall 2001): 304–10.

8. Mark C. Smith, *Social Science in the Crucible: The American Debate over Objectivity and Purpose* (Durham, NC: Duke University Press, 1994), 259.

9. Smith, *Social Science*, 256–57.

10. Morton Keller, "Social and Economic Regulation in the Progressive Era," in Milkis and Mileur, eds., *Progressivism*, 126–28.

11. Keller, "Social and Economic Regulation," 128.

12. Stephen Skowronek, Stephen M. Engel, and Bruce Ackerman, eds., *The Progressives' Century: Political Reform, Constitutional Government, and the Modern American State* (New Haven, CT: Yale University Press, 2016).

13. Charles R. Kesler, *I Am the Change: Barack Obama and the Crisis of Liberalism* (New York: Broadside Books, 2012), 231.

14. Ken I. Kersch, "Constitutional Conservatives Remember the Progressive Era," in Skowronek, Engel, and Ackerman, *Progressives' Century*, 130–54.

15. Stephen M. Teles, "How the Progressives Became the Tea Party's Mortal Enemy: Networks, Movements, and the Political Currency of Ideas," in Skowronek, Engel, and Ackerman, *Progressives' Century*, 453–77.

16. Kesler, *I Am the Change*, xii.

17. Kesler, *I Am the Change*, xiii.

18. Kesler, *I Am the Change*, xvii.

Index

Bradley C. S. Watson

is the Philip M. McKenna Chair in American and Western Political Thought at Saint Vincent College. He is the author and editor of numerous books, including *Living Constitution, Dying Faith: Progressivism and the New Science of Jurisprudence* and *Progressive Challenges to the American Constitution: A New Republic*.

Charles R. Kesler

is the Dengler-Dykema Distinguished Professor of Government at Claremont McKenna College and Claremont Graduate University. He is editor of the *Claremont Review of Books*.

CPSIA information can be obtained
at www.ICGtesting.com
Printed in the USA
LVHW081228230821
695894LV00003B/289